Tales out of Flying School

THE AUTO-BIOGRAPHY
OF AN INSTRUCTOR
IN SERVICE AND CIVIL FLYING

by Stanley Ward

ISBN 0 9528094 0 0

UK PRICE £10

Published in Great Britain by
OAK HILL BOOKS
4 Oak Hill Lane, Ipswich, Suffolk IP2 9AL, England

Cover Picture by John Castle

Printed in England by
The Five Castles Press Limited, Ipswich

Introduction

During conversations about aviation, there were few items on which I was unable and unwilling to add some snippet of my experience as an Instructor in RAF and civilian flying.

Friends were aware of my readiness to talk about the joys of learning to fly, and consequently I was invited to address sundry societies on various aspects of flying. It followed that suggestions were frequently made that some of the anecdotes should be recorded in writing.

It was not difficult to get into the habit of making notes to remind me of items that appeared to excite most interest or get most laughs. Add in the facts contained in 22 flying logbooks and hundreds of photographs - and we have the material for this book.

Author

Acknowledgements

There are many former students to whom I am indebted for providing, albeit unconsciously, some of the material for this book. In a similar manner, many of them demonstrated antics with aeroplanes that became part of my stunt-flying displays.

My lady, Enid, came into the picture late in the production, at a time when the writing was doubtful, and enthusiasm was lagging. I have to thank her for suffering the repeated hearing of numerous anecdotes, and for the later editing of the same, which saved me from making a complete fool of myself. More important, it was her encouragement which brought about the completion of the story.

Son Christopher helped considerably in tidying up the computer work, and in supplying print-outs for my many revisions.

I am sincerely grateful to John Castle for his cover picture, and for the use of photographs of his own posters.

My thanks for the kindness in allowing me to use their photographs go to the Ipswich Evening Star, Jim Empson, Peter Warren, Derek Simmonds and the Ipswich Parachute Centre.

Stanley Ward

Foreword

by

Air Marshal Sir Ivor Broom KCB CBE DSO DFC AFC

Stanley Ward learned to fly with the Royal Air Force in the U.S.A. in World War 2. He passed out top of his entry and, like others who distinguished themselves in training, was immediately earmarked for flying instructional duties which were to alter the pattern of his whole life.

On release from the Royal Air Force he returned to his pre-war employment in the local Government offices at Ipswich, but all his spare time - weekends and summer evenings were devoted to his great love of flying. He covered a wide spectrum of flying in small single engine aircraft. First and foremost he was a qualified flying instructor, but in addition he gave crazy flying displays at air displays, was an approved test pilot for the renewal of Certificates of Airworthiness for light aircraft and became involved to a limited extent in glider towing and parachute dropping. On retiring from the County Hall in 1981, he became a full time flying instructor, but it is rather ironical that about a year later he lost his flying license on medical grounds. His all consuming interest in flying remained unabated and although he no longer could act as a qualified instructor he completed a further 2,000 hours in the next 10 years - riding shotgun as he terms it. He accumulated some 13,500 flying hours - virtually all on single engined aircraft. I wonder if anyone else has ever accumulated such a total on light aircraft.

The book is full of amusing stories and experiences which will intrigue and delight anyone with the slightest interest in aviation. Some modern pilots may cringe when they read of some of his exploits - particularly over nearby European countries - in small aircraft which were not equipped with radio, had no navigational aids, and only very basic instrumentation for flying in clouds. Despite the lack of equipment which is generally considered essential today he shows - perhaps unconsciously - how he achieved safe operations, and extricated himself from potentially dangerous situations by adhering to sound airmanship principles. A fascinating story.

Ivor Broom

To Enid

CONTENTS

CHAPTER 6

CHAPTER 7

CHAPTER 8

CHAPTER 9

Chapter One

THE SEEDS ARE SOWN

"YOU MIGHT have been making something a bit more imaginative and useful – like a pipe-rack", was the gentle criticism by my much-loved Uncle Wally, a woodwork teacher. This quiet and not unkind chiding in 1930 followed a visit by his headmaster to Uncle's classroom where I was guest for a day. Nine years of age, I was making a model aeroplane from the piece of wood intended to keep me occupied – it is this that fixes for me the earliest indication of my interest in aeroplanes.

I was the awe-stricken schoolboy who watched from behind the fence when Alan Cobham's air circus visited Ipswich before we had an airport, and I never did have the necessary five bob for a joyflight. I was also one of those who were regularly chased by Air Ministry police whenever we tasted the delights of forbidden loitering on the public roads through RAF Station Martlesham Heath where we would hang around to get a glimpse of something new being tested at this Aeroplane & Armament Testing Station near Ipswich. Sharp-eyed lads at school could spot from the classroom any unusual aircraft circling the airfield, and the word was soon spread among the aviation enthusiasts who would be cycling out at the first opportunity, to have a look at it. Occasionally the aircraft was so interesting that the loitering had to be assisted by deliberately letting the wind out of a tyre and claiming a puncture so that the bicycle had to be walked.

I can clearly remember the thrill and delight of staying with my Aunty Gladys in Langer Road Felixstowe within sight of the Schneider Trophy seaplanes when they were being tested at the Marine Aircraft Experimental Air Station there.

The joy and endurance of cycling from Ipswich to London as an eleven year old boy is remembered mainly because I passed Blue Barnes Airport with a couple of Redwings in sight, on the left just before Colchester, and Hillman's Airfield on the right near Romford, where only a windsock was visible from the road.

I was one of five schoolboys who met at Barrack Corner in Ipswich at 1.30 am on a chilly morning in October 1934 to cycle the 37 miles to the RAF Station at Mildenhall to see the start of the Mildenhall to Melbourne Air Race. We arrived at 5.30 in good time to find a suitable vantage point from which to watch the takeoffs of aeroplanes that we could recognise instantly, flown by pilots most of whom were already heroes to us. I had a wooden model of the De Havilland Comet attached to the top of the front mudguard of my bike so that by day I could enjoy the sight of the two propellers being blown round at rpm which varied according to the speed of the cycle plus or minus the strength of the headwind, while at night I was flying the huge aeroplane which was in shadow on the road under my headlight.

This was of course the 1930's Comet powered by two Gypsy Six piston engines and the latest thing in propellers with a device which allowed a fine pitch and thus high rpm for takeoff and climb, with a once-per-flight adjustment in level flight to coarse pitch for cruising speed.

The sight of that great takeoff which included three of these beautiful Comets and many other wonderful aeroplanes was worth every mile of pedalling that day. The misfortune suffered by us and Amy and Jim Mollison when their Comet gave out in India was balanced by the win by Comet G-ACSS flown by C W A Scott and Tom Campbell Black. But the five tired and hungry little lads who took the rest of that day to cycle back to Ipswich could only be sure at that time that these magnificent people must be travelling much faster than we were.

My many approaches to the Royal Air Force during the thirties resulted in the collection of leaflets and pamphlets of all descriptions – entry as a Boy or, better, as an Aircraft Apprentice because the top three of each entry were given the opportunity of pilot training. I also studied entry as a Sergeant-Pilot and entry on a Short Service Commission. But without getting maudlin about it, what chance had this bottom-of-the-heap lad of ever attaining such heights? It was simply reaching for the moon – a wild dream that could not possibly ever be realised.

Nor was there a lot of encouragement from a loving Mother with her horror of the armed forces, aroused during the first world war, who did not want to contemplate the possibility of her youngest son leaving home at such an early age. Father was no more help – any conversation with him on any subject other than horse-racing would be cut short by ramblings about what was likely to win the two-thirty. In any case there was some doubt about my leg length for the standard pilot's cockpit!

It was in October 1938 that I learned of the Civil Air Guard at Ipswich Airport so application to join was made without delay – to be told that I would not be old enough until February 1939. Excitement increased as that date approached and I made sure that I had the two shillings and sixpence (12.5p) for membership, fifteen shillings for the uniform and five shillings for the medical examination which I duly passed on Wednesday the 5th of April at 7.30 pm. I was enrolled as 'Pilot' with Air Ministry Official number 8061, and informed that all my training would be carried out on light aircraft for which the charge was two shillings and sixpence per hour as compared with standard aircraft which cost five shillings. The light aircraft was in fact the Hillson Praga and although Ipswich did not have any, the Tiger Moth was classed as a standard aircraft.

My training would probably start in three months time and in reply to my question came the information that the method of payment was that members normally deposited a sum and then flew it off – oh dear! I would have difficulty enough in finding the two and six for a single hour, but we'll worry about that when the time comes. My salary as a local government junior clerk at that time was £35 per annum, so I was now aware that I was moving in with the 'nobs' who had money – this did not help to reduce the feeling of inferiority which had resulted from being a poor scholarship boy in a school where the majority of the boys were fee-paying.

However we must not let such small matters deflect us from the main purpose. Ground training could start at once and my records show that I got 80% in an examination on Friday the 23rd of June 1939 at 7 pm in the lecture subjects of navigation, meteorology and air legislation. Expenditure in the clubhouse was minimised by my plea that I was teetotal. Lists of those whose flying was to commence appeared at regular intervals and these included the names of many well-respected elderly ladies and gentlemen, but mine never appeared!

However, a letter dated 30 August 1939 from the Commission of the Civil Air Guard informed me that "...should a war emergency arise, in view of my qualifications..." I had been noted for probable war employment, after further training "as......." and the magic word 'pilot' had been typed in the space. Just as well about the further training because I had at this time never been in the air.

During the early part of 1939 it was announced that the Royal Air Force intended to open No.45 Elementary & Reserve Flying Training School at Ipswich Airport for the training of pilots for the RAF Volunteer Reserve. The result of my immediate application was for me to appear before selection and medical boards in June – only to be informed that although my leg length and brain were considered to be quite satisfactory, I had a weakness in my right eye. They would therefore have to defer selection for three months, and if there were no further deterioration at the end of that period I would be accepted. Little did I know then what heartache this simple decision was to cause me: looking back some fifty years however it probably accounted for my survival! Nevertheless from that moment a large part of my meagre wealth was spent on bottles of 'Optrex' and I became an expert in eye-washing – some would say that I retain that prowess to this day.

The unit opened on the 3rd of July 1939, and had hardly got going before it was closed on the 2nd of September. The Civil Air Guard was ordered to attend for a compulsory parade at Ipswich Airport at 11 am on Sunday 3rd September 1939. But there was something up – instead of parading we stayed in the clubhouse to hear the Prime Minister on the wireless, and so we heard Neville Chamberlain announcing that this country was at war with Germany. It all went quiet for a bit, then some great sport shouted "drinks all round on me" and as it was unlikely that the obligation to buy a round would ever get to me, I had a half of bitter.

THE STRUGGLE TO GET INTO THE RAF

On the 5th of September I received a letter from the RAF Volunteer Reserve at Ipswich stating that all enlistment into the Reserve was closed but that my papers had been sent to Headquarters. A letter from the Air Ministry 13th October advised that we could only be considered for an engagement to serve for the period of the present emergency and if I wished to be considered on this basis I should tell them so: in due course I would be required to report to a Receiving Centre but in the meantime I should carry on in my normal civil occupation. I could hardly wait to serve for any period so my reply said yes please, but on the 31st December I felt the need to write complaining that I had been waiting for over two months.

At the start of the war I had a second iron in the fire by way of the Civil Air Guard but this gave no greater promise because my letter of September 19th 1939, impatient at not having been called to serve as a pilot, received a reply from the Office of the Commission of the Civil Air Guard stating that I would have to wait "...at least until the end of the year". Visits to the Recruiting Office in Ipswich left me in no doubt that pilot training facilities were flooded with reservists and partly-trained servicemen and that they would not be recruiting any pilots for some time to come. On the 31st of December I wrote also to the Civil Air Guard reminding them of their promise that I would serve as a pilot.

The reply from the RAFVR explained that it would be a long wait although "...every effort is being made to expedite the matter" but the CAG reply was a little more hopeful in that it informed me that it had never been intended that the CAG should function as a complete unit in time of war so you should now pop along to the nearest Combined Recruiting Centre, show them this letter and offer yourself to the Royal Air Force! I had expected VIP treatment on the strength of that letter but although the recruiting Sergeant did not exactly say "What you again?" he did give me the January 1940 equivalent of 'No-way' regarding immediate entry as a pilot.

So I explained the predicament of my shaky eye – that I may be waiting in vain for pilot training. His eyes must have lit up with eager recruiting anticipation because my feet did not touch the ground again until I was downstairs in the medical centre having an eye-test. "Not a hope for pilot" was the verdict of the examiner who might have been a ground trades recruiting officer for all I knew because I then had to ask what was I good for? They didn't tell me in the way they might have done if I had already signed up but explained that they had a nice line in Armourers – yes armourers did work on aeroplanes – yes I would be crawling all over aircraft, putting guns into Spitfires and bombs into Wellingtons – yes of course the pilots would give me rides.

JOINING UP

And so it was that on the 10th of May I climbed into the train to report to RAF Receiving Centre at Cardington Bedford as a potential Armourer-under-training. I soon realised something of my new importance because my travelling companion, also an intending recruit, was no less a person than Jackie Little, the Ipswich Town footballer, and he was actually speaking to me as if I were an equal!

It was explained to me that it was no longer possible to train armourers in all aspects of the business so the trade had been divided into Armourers Guns and Armourers Bombs and they could offer me a good line of training in the latter – thus it was that I signed up to become 1151597 Aircraftsman 2nd Class Ward S W Aircrafthand u/t Armourer (Bombs).

ACTING GROUND GUNNER

After recruits' training at Morecambe we were informed on parade that in the light of the war situation (the fall of France), further training was cancelled and we would be posted as necessary to defend the country. So on the 31st of May 1940 I was posted to RAF Church Fenton in Yorkshire to man a 20 mm Hispano cannon on the aerodrome. The duty hours were four on, four off and four on standby in the tent beside the gun emplacement, with an occasional day off. We were permitted to practice swinging the gun around when Hurricane fighters practised attacks on us, but we were not allowed to fire the gun without specific orders.

After five weeks of this, a firing range strong enough to take 20 mm had been completed so we happily carried our gun down for firing practice. In the hands of the Armament Officer it fired just one round from the drum of ammunition and then stopped. It transpired that the ejector was wrongly positioned so that it failed to get rid of the spent cartridge case, with the result that this sharp-edged piece of metal cut through the next round which was waiting in the drum, spraying the Officer with the tiny grains of neonite, the propulsive charge. It was really only a bit of luck that the percussion cap was not detonated because this would have exploded the round in the mouth of the drum which was just beside the Officer's right ear – nasty!

Adjustment of the ejector was the work of minutes, and then we were treated to a fine display of 'after you Claude' when the Officer invited the Armament Warrant Officer to have a go this time while the latter tried to decline on the basis that the Officer had not had a real go. The Officer won the argument and the Warrant Officer duly survived the second test, after which we all had a go. But five weeks! Lucky we weren't attacked for real.

ON A COURSE OF TRAINING AT LAST

We were not attacked for the next three months, so A/C 2 Ward S W u/t Armourer (Bombs), Acting Ground Gunner, was able to drop the last bit of his trade description on the 8th August to start training at the Air & Ground Armament Training School, Manby, Lincolnshire. Seven weeks later I was a duly credited Armourer (Bombs) in pay group 2. The only crisis during that time was a panic when we were given an hour to pack our kit for immediate departure elsewhere because of a suggestion that the Germans had landed on the coast at Grimsby – but after parading in full kit in the sight of many buses and trucks, we were dismissed and we never heard anymore about it.

My course result was good, particularly the work in making a small adjustable spanner, so I was offered further training on a six-month course to Fitter-Armourer in group one which meant a higher rate of pay. This I accepted and was then packed off to No 8 School of Technical Training, RAF Weeton in Lancashire with reclassification to Aircraftsman First Class.

I was fairly clever on the fitters' course because my work jobs averaged 88% with the final test job awarded 94% – some of the pieces found their way into the show-case of specimens. It was not too surprising therefore that I was invited to become an instructor, with the inducements of Leading Aircraftsman immediately and the rank of Corporal within two weeks. Me, a Corporal! Yes please.

RE-MUSTERING TO PILOT

During 1941 after the thrill of being a Corporal instructor had worn off, it occurred to me that this was going to be a remarkably dull war because I was now 'screened' as a group one instructor and was therefore denied any other form of service for the duration of the war. That is excepting aircrew so my thoughts again turned to the possibility of getting into the air.

My application to re-muster as a pilot was met with a frown by the Station Commander, himself wearing wings, and brought comments from him such as "silly boy – anybody can fly an aeroplane but few can do what you are doing". However, after some discussion he seemed to appreciate how I felt and agreed to put my application forward.

The appropriate form had a question "have you ever applied for aircrew training before?" I could not see why I should draw attention to a possible point of failure, so "no" was entered without hesitation. Selection and medical boards followed soon after at RAF Padgate, but this time there was no problem with eyesight – I shall never know if it was because my eyes had improved or that they were getting a bit short of aircrew in 1941 – but not a word to anyone, we were away!

Not yet though, it was May 1942 before I was posted to Arcy-tarcy as the Aircrew Receiving Centre (ACRC) in St Johns Wood London was known. This was a dangerous place to be after the peace and quiet of mid-Lancashire, but we did have the distinction of standing naked in the Long Room at Lords cricket ground while a medical officer inspected us at the front and rear to ensure that we were free from infection.

Shortly after this we were informed that we could no longer be considered for one particular job in aircrew such as pilot or navigator but would in future be known as aircrew trainees, and 'they' would decide who were to be trained to become pilots, navigators or bomb aimers and we must sign to say that we accepted this. Oh misery, I wanted to be a pilot and nothing else – but we had to sign or go back to groundcrew.

INITIAL TRAINING WINGS

These were units at which the basic facts of life in the RAF were taught which included Kings Regulations, drill and physical training together with an introduction to flying matters such as air navigation, meteorology, principles of flight and the Morse code – audio and visual. Many of these units were sited at seaside resorts where hotels and boarding houses could be used to accommodate the cadets. One of the joys of aircrew training was that marching around the streets of these towns was done at 130 paces to the minute instead of the normal more leisurely 120 – it was claimed that this would quicken our reactions.

Aircrew training courses included direct entry cadets from civvy street as well as serving airmen like myself who had been 'in' for some time and whose ranks ranged from AC2 to Warrant Officer. It was one of the irritations of this training period that we were all classified as cadets and if any distinction at all was made between us, it was usually that some ignorant drill corporal was rubbing the old sweats' noses in it. It was a bit galling having to undergo basic drill again but we could at least doze a little during lessons on RAF ranks and badges.

I had the good fortune to be posted to No.10 ITW at Scarborough Yorkshire, and to be housed in the magnificent Grand Hotel which dominates the town. No.2 Flight of No.2 Squadron boasted 3 Leading Aircraftsmen, 4 Corporals and 2 Flight Sergeants – the latter two being air gunners who had each just completed tours of thirty bomber operations.

We were there from May to August 1942 and despite the war there were plenty of folk on holiday so we enjoyed life with good Yorkshire beer and jolly dance halls. The civilian folk were undoubtedly thrilled by the sight of squads and flights of young airmen marching around the town at 130 to the minute or drilling in the open spaces or having fun and games in shorts on the sand as a part of physical training. They must have been fascinated by the sight of Morse signals from Aldis lamps on the end of the pier which were being read or otherwise by cadets on the balcony of the Grand.

Chapter Two

GRADING SCHOOLS

A NUMBER of the airfields operated by flying clubs and schools before the war were taken over by the RAF to become Elementary Flying Training Schools, and by 1942 many of these had become Grading Schools. These were a part of the assessment procedure used in selecting potential aircrew into the next stage of training as pilots, navigators or bomb aimers.

On therefore to No 15 EFTS RAF Carlisle for twelve hours flying on Tiger Moths – a biplane with two open cockpits in tandem and a Gypsy Major engine of 120 horse-power. At last an aeroplane – it had been a long road, but here we were and whatever happened I would get at least twelve hours of pilot training. The thrill of meeting my first flying instructor, Pilot Officer Airey, was quite indescribable. I believe that I expected him to have two heads or something to indicate that he was quite different from other mortals. I still remember as clearly as if it had been yesterday, the moment just after 0900 on the 24th of August when the Tiger Moth passed above the hedge at the boundary of Kingstown aerodrome – a sight that served to convince me that I was actually flying.

Pilots are issued with logbooks in which to record every flight, but there was no guarantee that we would fill more than the first page so we were given a double page torn out of a standard logbook on which to record our flying at Grading School. I still have mine and it shows that I flew seven hours and forty minutes with P/O Airey before I had to undergo the 7/8 hour test with P/O Woodley. Airey then went on leave so I was transferred to Sergeant Lancaster (that was a good wartime name) for three trips before flying on a solo test with P/O Woodley on the 7th September. I did not know the result of the test at that time – instructors tend to keep secret the fact that they intend to send a student solo, until a few seconds before they get out and send him off – it has something to do with the build-up of nervous tension, and it still applies today.

The test had been flown from our satellite airfield just over the

Stanley Ward – re-united with his first 'mount', a Tiger Moth, at a Fly-in, Holbrook, Ipswich, June 1995.

border into Scotland (used to reduce the traffic at the main field), and unfortunately the weather was deteriorating so we were forced to hustle back to the main field. I had to wait until the 9th when Sgt Lancaster rushed us over in a ten-minute flight to the satellite where he got out of the aeroplane and ordered me to do one circuit (takeoff, circuit and landing) and to bring the aeroplane back in one piece.

Again the memory is quite clear – as the wheels left the ground my fleeting comment to myself was "well – you're airborne now old mate so you've got to get it down". Absolute elation – I was singing on the downwind leg. As I 'held-off' to land, the wheels clipped the ground just a split second too soon so the Tiger ballooned a bit, it was nothing, but a tiny squeeze of throttle reduced the bump on the second touchdown and resulted in a perfect three-pointer.

On the same day, a further 20 minutes with Sgt Lancaster, and a final 30-minute flight test with the Flight Commander, completed my Grading Course – I had a total of 12 hours and 10 minutes flying time.

Back at the main field Cadet Pidsley took my photograph on that very day, in full Sidcot flying suit and leather helmet complete with Gosport voice tubes dangling from the ears.

The skies over the United Kingdom were a bit crowded with aircraft of all commands of the RAF as well as those from the Dominions, the USA, Germany and even one or two from Italy, so it was obviously easier to take trainees to the aeroplanes and instructors than to bring aeroplanes and fuel to blockaded Britain where there was a shortage of everything including instructors.

So we were packed off to an Embarkation Centre at Heaton Park Manchester to wait for a boat to take us somewhere for something and we were billeted with good Lancashire families around and about. We were kept alive and active by various fun and games like drill and marching. It may be that it all takes time to assess aircrew or that there is just a slight touch of cruelty in the sorting circles, because we were left waiting for some time before being advised of our future role in this war.

The film 'Journey Together' faithfully showed the scene of hopeful airmen waiting in the rain for their names to be called. Coming top in ground subjects at ITW and going solo at grading school should have made me reasonably confident as hundreds of us paraded similarly in the rain in November to hear what we were destined to become.

As a 'W' I had a long wait during which I saw many a strong men burst into tears at being selected bomb aimer, and there were even a few who took a poor view of being selected pilot when all they wanted to do was to bomb the bastards! My name was eventually reached – pilot!

Stanley Ward on the day of his first solo flight, 9 September 1942 at Carlisle.

OVERSEAS

So, we were still on the rails but did not get on the move again until the 18th December when in the dead of night we assembled with full kit – that is, one kitbag of ordinary gear plus one packed with flying kit. Almost secretly we marched to a small railway station on the other side of the park to board a train to where we did not know. It was not long however before the more-travelled types were speculating on our progress and muttering about the north, to be proved correct as coming daylight revealed the approaches to Glasgow. Down at the docks we boarded the Royal Mail Ship 'Andes', a very new liner of 25,000 tons which had been intended for the South American luxury cruise trade but was now a troopship.

The next day we were waved off by dock workers and others as the ship crept down the Clyde to Gourock where after a compass swing in the wide river we joined a convoy of ships going out to sea. We still had no idea of where we were going but we knew that flying training was carried out in Rhodesia and South Africa and in Canada and the United States of America so we could get some idea if we watched to see whether we turned left or kept straight on after leaving the Clyde. In the light of dawn next day it was plain to see that the ship was getting ahead of the others in the convoy and would soon be alone with its superior speed; the Captain confirmed this as he issued dire warnings over the public address system of what would happen if we did not obey the strict rules about keeping off the open decks after dark and not throwing anything over the side at any time – we still did not know where we were headed.

Many troops had their first experience of sleeping in hammocks but as a Corporal I was appointed as a guard commander for the period from ten until one by day and by night, so I had the privilege of a bunk. My duties involved the placing of ten guards at various points about the ship, keeping an eye on them and bringing them off again. Their job was to ensure that all was well and to see that there was no infringement of the rules about security. It followed that I had a free run of the ship even at night – but it was not always easy; a chap dying of seasickness in his hammock was not interested in going on guard duty, because death was an acceptable option. It follows that a Corporal laying down the law was of no consequence.

In addition to troops going out for training there were others going home and as I soon discovered, many wives and families travelling to be with their men who were stationed in Canada – so we must be going to Canada!

Duties with the guard took me into the galley where I was able to make a good friend of Cliff, the first-class chef with whom I discussed many things and from whom I learned that at around midnight, dishes of unwanted food came down from the first-class section of the ship and that if I were there at the time I might find some tasty morsels to supplement the two meals a day from our galley which was the lot of the ordinary troops. I should say that Cliff fed only the service officers and the families referred to above.

I must have appeared a bit naive when I told him of my disgust at having to chase a Major and a woman caught snogging in various forbidden parts of the ship; were not the civilian ladies on board all going to join their husbands? "Stanley my boy" he said "take it from me that when a lady goes on board a ship she leaves her morals on the dockside". I raised the question of survival in his position below decks in a ship like this sailing these dangerous waters on her own. He had been sailing since leaving school, and from the start of the war had been moving troops to and from various theatres of lively activity. "They'll get me one day but it is pointless to worry about it so we just carry on". I am happy that they certainly did not get the RMS Andes on this trip – in fact she survived the war.

Our eating arrangements involved bunches of 21 of us at a table, and two of these had to go to the servery to obtain the trays of food for the group. We ate out of our mess tins with our own eating irons. Tea was collected individually from urns in our personal mugs. At times the sea was a bit rough so one or two could not face the galley – the best of these was when there were only three of us to share the sausages and mash for 21 – the anti sickness secret of at least two of us was to keep eating and to play portable chess while we queued at the wonderful shop which sold all those lovely sweets we had not seen since the start of the war – I rather liked almond creams.

At sometime during the voyage all sterling cash had to be handed in on the assurance that the receipt would be honoured in the dollar equivalent after arrival in Canada. In the early hours of Christmas day the cry went around that the lights of land had been sighted, and most of us got up to watch the port of Halifax Nova Scotia come closer until we were docked. There was hardly any delay in getting us ashore and aboard a train for the journey to No 31 Personnel Disposal Centre at Moncton New Brunswick. Unhappily the journey took most of the day and there was no food aboard. On the few occasions that the train did stop in the middle of a township sustenance was not available because it was Christmas Day, and in any case we were all penniless!

Whatever sort of welcome we may have expected at Moncton, most of us had to be disappointed because if they had known that we were coming they had forgotten it during the Christmas festivities, so there was no pudding for us. However, after finding beds in barrack blocks a few still-sober stalwarts hashed up a not very Christmassy but nevertheless very welcome meal.

BY TRAIN TO PONCA CITY

We left in mid-January by train to Chicago taking about a day and a half and giving most of us the first experience of living on a train. In Chicago we looked around doubtfully for Al Capone or Jack Dillinger but did not see a single gangfight in all the five hours we had before embarking on the Atchison, Topeka and Sante Fe railtrain for a two and a half day journey to Ponca City in Oklahoma.

The coaches of this train were far more plushy and up to date than the Canadian one but they were smaller and they lacked the wonderful sleeping facilities provided by pulling down part of the ceiling to make a bed for two of the four sitting below – the other two were accommodated by switching the seat backs to the gap between the seats. In the American train we had to make do with recliners.

Apart from the sight of the negro train crew shooting dice on the floor of the carriage perhaps the most amusing part of the journey was the behaviour of the American passengers who appeared to have a permanent glass of Coca Cola in front of them. The train passed through 'wet' and 'dry' States on its way south and we quickly learned which was which because the glass was accompanied by a bottle of rum while we were in a 'wet' State but the bottle disappeared whenever we crossed the border into a 'dry' State.

PONCA CITY

We reached our destination to what was almost a civic reception with an extraordinary variety of people assembled to greet us! The minority were ordinary American white people while the rest included cowboys, real red Indians and negroes. It did not take long to get used to being treated as something of a celebrity, shining, unashamedly I'm afraid, in the reflected glory of those who flew in the Battle of Britain and those who were then flying in the steadily increasing bomber raids into Germany. The Royal Air Force was still a novelty to most of the people of this small mid-western town of perhaps 35,000 population, and each new course was welcomed with open arms – a credit to the behaviour of earlier courses. At the start of every period of liberty from camp the road outside was lined with cars, and anyone who did not already have friends to go to would soon be taken aboard. If he wished he could in most cases then remain the guest of that family throughout his stay in Ponca City.

The hospitality was outstanding and all of us were left hopelessly in debt to the people of this town. I was fortunate in getting to know a large number of individuals and groups and they were without exception always friendly and generous. The group with whom I spent most time were met when I happened to answer the telephone in the barrack block and was asked by a young American lady to "say something, anything, just speak". I expect that I talked about the weather. She followed with "you've got a nice voice – will you come to a party tonight?" A dubious introduction but who is worried? I accepted the offer of the car at the gate at six o'clock, and so started a friendship with a group of families and other cadets which lasted the remainder of my time there and continues to this day.

Off duty periods were eagerly awaited perhaps because they were a bit limited and there was a great deal to do. American girls are really no different from girls at home and it has been said that they had nothing that our girls did not have, but they had it there. So while the G.I.s snapped up the spare and not so spare talent at home the boot was on the other foot in Ponca City. British boys in the RAF were considered to be quite attractive and although we did not have the cash advantage of the G.I.,in Britain, we wanted for nothing in female attention. We did in fact receive an extra allowance to meet the higher cost of living in the USA which amounted to no less than seven shillings and sixpence (37.5p) per week.

We were allowed out only on Wednesdays evenings until 2200 hours, Saturdays to 2359 and Sundays after Church Parade until 2200 hours. There was no messing about on a flying course in the USA – they could not have the cream of British youth gallivanting about with all that lovely American womanhood every night of the week, and woe betide you if you got any ideas about international marriage. The complications of the payment of allowances to the wife and perhaps the widow were far too much, to say nothing of the distraction to the pilot under training who would shortly have to leave the side of his bride to go and fight the war.

So although King's Regulations could not rule against human nature in this sort of thing, nevertheless anyone thinking about it would soon find himself back in Canada either to continue his training there if he were lucky or, more likely, to start a navigator's course because he was clearly unsuitable for pilot training.

Oklahoma was a dry State at this time so it was no great problem to stay off the liquor. There was a local bootlegger where you just knocked on the green door, and if your eyes were the right colour you were admitted to pay half a dollar for a small glass of doubtful looking liquid with a flavour not unlike what I imagine oil to have. It was not so much the booze that put most of us off as the atmosphere in which it had to be drunk, and many like me were satisfied with the one visit for experience.

A near-beer was also available in beer bars and we enjoyed that in the absence of anything better. It was a gassy lager type of beer into which the locals gaily sprinkled salt and accompanied it with numerous hard boiled 'cackle berries'. This stuff was always sold off the ice – we were once refused a beer in such a bar when the barman said "I don't have any" – when asked about the crates of bottles clearly visible he replied that they were warm. We surely added to the numbers of those who considered the British to be a little peculiar when we said that we would have some anyway.

NO 6 BRITISH FLYING TRAINING SCHOOL

But to go back to our arrival when we had got down from the high train which had stopped dead across the main street of the town. Buses took us the four miles to the Darr School of Aeronautics which was No 6 BFTS, one of six such schools in the USA set up for the training of RAF pilots during the war. The school was equipped with US Army Air Corps aeroplanes and ground training aids, the instructors were approved American civilians and the aeroplanes were maintained by civilian personnel.

Administration of the cadets, and discipline, was entirely RAF and the final check flights were conducted by RAF Officers. The RAF staff consisted only of a Wing Commander Commanding Officer, a Flight Lieutenant Station Adjutant, one Flight Lieutenant and one Flying Officer who were check pilots, and a Sergeant physical training instructor – and a right doddle it was for the lot of them. Two U S Army Air Corps Captains were included in the establishment, one was a pilot and the other a surgeon.

Although six such schools had been set up, there were now only five because the one at Lancaster in California was closed in January 1943 – it appears that the attraction of nearby Hollywood became so much of a distraction for the RAF cadets that it was considered wiser to close it.

The camp guards were American civilians who each carried a six-gun in a holster on a cowboy type belt, and we were warned in no uncertain terms that they would not hesitate to use them on anyone trying to get in or out other than through the gate. The cookhouse was all American, so chow-time was to me anyway always a time of keen anticipation and I was never let down by the exciting food which was served there. Except for the hangars the camp was built entirely of wood in single storey blocks and it had its own swimming pool. Barrack huts were generously fitted with showers, drinking fountains and salt dispensers, and each had incredibly efficient hot or cold air blowers which operated automatically to maintain an acceptable air temperature in a place where the outside air temperature could vary between 20oF below to 120oF in the shade.

For those who survived it, the course here would take us through to RAF wings so we could look forward to 200 hours of flight training plus innumerable hours of ground school and 'link' trainer time. We would start on the Stearman PT17 for the primary stage of 70 hours and then proceed to basic and advanced on the AT6 Texan or as the RAF knew it, the Harvard, for a further 130 hours. The basic stage of 60 hours was earlier done on the BT13 Vultee which was a halfway aeroplane between the biplane PT17 and the hot ship AT6 but this had been withdrawn, probably because that stepping-stone proved to be unnecessary. The stages covered periods of nine weeks with a week of leave in between, but as I remember it the week between basic and advanced was dropped in favour of moving it to the end of the course.

The school had three courses running at the same time, one on each stage, and each course was divided into two Flights which alternated with the use of the aeroplanes and groundschool facilities so that we would fly in the morning of one day and be at groundschool in the afternoon switching to the opposite on the next day. Numbers and content of each course varied as time went on but by the time of No 12 there were eighty-six cadets – made up of sixty-nine from the RAF and seventeen from the US Army Air Corps. No 13 course had ninety-nine with eighty-one RAF and eighteen USAAC.

PRIMARY TRAINING

The Stearman PT17, also named the Boeing Kaydet, was a fabric covered biplane with fixed undercarriage, fixed pitch propeller and two open cockpits in tandem, the student occupying the rear seat for both dual and solo flying. It weighed 2600 lbs at maximum and was powered by a Continental seven cylinder radial engine which could develop 220 horsepower. This was started by two sweating individuals who cranked up a flywheel with a large two-man handle; at the appropriate speed, judged by ear, one of them would engage a clutch which turned the engine, and if that was in the mind it would start – always providing that the occupant of the cockpit had remembered to switch the magnetos on. If he hadn't he would learn some new language before the crankers started to wind it up again.

But this was one hell of an aeroplane and I enjoyed flying it very much – its nearest equivalent in the RAF was the Tiger Moth which could boast only 120 horsepower and weighed only 1900 lbs, so it was but a child compared with this monster.

The instrumentation of the PT17 was a bit primitive so present-day students may be surprised to learn that it offered only an airspeed indicator, sensitive altimeter, engine rev counter, oil pressure and temperature gauges and magnetic compass. They may be more surprised to learn that the version used for instrument and night flying described as 'instrument ships' and officially designated the PT17A had in addition just a 'needle and ball' and that was in the rear cockpit only. The needle indicates the rate of turn while the ball tells you whether or not the turn is in balance – these two indicators contained in a single dial are the absolute minimum for the maintenance of control without outside reference, that is when flying in cloud or other conditions under which vertical and horizontal references are obscured.

I believe that many of today's pilots would consider themselves deprived if they did not also have an artificial horizon (attitude indicator), a gyroscopic direction indicator and a vertical speed indicator, to say nothing of a 720 channel communications radio and perhaps thousands of pounds worth of radio-navigation aids.

My instructor on the PT17 was Noel Houk a young man so keen on flying it just wasn't true. He had worked his way through to his civilian flying licences and to this job which kept his eyes shining with sheer enthusiasm and the joy of living. He celebrated his first one thousand hours flying time while I was with him. One of nature's gentlemen, he felt very keenly the responsibility he had in his task of training these young lads who would go on, well some of them, to pit their skills and risk their lives flying against the enemy. His affection for his students, four British and one American, was obvious even to us. I met him again in 1992, in retirement after many years as a training captain on the Boeing 747!

Flying at 6BFTS started for me on the 21st of January 1943 with one or perhaps two trips each day going through the routines of effects of controls, straight and level flight, climbing and descending, taxying, medium level turns, further effects of controls, stalling and spinning, taking off and landing into wind, co-ordination of controls and so on to first solo on January 30th after seven hours and thirty five minutes dual instruction. Only it was really my second first solo because I had done the one in Scotland on a Tiger Moth, but that was only a ten minute affair whereas this was a full thirty five minutes of supervised takeoffs circuits and landings.

Things now moved pretty rapidly because we no longer had to wait for the availability of the instructor to fly with us, so hours and experience built up, and by February 6th when we started instrument flying training I had ten hours and forty nine minutes dual and four hours and seventeen minutes solo on the PT17 including solo stalling and spinning. This brought the first life or death decision for the trainee – the moment of deliberately going into a spin alone without the comfort of an instructor to help if anything 'like went wrong'!

Dual instruction was given roughly alternately with solo practice and in addition there were regular visits to the Link Trainer for simulated instrument flying. The Link trainer was the forerunner of the present-day simulator but it was a much simpler machine operated by air pressure so that the whole thing floated on air, and reasonably faithfully produced the movements of an aeroplane, any aeroplane, by the operation of similar controls. It could not produce "G", that is there were no acceleration forces, so we got no feeling of pressure down onto the seat in tight turns or in pulling out from dives and we got no push in the back on opening the throttle. Also although the Link banked in turns, the forces were not balanced so there was a feeling of falling towards the lowered wing which is not present in the real thing – that is, if the real thing is flown accurately!

The Link could be stalled and it was capable of spinning, which was quite frightening on instruments under the closed hood with an indicated high rate of descent, although the machine was of course securely fixed to the floor.

The use of the Link was however invaluable in the learning of instrument appreciation and procedures. A "crab" crawling across a chart on the instructor's table indicated the path flown, so that accuracy in flight and in carrying out instructions could be checked directly. It was possible also to simulate rough air so that the machine rocked about quite alarmingly and it became extremely difficult to maintain control – which was what it was intended to be all about.

Probably the most easily remembered fact about the Link trainer was the beauty of the instructors. Sex equality had already reached this scene, and these ladies must have been chosen for their physical attributes as well as prowess in their jobs – something which did a great deal to reduce our hatred of the dreaded Link.

Night flying began for me on February 11 with general handling and four practice landings with my instructor. This programme continued until by March 10, I had 4 hours 45 minutes dual and 45 minutes solo at night.

It was a Wednesday which was a liberty evening so, following usual

Stearman PT 17A B227 before and after the author's night flight, 11th March 1943.

habit, the group of us spent this at a roadhouse talking, dancing and sipping coke. Coke was normal not only because of night flying scheduled for that night but also because it was cheaper and because it was the stuff that everyone around you was drinking in this 'dry' State – many an evening was enjoyed at such a roadhouse where we could occupy a four or six-seater cubicle, drinking coke from the inevitable tub of ice, and dancing on the tiny floor in the middle of the room. Not very costly so we had to conclude that the proprietors made their money out of the nickels which were put into the remote coin-box selectors with which each of the twenty-odd cubicles were fitted and which operated the huge and ornate juke-box.

Anyway, burping with coke but nothing else, we duly reported back at base shortly after 2200 hours and after picking up flying clothing and parachutes, we were whisked away in a truck to a satellite field about five miles distant. At night the main field was used for the advanced courses with their bigger and faster aeroplanes and their much more extensive night flying programme. Also they were subject to air traffic control by radio which the primary trainers did not have. Primary night flying was mainly concerned with takeoffs and landings so we were pushed off to an extensive area of grassland on which the takeoff and landing path was indicated by two lines of paraffin flares.

The first student on each aeroplane would start his detail from base with his instructor, and they would finish up at the satellite where the flarepath had already been laid and lit by the ground crews. The rest of us would be there and ready in time for the second detail.

On this particular evening my flying started on a check ride with my instructor who was satisfied after one takeoff, circuit and landing – ten minutes – that I was fit to fly solo again for practice landings. I duly completed the first without any evident difficulty, because as I stopped at the holding position the instructor gave me the traditional thumbs-up signal made visible by the flickering light of number one flare. This indicated his satisfaction with my performance and cleared me to do another one. A green light from the control position was the okay to taxi on to the flarepath, line up and hold – on the second green I opened the throttle and was soon tingling with the thrill of the surge of the 220 hp as the Stearman trundled down the grass runway and lifted into the dark sky.

Immediately after takeoff it was necessary at night to concentrate on the instruments – particularly the turn indicator – to ensure that the nose of the aeroplane did not yaw to left or right during the climb out when there might not be sufficient external reference by which to keep straight. At 200 feet, less than half a minute, a look back was needed to ensure that you were still in line with the two rows of flares – any attempt to look back earlier could easily result in some small loss of control with insufficient height for recovery. On this occasion my casual glance back revealed nothing! The flarepath was not in sight! Strange! Where could it have gone? A quick check of the instruments indicated that I was keeping straight, and my compass heading was still that of the takeoff direction – well, within a few degrees anyway and certainly not enough to lose the lights.

They were gone however, and to make matters worse there was no sign of any lights anywhere. There was no blackout here in the mid-west but the normally warm glow of the city had also disappeared and there was not a single light visible anywhere on the ground; a glance upwards did nothing to help because not one of the millions of stars could be seen. Quite suddenly I felt very lonely – the aeroplane was cut off from everything, there was just nothing to be seen, the earth and the sky had disappeared.

One must stay relaxed at times like this and that was no problem because the concentration required for flying 'with sole reference to the instruments' kept me busy enough to ensure that panic could not take over. The circuit pattern was a square, or rather rectangular, path over the ground made up of a straight climb out in line with the flarepath to 200 feet followed by a ninety degree level turn to the left on to the cross-wind leg and a further climb to 500 feet. Another level turn to the left brought us on to the down-wind leg which was level and parallel to the flarepath for about two minutes before another level left turn was required on to the base-leg from which the descent was started and during which a left descending turn was made on to the final approach towards the landing path in the same direction as the takeoff.

Nothing to it as they say, but – with no visual references there was no possibility of squaring up with the two lines of lights that formed the flarepath. The only means I would have of keeping square was the magnetic compass, and that was no easy task with my modest five hours of instrument flying training. The Stearman did not boast an artificial horizon nor a gyro-driven direction indicator (instruments which give a direct indication of the aeroplane's attitude in pitch and roll and a positive reading of its heading), so all I had was a turn and balance indicator by which to judge whether or not my wings were level.

By this famous 'needle and ball', the needle would be upright if I were not turning and if the wings were level as well, the ball would be nicely in the centre. If I could keep it all like that and avoid either accelerating or decelerating the aeroplane, then the magnetic compass needle would be showing the correct heading.

So, this was no time for night-dreaming, I had to do something about it because with no radio communication nor navigation aids I would soon be lost without hope if I did not get my finger out, and fast. The only thing to do, was to complete the circuit on instruments as if nothing had happened and then perhaps the flarepath would come up okay under my nose on the final approach. My present heading of 080 degrees was good so a ninety degree turn to the left would be 350 degrees – and that took some working out because mental arithmetic is not easy in the air – but what is the compass turning error at the completion of a turn towards the North? Do we turn beyond the required heading or is it the one where you have to roll out before you reach it?

Couldn't think that one out at that moment so decided to turn and roll out early – it could be corrected later. Turns made by reference to the magnetic compass must not be at more than rate one which is achieved by keeping the bank angle at less than 15 degrees, more than this and the compass goes mad because of the vertical component of the earth's magnetic field – and if you expect me to enlarge on this subject here then you are reading the wrong book. But I have no instrument to indicate the angle of bank so aileron has to be applied very gently watching the dreaded turn needle and taking off the aileron at the right time.

The heading on roll out was incredibly enough not far out so I climbed up to 500 feet, levelled out and turned left again, to 260 degrees. Confidence was growing rapidly, this was after all the first time I had flown on instruments for real – up to now all such flying had been simulated, with the outside blanked out artificially by a hood over my cockpit while the instructor remained in the clear. Well I was still flying so I must have learned something about it, and I was even holding reasonable headings so the flarepath lights must come back into view in just a few minutes from now and all will be well.

Another level turn to a heading of 170 degrees put me on to the base leg where I started a gentle descent before the final approach turn on to the heading of 080. Now was the time that things should be coming into sight again, but there was nothing to be seen! Check heading good, still descending but now at 150 feet, we (me and the aeroplane) cannot go down much more – thank heavens this is wide open flat country – ease in some power to level off, suddenly – lights!

But they are directly below me – my circuit had been spot on directionally but I am too high, and there is no hope of getting on to the flarepath from here. The only possibility is a tight 360 degree turn and the hope that the lights come up again in a better position. I duly started a turn as steep as I dare to the right, then a sudden fear grabbed me that there may be other aircraft trying to get in, but I dismissed this thought as quickly as it had come because there was nothing I could do about it anyway. If there were others they could be anywhere so there was not much point in following strict circuit procedures, and in fact I must have been the last aeroplane to takeoff so the chances were that anyone in front of me had been cleverer than I and had got down by now.

With eyes standing out like chapel hatpegs searching for the glimpse of a light I stopped the turn on a heading of simple guesswork, but there was nothing in sight. This was now bloody dangerous, the 'this' being the matter of wandering around at about 100 feet on instruments, so I elected to climb. At 800 feet there was more room to correct any mistakes I might make and it was possible to breath again and to give some serious thought to the predicament in which I found myself.

Whatever was it? It could not be fog because I would probably be above it at this height. It was unlikely to be cloud to creep in right down to ground level. There was nothing giving a clue from the open cockpit. The extraordinary thing was that I felt remarkably calm about it all – probably a touch of the optimism of youth that something always turns up, my guardian angel would see to that. But be sensible about it young fellow, you must try to stay in the area, otherwise when the clearance comes you will not be able to find the flarepath. Also, remember that Oklahoma is a very big place, sparsely populated and with vast areas of nothing. So it seemed to be a pretty good idea to stay around here otherwise if I did eventually have to use my parachute, it would be a hell of a job to find me.

So I started a gentle turn to the left and continued going round and round. Now this can become very boring to an impatient young man with nothing to see but the phosphorescent glow of the instruments under the meagre instrument lighting – and eventually the curiosity aroused by the feeling that there must by now be something to see lower down became overwhelming and I could not resist the desire to throttle back a bit and start a descent. I might after all be in a layer of cloud which was now clear of the ground.

But this was where my limited instrument experience let me down – well something has to be blamed – because as we progressed into the descending turn to the left the nose of the aeroplane gently yawed left towards the ground and the bank gently increased – it is at least reasonable to believe that this is what happened because the instruments soon indicated that we were in a spiral dive with airspeed and rate of turn rapidly increasing, and this was costing height and we did not have a lot of that to start with.

Now what was it that I had been told? If you get into a spiral dive on instruments, throttle back and take off the bank before you pull out of the dive. Oh yes, I had done this many times in simulated conditions so here we go, move the stick to the right and push in a bit of rudder, watch the needle and ball – there we are, turn stopped and the ball is in the centre so the wings are level. Great stuff Ward, now ease out of the dive, gently, keep straight, how much height have we got left? 150 feet, that's good.......

I didn't even feel the bump! It was sometime afterwards that I found myself sitting, at least I thought I was sitting, in the cockpit of an aeroplane, with nobody nor anything else around. It was very quiet and I wondered why I was there. It seemed a bit foolish to remain where I was so I might as well get out.

That was where I made my second mistake. Would you believe that you could think that you were sitting the right way up when in fact you were hanging upside down? In those days we secured ourselves in the aeroplane by means of a simple lapstrap which had a quick release lever, so all that I had to do was to shift this lever....and that is how I fell out on to my head and became unconscious for the second time that night.

The next time that I came round from blissful oblivion I found myself lying in a heap on the ground with a lot of mud around and a light coating of snow. It was when I tried to get up that I realised that there was something wrong – an agonising pain in my right hip made it clear to me that I would not be walking far for sometime to come. I dozed off and woke again at intervals and it was much later before I became aware that my right foot was very cold – the rest of me was warm enough because I was wearing a full Irvine suit (sheepskin zip-up jacket and trousers) flying boots, leather helmet and gloves, scarf and goggles.

The cause soon became apparent, there was no boot on my right foot. It must be here somewhere so I groped around and eventually found it, but unhappily it was impossible to reach down to put it on, nor could I move my leg to manoeuvre the foot into it.

But I did have the common sense and ability to drag myself away from what was obviously the result of a most enormous prang. A painful yard or so enabled me to remove the parachute harness with its seat pack attached which was not doing anything to increase my personal comfort. Somehow I was bright enough to position the pack into use as a pillow and thus I was able to fade away again in a much more conventional posture. It was very dark, damp and extraordinarily quiet.

I may have applied my long held simple principle of not worrying about any problem if there is nothing you can do about it – although it is probably more correct to say that I was too dopey to apply too much practical thought to what my next move should be. It was clear that I had a distinct discouragement in the form of real pain, to any idea of physical movement, so I just lay there.

The quiet of the night was eventually disturbed by the noise of a truck engine in the distance and eventually I was able to see some lights moving along a road some way away but definitely coming closer. Then I saw what looked like a searchlight scanning all over the place, and I clearly remember delving into my suit to find a handkerchief which I got ready to wave in the beam as it reached me – it must reach me! But I might as well have saved the effort because when the light did reach me it illuminated a huge silver wing which was sticking apparently vertically out of the ground just behind me, giving me for a brief instant some further evidence that I had not done a lot of good to Uncle Sam's Stearman PT 17A number B227.

The light passed on but it could not have missed that lot, and true enough it stopped and swept back finally locating this grotesque monument to my flying skill. I had no idea of the time, either because I could not be bothered or because my watch had anyway stopped at 0130 which was the moment of impact, but the relief at being found was quite something. I suppose that I had secretly thought that nothing much would happen before daylight when with a bit of luck the wreckage might one day be sighted from the air by a searching aeroplane, rather like Ralph Graves was found by Jack Holt in the film "Flight" – circa 1933 – although I was not sure who would be the beautiful girl who, like in the film, pleaded with Jack to go up and search. The light went out and I lay in eager anticipation of the arrival of human beings who obviously cared about me enough to be out on a night like this. Soon I was lit up by a very bright torch held by the truck driver who was alone and who became very concerned about the state of my health. I told him that I was okay but that a stretcher would be necessary because there was something wrong with my right leg. He was however adamant that he would stay with me until someone else turned up – "It won't be long because there are dozens of cars and trucks in the search".

"Please, do go now, I am quite frozen and my leg hurts. I've been okay on my own until now and I can manage a little longer while you go and find a telephone". "But I don't like leaving you alone again". This fine fellow, who without doubt saved my life, visited me in hospital afterwards and told me that he had thought that I must be dying. He was Farrel Watson, Assistant Superintendent of Maintenance, and it was a wonderful and breathtaking experience to meet him again, with his wife Zella at their home, during a visit to Ponca City in 1989. The next day he became a celebrity in the local newspaper and on radio and t/v, where he showed the huge torch (flashlight) he was using that night – which he had modified so that it would take twice the original number of batteries.

The fact was that when the PT17 first hit the ground, my head had gone forward into the instrument panel knocking me out, severely damaging my front teeth, and breaking the right lens of my goggles from which a piece of the glass had cut my face somewhere near the eye; when I came round and released the safety strap I fell on to my head and my face became caked in mud – then when I had settled down propped against the parachute, my head had fallen to the left, and blood had run from the eye across and down my face. It had thus washed a line through the mud before congealing so that when my finder had shone his torch on me it appeared to him that my face had been cut across from the right eye to my throat on the left side. He did not want to leave me to die alone in the field!

However I prevailed upon him to go, and as he sought a telephone

Farrel Watson, who found the author after the night crash in 1943, talks it over with him at Farrel's home in Ponca City in 1989.

he met other searchers and directed them to the scene, so that long before the base Doctor arrived I was surrounded by fellow students, instructors and ground staff, and was soon underneath a huge pile of sheepskin clothing as they stripped off to help keep me warm. I heard efforts being made to break off a piece of the aeroplane big enough to carry me to the road while we were waiting for the ambulance, but this didn't work so they then tried to jolly me up with conversation. Some said that I was quite witty in my position as the centre of attention.

The Flight Surgeon duly arrived and gave me a shot of morphia to ease the pain from the hip. It seems that it was about 0430 when I was found so I had been there for three hours, but it was 0630 when I was wheeled into Ponca City civil hospital. The local press reported that I had "...come to ground about a mile from the flying field" but it was actually bit more than that although it did indicate that my steady turn had kept me in the vicinity, because I had in fact been airborne for forty minutes.

From the wreckage and marks on the ground it was estimated by the experts that I had hit the ground at about 120 mph in a nose-down attitude with the wings level. The main wheels of the fixed undercarriage had gouged two huge grooves in the earth of the ploughed field causing the aeroplane to go up on to its nose where the radial engine had been wiped off. I and the remainder careered onwards actually leaving the ground again still rotating so that it landed this time firmly on the tail from where it twisted and toppled over to finish up inverted and facing the way it had come. The tail-wheel was in fact just behind my cockpit and the front cockpit was completely wrecked.

My right flying boot had been jammed in the wreckage of the front cockpit so that when I released the lap strap I fell only until my weight was taken by the right leg – resulting in a dislocated hip. My foot then slipped out of the boot and I fell on my face into the mud. The boot obviously then fell by itself. The shock and exposure resulted in pneumonia which all but stopped me from breathing by the Friday and it was reckoned that I would pass away during the weekend – when I did eventually get back I had to do some retrieving of my toiletries and civvy underpants and vests which had been swiped by my barrack room-mates.

The 'ifs' are interesting – if the engine had not been knocked off so early we might have burned and you would not be reading this. If I had not released my lap strap so carelessly I might have walked away with a cut eye and a headache. If my leg had not been trapped I might have fallen on to my head from a greater distance and broken my neck....ah well!

The Court of Enquiry conducted by the Commanding Officer, the Adjutant and the Chief Flying Instructor began its work in my hospital room later in the day so as to get my story before I had a chance to die with my secrets. I was however quite coherent in spite of much morphia and other delights and my hip had been relocated. The story was told and although I could remember every incident, there was no recollection whatever of the bump when we hit the ground.

The finding of the Court was that the accident was caused by the inclement weather and my lack of experience. I had 62 hours and 28 minutes flying time.

The snowstorm, for that is what it was, had been forecast but the decision on night flying had been that flying could start and would continue until it got nearer. I was the only student solo at the time. Two aeroplanes in front of me got down because the instructors, knowing that it was coming, recognised it as soon as the visibility started to reduce. The first one landed on the flarepath, while the second one cut the corners, found the flarepath occupied by the landing aeroplane so he landed on the unlit field to the left of the flarepath – safely by luck. I continued on my happy and ignorant way, flying the disciplined circuit to arrive on the final approach too late. My glimpse of the flares was possible only when I was in a position above them that allowed me a sight line along the path of the snowflakes.

In the light of experience since then, it has seemed to me that the decision to continue flying until the weather arrived, especially with an inexperienced student out solo, was perhaps not one of the better decisions that could have been made.

But at least it gave me my first real experience of being a celebrity – can you imagine the curiosity value of a British boy from the Royal Air force, lying in a small Church Hospital in the mid-west of the USA? As soon as I had recovered sufficiently to appreciate what was going on, I began to enjoy every minute, flattered by every face that appeared around the door to get a glimpse of this marvel. I could get a tray of coffee from the nurses at any time of the day or night and I am sure that there was a bit of competition to get in to do for me. I could not fail to enjoy this sort of thing. But of course all good things have to come to an end, so after three weeks they considered that I was well enough to be moved to and treated at the sickbay on the camp – oh misery!

Discharge came after a total of five weeks and I was sent on leave for three weeks to convalesce – and incidentally to learn to walk again. Bob and Joey Ratliff took me into their home without hesitation and brought me back to full fitness. Joey was one of the gang and she flew as a private pilot from the civilian side of the same airfield, so I occasionally spent time on the balcony of the flying club enviously watching my colleagues continuing their training. On one such occasion one of our school flying instructors passed me on the balcony, stopped, came back, looked at me and asked "Say aren't you that guy Ward?" On my assurance that I was indeed, he made the never-to-be-forgotten-by-me observation "I wanna shake your hand man. I ain't never seen such a wreck that anyone lived through. Brother, you're sure livin' on borrowed time."

It was May 6th before I was pronounced fit to start flying again and I was taken up for a check ride with the Flight Commander, Mr Freye, a middle-aged, kindly, experienced instructor. I may have worried about my reaction to getting back – films I had seen in which the hero crashed an aeroplane had always indicated that you have to fly immediately after a crash otherwise your nerve is lost for ever. But come to think of it, I did not remember being frightened at any time during that night – I would be now – but at that time I was not haunted by any sort of imagination, and even as we hurtled towards the ground I was still oblivious of any impending calamity, so I had no dreadful visions to come back. And none did, so after fifty minutes of re-familiarisation, Mr Freye sent me off solo for twenty minutes of circuits and landings.

Training then continued through steep turns, formation flying, precautionary landings, aerobatics, taking off and landing out of wind, revisions and reviews, to the completion of the 70 hour primary stage of training. I could not catch up with my old course mates on number 12, because they were now eight weeks ahead of me, so I had to join the following Course 13. There was no more night flying for me because my flying programme was out of phase with their's, and no more primary night work was scheduled – it could hardly be laid on for a single cadet, even if that cadet was me! I now had a total of 82 hours and 11 minutes flying time.

Chapter Three

ADVANCED TRAINING

FLYING the mighty North American AT 6A started for me on the 6th of June 1943. What a thrill that was – but not before many hours had been spent sitting in the cockpit of one in the hangar, getting the atmosphere and learning where the 40-odd dials, tits and knobs were until I could find any one, blindfolded and without hesitation.

The AT 6A was a single-engined advanced trainer with a 550 horsepower Pratt and Whitney 'Wasp Junior' engine, retractable undercarriage, constant speed propellor and a tail-wheel. It was a low-wing monoplane, two-seater in tandem with the instructor in the rear seat and both of us under a sliding canopy. We were fitted with an all-purpose two-way radio which was tuned in by cranking a handle to find the various frequencies, including the local radio station which allowed us when solo to fly to the tunes of the day, like 'That Old Black Magic', and many an AT could be seen yawing about in the sky in time to the music as the student beat it out on his feet.

My advanced training was in the hands of Mr Neumann, a short thickset civilian of immense experience, who proved to be quite tough, was a great flyer and enjoyed the essential quiet sense of humour. Unhappily, throughout this period when so many souvenir photographs were taken, I never got one of him but I can still see him in my mind's eye. He stopped me from killing both of us on many occasions but I learned shortly after my return to England that he had died with a student in a flying accident.

I loved the AT 6A and had no difficulty in going solo from a satellite field for 25 minutes of supervised circuits and landings on the 14th June after five hours and twenty-two minutes of dual instruction and masses of encouragement from this man.

I do not remember any problem from the crash in the Stearman at any time during day flying. I was happy in the AT, not afraid of it and I flew it moderately well, receiving as many smiles as frowns from Mr Neumann. The first night flying for me since the accident was in an AT on the 6th July when I did 37 minutes of dual night familiarisation which included three takeoffs, circuits and landings – I thoroughly enjoyed the thrill of this in the monster with its exhaust flames lighting up the darkness, and it was a relief to note that I had no haunting memories or fears of that previous time in the air at night.

On July 12th Mr Neumann and I did a further one hour and two minutes which included four landings and some practice overshoot procedures – this is the art of converting an approach or a landing attempt into a climb away as would be necessary if you failed to get down on to the runway early enough to stop the thing, or if you managed such a bad bounce that the only way of saving anything for further use was to abandon that particular attempt to land, and to go round again. In his wisdom, my instructor did not send me solo that night. This was not outrageous – but some chaps were in fact already solo by now!

On the 14th July we again went night flying together and did thirty-five minutes and four landings, but again no solo! And many more of my course-mates were piling in the night solo hours by now. I did not mind being behind but it was an unpleasant, and unusual, position for me to be in. Was my nerve letting me down with some deep-seated memory haunting my sub-conscious? Were unseen visions of my last night-solo flight causing me to tense-up and fly badly, unconsciously, so as to avoid being sent up there again on my own?

On the 22nd we did another hour together with five landings – and no solo. Now it was getting serious. Mr Nuemann slapped me on the back and joked about it but it was no joke to me. I knew how easy it was to get CT'd – the dreaded endorsement of 'ceased training' – the threat of which hung over us all continuously, glowing bright red whenever a performance faltered or indicated a weakness somewhere. "Better to chop them at that stage than wait until they have an expensive bomber and a crew in their hands" was the quite reasonable philosophy, and there was a limit to what the most kindly instructor could do to save a student.

Soon I was the only one on the course who was not solo at night so my poor performance must by now have been brought to the notice of those above my instructor. Worse, the night flying programme must by now be nearing its end so that I might not be able to get the necessary solo flying done in time – that would be the end for me. The object of night flying training was, after all, not solely to pound around the circuit doing takeoffs and landings with your instructor, but rather to get on to night cross-country flying on your own or with another student.

There was no more night flying scheduled until the 28th July and during that day I had done two good solo trips and a dual formation flight with Mr Neumann. It happened to be graduation day for course 12 with which I had started back in January. There were my old comrades, resplendent with the beautiful RAF wings on the left breast of their uniforms, and they were celebrating their last evening in Ponca City. In spite of the fact that Oklahoma was a dry State there was plenty of Bourbon whiskey around, and one or two of the chaps were showing the unmistakeable signs of having had one or two too many. Desperately trying to hide my aching jealousy I joined my former mates, envious of their success and bitterly disappointed that I had fallen behind them but I was looking up to them as undoubted heroes – they were wearing pilot's wings weren't they?

Of course I could not have a drink with them – I would be night flying in a few hours time! What? Not join in a toast to us on our farewell? It may be the last time you see some of us, we could be dead before you get back to England. This went on a bit until eventually it was "Oh well, put like that how can I refuse – but only a small one please". Somehow or other that one was followed by another small one before some sense of responsibility, encouraged perhaps by fear of putting myself further into disfavour, gave me the moral courage to refuse any more. It would certainly be the end if I were not able to fly because I was pickled. It may have been the boisterous good wishes, the boozey encouragement of my devoted ex-course mates or the false courage instilled by the liquor, but I went solo that night!

Each year the RAF put on a Vaudeville show in the City Auditorium on the main street of Ponca City, and 1943 was no exception. The task was delegated to a Flying Officer on the staff who for one reason or another passed on to me the job of compiling and producing the show. Perhaps I talk too much about myself, because he had evidently learned that I had some experience in amateur shows before the war and in camp concerts in the RAF.

But this job was right up my street – I carried an extensive file of scripts, and was soon involved with the whole paraphernalia of show business, leading to the evening of Saturday the 3rd July which was well advertised by posters all over the city inviting people to 'See the Belle of Ponca' at the Grand Vaudeville, and ordering them to 'Be There' at 7.30 pm.

The 'Belle' was an old English melodrama in which I had played the belle, the hero and the villain in various performances called the 'Belle of...' wherever I happened to be at the time. On this occasion I played the female, as well as singing with the glee club, keeping the show going

6 B. F. T. S.

GRAND

VAUDEVILLE

By Kind Permission of Wing Commander C. A. Ball

At The City Auditorium, Ponca City

Saturday, July 3, 1943 at 7:30 P. M.

Adults, 45c; Federal Tax, 05c; Total, 50c.

Author dressed as the Belle of Ponca, for the RAF Vaudeville in the City Auditorium, July 1943. Inset: Copy of the ticket to the Grand Vaudeville at the City Auditorium, Ponca City in 1943 – note total cost of 50 cents.

and sharing the job of compere. The programme of 16 items ranged from a bunch of 'Gremlins' invading the auditorium and opening the curtains, to Cadet McMeekan in full highland costume playing the bagpipes initially in the road outside so that the sound gradually got louder as he entered from the foyer and marched down the centre aisle to the stage where he accompanied a group of dancing cadets in their 'Eightsome Reel'.

The only discordant note came at the start when I was showing concern at the small number present at 7.30. Mr Woodson Tyree, who had helped me enormously with the production, told me that I had made a mistake in timing the start so early because the theatre-going public in Ponca City were used to 8.00 pm and would probably not change their way of life for an RAF show!

I took his advice and surreptitiously delayed the start to 8.00 with the risk that some of the audience would be expecting things to move at 7.30 – so I should not have been surprised to receive a summons at 7.40 to report to the CO who was sitting in the front row with his wife. He was not amused about the delay and left me in no doubt that my explanation did not cover the case and that the thing should have started at the stated time regardless. His devotion to punctuality was to be tested on at least two more occasions within the next month to my own discomfort, but more about that later. However, the show was deemed to have been a success and received a full column appreciation in the Tulsa Tribune of Monday the 5th July.

After the trauma of my night solo problem, rapid progress was now possible and it was not long before contempt crept in with familiarity, but I was pulled up sharply by a quiet little incident at night. Night landings were practised from the main airfield using an electric flarepath laid on the grass unless the wind happened to be in line with the single concrete runway. I had been briefed to carry out circuits which involved the takeoff, a square circuit followed by the approach and landing.

After landing, the procedure was to taxi the aeroplane off the flarepath to the right, at which point the after-landing checks were carried out including raising the flaps from their down position in which drag was at a maximum to produce a steep approach, a shortened hold-off to touchdown and a reduced landing roll to a standstill. The careless could miss a part of these checks, but if a further takeoff were intended, it was likely that any omission would be detected during the pre-takeoff checks – that is, provided that the pilot was not again guilty of carelessness.

At the pre-takeoff point, with checks completed to my satisfaction, I radioed my readiness for takeoff again and duly received the necessary clearance, so I taxied the AT6 out on to the runway while my place at the pre-takeoff point was taken by another aeroplane which had just landed. With my left hand pushing open the throttle, the thrust of all 550 horse-power was released and the big trainer moved forward at the start of its takeoff run into the night.

The story would have ended at this point but for the sharp observation of the instructor in that aeroplane I had just left behind. His quick reaction produced a radio call "Aircraft taking off – your flaps are down". He had spotted the fully down flaps reflecting the light of a flare as the AT thundered past! It took only a moment to pump the pressure button and lift the flaps lever with my left hand to get the flaps going up as we accelerated to takeoff speed and a normal lift-off. Without that call, the drag of the flaps would have so reduced the gain in speed that we would not have had enough to provide the lift to balance our weight, and we would have hurtled on into whatever existed beyond the end of the flarepath. It is amazing what a lot you can learn about flying from an incident like that!

Many of the procedures so vital to flying an aeroplane become so instinctive that rigid adherence to them can lead to trouble. The day came when, as quite an advanced student, I taxied out by day in an AT6 with instructor Neumann in the rear seat. We taxied to a down-wind position which on this day was on the south side of the field giving us a takeoff over the hangar to which our flight office was attached – this would take us over the heads of our colleagues who would be sitting awaiting their turn in front of the building facing the airfield.

Pre-takeoff checks were completed meticulously to impress the instructor, and clearance was obtained by radio so we turned, lined up and opened the throttle to produce as efficient a takeoff as any reasonable eagle could have wished to see. Takeoff was now just a routine that had to be carried out before we could do any flying but it was always a good thing to behave well when the instructor was aboard so as to indicate that you did work hard when you were away practising solo. So, airborne – stop the wheels, select undercarriage up, throttle back to steady climb power, reduce the revs by adjusting the propellor pitch to cut down the dreadful noise – all done so fast that the instructor must be feeling that the front seat is occupied by none other than a 1943 Biggles!

But wait a second, because with equal lightning speed I had observed that we still had green lights indicating that the wheels were still down. "Wheels have not come up, Sir". In a split second came "Okay, select down and try them up again", and that is when it all went wrong! You see, there is a standard procedure in connection with the selection of ‘wheels down’, and the trained mind, well Ward’s trained mind anyhow, did not allow for any exceptions.

The problem was and still is that pilots, given the slightest chance, will land aeroplanes with their wheels up, and this makes a very expensive noise. So things are done to try to stop this habit. Today there are even some aeroplanes which have a jolly device that puts the wheels down automatically if you forget, but we enjoyed what is still more common these days, a horn which blares out its warning if the throttle is closed, as for an approach to land, while the wheels are still up or indeed if they are not actually locked down. The story is told, to emphasise the noise level that is experienced, of the character who was approaching to land with his wheels up and continued through the whole expensive exercise, in spite of repeated and increasingly frantic calls on the radio from the control tower where the controller had observed the forgetfulness. When asked why he had not taken any notice of the radio calls advising him that his wheels were not down, the luckless pilot pleaded that he could not hear anything but the noise from that bloody horn.

However, this is digressing – perhaps in an attempt to reduce by comparison, the level of the idiocy of my own behaviour. The fact is that the horn action can fail and the silence could then falsely indicate that the wheels were locked down leaving the pilot without any warning to save him. So, a procedure is used to cover even that contingency. As a part of the prelanding checks – without which no self respecting pilot would ever dream of starting his approach to land – we were required, before selecting wheels down, to close the throttle with the wheels up, in order to check that the horn made its noise. If it did, then the throttle was re-opened and the wheels were selected down. We waited then for the wheels to lower and lock, and the indicator lights to change from out to red to green which indicated that wheels were down and locked. But were they? Well we had to be sure, so the next move was to close the throttle again and observe no noise from the horn.

We could now safely assume that the wheels were waiting for the pilot gently to transfer the weight of the aeroplane to them, from the wings, at a reasonable rate of exchange. So you see, the computer between the ears is programmed to set the sequence in train as soon as the necessary stimulus is received. “Select down” said the instructor, so what is the first thing you do? Answer – close the throttle!

In the early climb just after takeoff, wheels down with all their drag, going towards the hangars, power already reduced – oh dear! What a time to close the throttle! In fairness, it did not take very long for the truth to dawn upon me that I had blundered, and it did not take long for me to get that 550 horse-power working for us again, but the reactions of the folk on the ground were even quicker because they were already fleeing left and right in front of the hangar to get out of the way of our probable crash-path. Of course, we made it over the hangar roof, but they did not often have aeroplanes as near to it as that.

Another piece of delicate mishandling on my part occurred when with Mr Neumann, I was practising side-slipping with wheels and flaps down. It was an uncomfortable exercise, with the nose held high, the right wing well down and bags of left rudder to prevent the aeroplane from weather-cocking towards the lowered wing. We had descended below 1,000 feet when I clumsily allowed the nose to come up too high; we instantly buffeted at the stall and the aeroplane started to yaw left into what would have been the entry into a spin.

It all happened so suddenly that it was only during the analysis back on the ground that I learned how close we were. Instructor Newmann had acted so quickly that we were climbing away before I had even reacted to the danger. In that time he had raised the flaps, retracted the undercarriage, opened up to full power, broken the stall and got us into the climb.

Then his quiet comment was, "I don't know what these ships are like in a spin below one thousand feet with gear and flaps down, but I was as sure as hell that weren't the time to find out."

CUMULO-NIMBUS OVER PONCA CITY

It was probably because unexpected bad weather was a little unusual in Oklahoma that we were caught out more than once. Secretly I, and probably many who knew about my first night adventure, must have given a thought to how I would react if faced again with adverse conditions while the memory of that night was still fresh in my mind.

It is in fact true to say that nobody really knows how he will behave when the pressure comes on, and a great deal of money is spent in trying to produce the best pilots in both the military and civil flying-world so that, with good training and equipment, they will have the greatest possible chance of surviving if something serious goes wrong. But we know that after all this it is still possible that a pilot will crack, and there is no way in which a pilot can be put under the strain of real stress, outside of the real thing. Many may survive a lifetime of flying without ever having such a weakness revealed and they may never know whether or not they would have stood up to it. Some are found to be wanting only in the actual awful moment, and then it is too late.

The high level of pay of airline pilots does not reflect the amount of work that they do, because there can be few jobs which require so little real effort. To some extent the pay rewards the high endeavour required to obtain and retain the necessary licenses. But to a large extent the rewards owe something to a myth – the myth that pilots are a rare breed who must be qualified for, and rewarded because of, their ability to remain cool in a crisis, and accordingly be able to bring that aeroplane down safely even if it loses a wing. The public who fly as passengers are happy that these pilots are highly paid – it helps to perpetuate the myth.

It is however a lot of nonsense, and most pilots are happy to allow to it to continue for obvious reasons. The evident proof of the fiction is displayed on every possible occasion by a popular press ever ready to find a hero in the pilot who survives in adversity, and if he dies, then it can usually prove well in advance of any inquiry and regardless of the fact that the aeroplane was completely out of control, that he gave his life avoiding a village, preferably one with an infants' school nearby, during the final plunge. Who is really going to argue with the press before the inquiry, and who remembers after it? Who wants to overstress the possibility of 'pilot error' when the pilot is dead, and absolute proof is impossible. The pilots' unions quite rightly make sure that the benefit of any doubt is given to the pilot. After all there is benefit in maintaining the myth so that pilots and operators would not want to do anything to bring it into question, provided that it does not interfere with flight safety.

However I am allowing my slip to show! I started this story in order to recall another eventful night flight in Oklahoma. Somehow we had some bad luck with weather in this part of the world where it should have been comparatively easy to get accurate forecasts – the middle of large land masses should not be areas of weather surprises. Perhaps because of this fact, weather briefing, which is so much a part of pre-flight briefing procedures in England, was not given there. The unexpected was not expected. So as usual, off we went this night, safe in the assumption that all we had to worry about was the serviceability of the aeroplane and our own competence. The aeroplane was the wonderful AT6 so there was no doubt about that, and – were we not the very cream of the flying world?

So it was, that on the 13th September, after the usual night flying check ride of ten minutes for a circuit and landing with my instructor to satisfy him that I was 'on the ball', I set out for the first solo local cross-country flight of four legs with turning points at Kaw City, Winfield and Harper, landing back after one hour and forty-five minutes. All very satisfactory and followed by a short break for a drag – yes we were daft enough to smoke in those days – then I was off again, this time a longer three-leg trip from base to Alva, to Harper and back to base.

Something under an hour later and before the airfield lights came into sight, it was evident that something was amiss because I could faintly hear on the radio other aircraft being directed not to land but to go to 'holding zones' where they would fly in circles. The zone system was a simple method of stacking aeroplanes to keep them out of each others way at night while they waited for their turn to land on the flarepath. The four zones were roughly located by imaginary lines drawn north to south and east to west through the centre of the airfield – thus zone one was to the north-east, two to the south-east and so on. If there were more than four aircraft, then vertical spacing was used and two in the same zone were separated by 500 feet.

As I got closer to base the radio volume improved, and my interest in the prospect of landing increased, so I took more careful notice of what was being said in these conversations. It seemed that because of a sudden increase in the wind strength and a change in the wind direction, all returning aeroplanes were being held off until this strange phenomenon passed away and safe landings became possible again. So it was easy to anticipate my own refusal to land and it was no surprise to be ordered into zone two at 2000 feet – I was in fact the sixth aeroplane to join the queue and was stacked 500 feet above some other character. One more was to join the happy band making a total of seven aeroplanes, all piloted by students because this was a time when the course was nearing its end and we were all getting our solo night hours in. It was after all, a bit late at night and time for most good instructors to be tucked up in bed with their ladies.

As I approached the airfield which was now clearly visible, some increase in turbulence became evident or in other words, it was becoming as rough as hell, but with lap strap tightened I soon located my zone and entered at the allotted height. Zone two was to the south-east of the airfield and was therefore largely over the city which was still well lit up. Strangely enough the visibility was quite good and there was no precipitation but it was of course quite dark and it was not possible to see what was going on down there on the field. Any radio enquiry from the circling aeroplanes was answered by a simple "Standby, we'll git yer down in just a little while".

After a lotta while, the requests from aeroplanes became more urgent – priority to land was asked for by one, and immediate landing permission was demanded by another but these were met with the routine answer. All this time, the air was getting rougher and the aeroplanes were being tossed about quite violently. In addition to the general roughness my machine like the others was continuously being rolled first one way and then the other, sometimes to the vertical, often so sharply that my head was frequently banged heavily against the side of the canopy. At one moment an off-the-clock rate of climb would be indicated, to be followed very quickly by a descent that could not be stopped in spite of full throttle being applied and the nose being pulled up way above the climbing attitude. The most outstanding effect of one of these up-currents, at least the one which was firmly recorded in my mind, was such that with the throttle fully closed and the nose stuffed down into the diving attitude so that the indicated airspeed was 200 mph, the rate of climb indicator showed that we were still climbing!

Something similar was clearly happening to someone else because a panic-stricken voice screamed over the radio that he was going up at 2000 feet per minute and he had another aeroplane 500 feet above him. A very calm voice came back, "Relax brother, I'm going up too".

It was at about this time that the terror that most of us must have felt began to show in some radio calls. Raised voices pleaded to be allowed to land, low fuel states were claimed to try to get some action, and one chap, mercifully never identified, was actually weeping over the radio.

The cool voice of the duty instructor now came from the control tower to all aircraft. The position was that the gale force winds seemed to have settled in one direction, but the flarepath was unfortunately now across and down-wind so it would be necessary to move the flares to re-align the landing path into wind. Work had started on this and, all being well, they would soon be bringing us down.

Few of us needed to be told that this was quite an operation. It was now pouring with rain and one could imagine the problem of getting this job done in a howling gale with the modest numbers of ground staff on duty at night. Two lines of lights 4000 feet long, with the essential lead-in and out paths, could not be re-sited in five minutes, so you buggers who are crying might as well dry your tears. Yes, my mouth was dry, and the hammering the aeroplane was receiving and passing on to me seemed to be getting worse, and yet faith in the AT 6 was undoubted because there is no recollection of any worry on that score, but questions were now being asked in the mind -who will be the first to get in – and who will be the last?

As if to answer these silent questions, the Tower indicated that it was now planning the approaches because one by one we were being called as to our fuel state. One could have cheated here I suppose, but I do not remember even thinking of it, rather I remember the dreadful task of trying to read the fuel gauges in these conditions. The aeroplane had a tank in each wing, and the gauges were situated near the floor of the cockpit, one to each side of the seat. The lighting of these was not too bright and we did not carry torches (flashlights), they could after all be read quite easily in normal steady cruise conditions, but this was not a steady cruise. The danger from putting your head near to the side of the cockpit was something very real because we did not wear bone-domes in those days, so such a move was courting an even heavier clout against the rather hard metal side. It was also far from easy with the violent movement to focus the eyes into the gloom of the cockpit floor for long enough to get a reading.

It was difficult enough to ride the storm and keep the aeroplane in some sort of flying attitude when the eyes were glued to the instruments except for an occasional glimpse at the blurred picture of lights below, but with the head down there, chaos ensued for a few moments each time I had a try to get a reading. One could of course use the normally far more reliable method of ascertaining fuel remaining by calculating the amount used from time flown and rate of consumption, and taking this away from the amount we started with. But this was a bit difficult – the delay was considerable and the consumption could be wildly different in these conditions of large throttle changes.

The reading was eventually obtained, although the questioner on the ground must have wondered what was taking all the time in reading a couple of gauges. As far as I was concerned, even if the consumption was 30 gallons an hour I appeared to have enough not to have to worry about using a parachute for a little while.

I wonder what would happen in a parachute with such variable air currents – presumably there would be times when the parachutist would be going upwards – what an interesting thought, but I was not thinking along those lines at that time, the flight was too intense and the calls of some of the other pilots were quite distracting. In a strange sort of way, I was enjoying this – perhaps it was the fact that for most of my life I had suffered from some sense of inferiority, whereas during this hectic period I was able to feel just a little less inferior because I was not so frightened that I had to announce it over the radio. Or perhaps deep down I was recalling that I had already lived five months longer than is normally allowed – wasn't I after all, living on "borrowed time"?

Suddenly the authoritative voice of the duty pilot cut across all the other bleating, "B215, carry out your pre-landing checks and position yourself for an approach and landing on the flarepath heading zero seven zero." So the first one was on his way. "KPCD this is B215, wheels down and locked, mixture rich, pitch fully fine, gas on reserve, coming in to land." "Roger B215, approach and land with extreme caution, if in doubt go around." What a dreadful thought, to muff it after all this and have to climb out again and do a full circuit to get into position again for another landing attempt, with all those other folk waiting to get the chance.

Yes, it did happen and we sweated it out, but after the fifth one had landed I heard the wonderful words "B280, carry out your landing checks..." etc, and I was on my way down, soon to line up on the final approach with the welcoming twin lines of lights – but what is going on? Ninety on the airspeed indicator and hardly any progress towards the threshold – well, it seemed like that anyway. Now careful, boy, we don't want any mistake here – are you sure those wheels are down? That would be silly, fancy blocking the flarepath after all this, with a wheels-up landing – you would never live that down. 'What a panic he must have been in' they would say. Relax, they are down and locked.

What about flaps? Certainly we do not want full flap in this wind, but what is reasonable and how in these conditions can I see the indicator to tell how much is down – full flap doesn't need any reading, you just select and leave the lever down. No, that will not do, somehow I must get 20 degrees down – there now, it wasn't that difficult was it? Are you sure the fuel is on reserve? It would be silly to be on left tank and find the engine stopping with 25 gallons still in the tank, but fiendishly unavailable because it was protected by the reserve position on the fuel cock. Stop panicking Ward, of course you are on reserve. So what about the propellor, are you sure it is fully fine – pretty daft you would look if you had to go around and found yourself trying to climb in course pitch.

Extra careful now, boy, don't muck it up at this stage, I know it is rough and the wind is 'wholly' blowing, but if the others have done it so can you. Bags of power on to achieve a moderately shallow approach, line looks good, airspeed good, generous to allow for all the variations plus an extra five mph for the wife and child. I wondered if any genius is capable of keeping the airspeed steady in these conditions.

There is the threshold, steady now, height is good, round it out, be ready for gusting up, wheee – that was a gust and a half, lower it gently, keep the power on but milk it off gently, gently, she's settling, you've got the landing attitude, ride it, the nose is slightly lower than the three-point attitude but a bit higher than for a daylight wheel landing, hold the power, we must touch on during one of these lunges towards the ground, flarepath lights flashing past. For God's sake don't run out of runway, ease the power off a bit, not too much, steady, whoops, that was the ground, silly bugger, you were too late, we're off again, gently now, power again, ease it on, that's it, quick, nose down a bit, hold it, you're on, kill the power, keep straight, keep that nose down, forward, forward, forward on the stick as your speed dies away – you've made it, but remember that the landing is not finished until the aeroplane comes to rest. There you are, the tail is down and you are almost stationary relative to the ground, stick right back now to keep that tail from coming up.

"Whew, nothing to it" Look at all that runway remaining, I had plenty of room. Hurry up, get off the flarepath, there is still one more poor bastard waiting to go through all that.

The canteen was still open – real American black coffee never tasted so good. There were only three of us enjoying this relaxing moment, and one of these had decided that we could unwind more easily with the juke-box pounding out the inevitable "Hawian War chant", and it was all very blissful. We had proved that we were men – and we felt that we had done something for the Royal Air Force.

"Goddamit Ward, I was listening out to the radio in bed last night and heard what was going on. I telephoned the field to find out who was airborne, and when they said that you were one of them, I would have bet my last dollar that you would be having trouble after that previous night effort of yours. Let me shake your hand boy." These were the words of Mr Freye, that wonderful Flight Commander who had got me flying on my own again so soon, after I returned from sick leave the last time.

A LONG CROSS-COUNTRY

As we became more experienced, student pilots were required to fly with each other, particularly on navigation exercises during which the one in the rear seat would act as navigator. The stick in that position was easily removed and stowed so that he could carry a plotting board on his knees. With a map clipped to this he could plot the progress of the flight and even calculate the wind velocity from tracks and ground speeds observed.

This culminated in the long cross-country flight taking us a total of some 2000 miles to El Paso, Texas and return. These flights were arranged at intervals so that they did not interfere too much with local training at the base airfield. Mine for example included five AT6's with two students to each plus a control ship manned by two senior instructors whose job was to shepherd us around and generally look after us as students. This was a bit of a jolly for the instructors because the flight involved a night stop at El Paso, and that being a border town between the USA and Mexico, was quite a place for Oklahoma-based instructors to have a night out.

My companion was Cadet Greg Underwood and our exercise started on the 4th of September 1943. Soon after dawn on this Saturday the aeroplanes were checked out from Ponca City at ten minute intervals to ensure that we did not follow each other. Greg and I duly arrived in Amarillo in Texas exactly two hours and eleven minutes later, with me as pilot on this leg. After re-fuelling we took off and headed for La Junta in Colorado having changed seats so that Greg was now the pilot and I was navigating. My logbook indicates no problems and nothing of particular note except that we arrived one hour and thirty-four minutes later.

The next leg was to take us south just to the east of the Rocky Mountains – a new experience because Oklahoma is fairly flat country and we were not used to high ground. This was going to be quite different because at one point we would have to climb to 10,000 feet to fly through a pass in the mountains – and we must not miss the pass – most of us had never been as high as 10,000 feet before this.

Some explanation is necessary here in that all air navigation was done by 'dead reckoning'- a bit different from today's radio-beacon flying and computerised calculations. The term 'dead' is slightly unfortunate but that is its name and it means that we calculate the heading to steer and the speed over the ground that we shall achieve, by applying the forecast wind direction and speed to the track required and the airspeed at which we would be flying the aeroplane. When we get into the air, we fly the aeroplane as near as possible to the calculated heading by means of a direction indicator synchronised with a magnetic compass, and we read the map to see whether or not we are going where we intended to go.

Of course a lot depended on the ability of the pilot to fly the aeroplane roughly in the direction required and at about the speed used in the calculation. Some chaps had problems in this matter but Greg and I were not too bad, so the navigation suffered only from the natural vagaries.

If the forecast winds were not accurate we would wander off track and timings would go off a bit, then it was up to the student who was navigating to work out what the wind velocity actually was and then to re-calculate the heading and groundspeed from the off-track position in which we found ourselves. I was pilot on this leg so the dreadful responsibility lay with Greg, but he didn't let us down.

The time to turn to the right to take us to the west came up and we found ourselves at 10,000 feet flying between the walls of mighty mountains that towered above us on each side with the ground only about 1,000 feet below – I expect that in fact there was miles of distance between but we had to memorise something exciting to tell the grandchildren! I well remember the awesome sight as we cleared the high ground into the plain beyond when it suddenly fell away to a height above sea level of a mere 5,000 feet of fairly flat earth. It was not long before we sighted the airfield at Albuquerque in New Mexico which was our next re-fuelling stop.

With the runway so high above sea level and with the high temperatures in this part of the world, the air is a little thin, which meant that while we used the same modest indicated approach speed of the AT6, our true airspeed was in fact quite a bit higher, and the landing run was accordingly considerably longer, but we touched down two hours and nineteen minutes after takeoff from La Junta, not a little pleased with ourselves.

So we hung around a bit, enjoying the fame of being Royal Air Force in such a distant place as New Mexico. We even went into the city and walked the main street, only to have to face the wrath of the occupants of the instructor's ship who always had to takeoff last to ensure that everybody eventually got to each landing point and got away again without any trouble. With the next landing being El Paso, the Flight Commander was not amused at any delay in getting to the fleshpots.

So once again with full tanks we got airborne, this time with Greg up front and me with the easy task of navigating this leg which eventually ran along the Rio Grande, and this remained in sight until we reached El Paso. A radio call to the Municipal Airport control soon got us on to the correct runway one hour and fifty-five minutes after takeoff, and we were again able to preen ourselves before the presumably admiring populace in the terminal building.

Then we learned that one of our aircraft was missing! Oh, dear! Now the Flight Commander was really brassed. The trouble turned out to be that there is also a military airfield at El Paso, positioned about five miles from the municipal field – don't ask me why we in the RAF flying US Air Force aeroplanes with their insignia on them, used the civil airport when there was a military field close by, perhaps it was because our instructors in the control ship were civilians, but I don't know.

Anyway, to continue the story, I have to tell you something you will never believe – but it happened. Approaching El Paso, the missing pilot called the civil airport on their radio frequency and duly received details of the runway in use, pressure settings etc., and permission to join the circuit for landing. But he sighted the military field and joined the circuit there thinking it was the destination airfield. Having received permission to land from the controller at the civil field who, not having anything like radar, would have given them the benefit of the doubt even if they could not actually be seen in the circuit, they landed on a similarly directioned runway at the military field.

At rest on the runway, they asked for taxi instructions. "Where are you?" asks the controller. "On the runway" says our erring friend. "Well, I cannot see you." etc.etc., and so the mistake was discovered. It was quite a laugh, but also a bit lucky because it could have been tricky if a flight of fighters had been on their way in.

The effect on the Flight Commander can be imagined, but Greg and I caught most of their fire because of our indiscipline in hanging around and causing delays in the completion of the flight. Then came the extensive briefing on what we were to do that night in El Paso or rather what we were not to do – I believe that the two instructors thought out what they were going to do and then related it all to us in the negative. Apart from the horror stories about the women in this town, the most important thing was that in El Paso there was a bridge across the Rio Grande, and across that bridge was the Mexican town of Juarez. The problem was that Mexico was not in the war – it was a neutral country, so if we crossed the bridge we, as members of the armed forces of a nation at war, were in danger of internment for the duration!

Now discipline is all very well, but you did not join the RAF for pilot training if you lacked a bit of have-a-go spirit, even if it was a little dangerous. This is not a sex novel so we will not go into the details of any ignored warnings about the women. The desire to cross that bridge was something different, although it was not a matter of wanting to be interned in a place like Mexico, it was merely that we had been told not to do it, and it all looked so simple. With no problem on the US side we crossed to find everyone very friendly and rather disappointingly not taking any notice of us.

There was no doubt that these frontier towns were quite something, and it was not difficult to feel that we were indeed in a part of the wild west that we knew so much about from the films – there was a Leo Carillo on every street corner, and a noise and bustle that would have done credit to Picadilly Circus in peacetime.

We all survived the experience of something other than our hitherto cossetted world, and one group reported that the instructors had been seen in Juarez, but then as civilians they would not have been in any danger of internment!

After weather briefing we climbed into a clear Sunday morning sky heading for Midland in Texas via the Great Salt Flat. Greg was navigating this leg, a fairly easy task because the Salt Flat was so vast that it dominated the scene for quite a long time.

Flying over Texas was quite an experience in itself. It is a big place and there is a lot of nothing, so we frequently had to rely entirely on the heading being flown because there were no pin-points, that is, no features like towns or rivers or airfields or railway lines from which you can locate your position on the map. However, when you did spot anything like this there was no doubt about where you were because it would be the only one such for perhaps a hundred miles – a bit different from, say, Lancashire where a railway line could be any one of a dozen.

I was amazed to see a number of craters of extinct volcanoes but not surprised by the enormous cactus plants because these had been seen before in films starring Tom Mix or Buck Jones.

What a wonder was all this! Can anyone understand what it was like for me, a young man with so little going for him in his early days, with a sense of inferiority that you could photograph, sitting up there at the controls of 5600 lbs of beautiful aeroplane thrusting through the skies of Texas, USA at 140 mph, wearing the uniform of the RAF and giving as competent a display of airmanship and pilotage as anyone could reasonably expect. More than that he was showing a confidence in his ability to do just this – had he not been studying every aspect of flight in aeroplanes since he was nine years of age? How lucky he had been to be alive in time of war when your country needed pilots. How could this opportunity have arisen otherwise, for he could never have expected to be able to afford the cost of even taxiing the simplest light aeroplane from a flying club, even if they had allowed him to be a member.

One hour and fifty-two minutes into the flight we were touching down on Midland airfield, only to learn that a bad weather front barred our way to the next re-fuelling stop at Fort Worth. Oh, dear! All of our pre-flight planning had suddenly become useless. And we, the 'hang-about' ship, were ahead of the field. So we had to wait while all the others arrived and landed, until the instructors turned up to make the necessary decision as to what to do now.

Earnest consultations with the weathermen took place, followed by careful calculations taking into account the speed and direction of movement of the bad weather, and taking into account the performance of our aeroplanes to work out the time to reach a suitable alternative airfield, and whether or not we had the range to get there with a reasonable reserve of fuel in case we got lost or ran into other difficulties which might delay us en route.

The decision was taken – we would re-route direct to Oklahoma City, and don't hang about, get your flight plan worked out and checked, ensure that your fuel tanks are full to the brim because this is a long ride and we do not want any glide approaches to land.

Greg was pilot on this trip so the task of re-planning fell to me – oh misery! But we did not waste any time and were first into the air on this great unplanned adventure. However as so often when trouble is expected, it did not arrive and we eventually sighted the biggest airfield we had ever approached.

It is nothing out of the ordinary now to find yourself slotted in between very large aeroplanes, but the first time you are told that you are being followed in to land by a four-engined B17 bomber, you swallow a little harder and hope that the good Lord is watching over you. The air traffic controller's plea that you expedite your turn next right to clear the runway struck a terror never before experienced. It was only with the controller's continuous advice that we were able to find our way to park on what was one great mass of concrete, and it had all taken two hours and twenty-nine minutes from Midland.

The next and last leg was really just up the road to Ponca City, and this was mine. A mere forty-six minutes later we were flying over the City to our base on the north side, and I was being a naughty boy by making three wow-wows with all the noise that an AT6's propeller can make at high revs. This was the pre-arranged signal to our gang in the City that we were back and would be waiting at the gate for a pick-up within a half-hour. They had after all been without our desirable company for the whole of the weekend and it was now about four o'clock on Sunday afternoon – and we would have to be back in camp by 10 pm.

We were in fact being royally entertained before the instructors' ship had even landed, which proved that with the right incentive, we were anything but the "hang about" ship.

DISCIPLINE

At the topmost level of the RAF administration at the school, a decision had been taken that discipline must be tightened up, and particularly that strict time-keeping had to be observed by all pilots under training. This had come about through an unfortunate blunder by McComisky, a friend from my former course. All now proudly displaying their new 'wings', they were on their way back to Canada and England. Paddy evidently had some difficulty in saying farewell to his lady-love so that he missed the train at Ponca City, to the horror of the crowds who collected on such occasions – particularly of the Commanding Officer and other Officers present. This was indeed a bad show. The fact that the same lady drove like a mad woman, as she told me afterwards, and caught the train up at Wichita, crashing the car within the last few yards, did nothing to lessen the gravity of the crime. Many years later she told me that good old Paddy had reimbursed every penny of the car repair costs.

However, I was one of the first unfortunate victims of the purge that followed. I too sometimes had difficulty in saying goodnight even if it was only a few days to our next meeting, so it was at 2220 hours on the following Wednesday that I attempted to walk past the American civilian guard at the main gate. We had become quite friendly during the period of convalescence after my crash, and I had no doubt that he would not pull me up for this minor infringement by 20 minutes.

"Goodnight Joe", "Just a minute, cadet", "What's the matter Joe?" "You are late, I want your name and number". "Oh, come off it Joe, you're not going to book me, surely", "Just hold your tongue and come into the box where I have some light." This was his small wooden guard box at the gate – whatever was he up to? I advanced towards him, "Joe, you know jolly well who I am, but what is this all about?" He looked at me without his usual smile. "Just give me your name and number, now!" "Cadet Ward S W 1151597, but seriously Joe you are not going to turn me in for a mere twenty minutes?" "You just get off to your bed," and he almost pushed me out of the hut.

As I slowly walked into the camp a voice hit me – "Ward!" I stopped in my tracks, and turned around to see the RAF Commanding Officer sitting on a chair immediately behind the guard box. He must have heard all of our conversation – so that was what Joe was trying to indicate. "Sir" "You will report to the Adjutant at 1000 hours tomorrow" "Yes sir."

There were five of us. The Adjutant spoke briefly and to the point, advising us that we would all be confined to camp for two weeks with immediate effect. Oh dear, life in town was certainly going to be a bit dull – whatever would our ladies do without us, and more to the point what would we do without our ladies?

"You cannot confine me to camp Sir, I am a Corporal." "You have the option Ward, you can accept this punishment or elect to go before the CO and risk being sent back to Canada." Oh well, you can only try. I was correct in that it was contrary to regulations for the CO to confine a non-commissioned officer to camp, but what can you do. It was not that I disliked Canada or anything like that, it was merely that being

C.T'ed (ceased training) for disciplinary reasons was reckoned at that time to lead to your becoming a navigator or a bomb aimer. We were not aware at this time that most cadets sent back to Canada for minor offences were re-coursed for pilot training there, so the threat commanded immediate compliance with any dictate from these long-way-from-home RAF commanders.

LOSSES

On Monday the 21st of June 1943 we suffered a loss which badly shook morale for a time. For those like me who were airborne and listening out on the base frequency, it all started with repeated but unanswered calls from base to the aeroplane with the call-sign A1. Back on the ground we learned that our Chief Flying Instructor, Henry Jerger, was missing in an AT6 on a test flight. Shortly after this, the unbelievable news broke that he and the mechanic on board for the test flight had both been killed. We saw the dreadful wreckage later on as it was brought back to base on the back of a truck.

On the following day, sixty of us formed a guard of honour at a short local service before his body was taken to his former home in Illinois. The most used phrase for a while was, "If it can happen to him, what chance have we got?" – but we were not on this course because we got frightened too easily. I felt it particularly badly because not only was he liked and admired by all of us for being the great person that he was, but I looked upon him as a personal friend since he had visited me in hospital after my accident, and had helped me very much with his encouragement and tales of his early flying days.

Losses from the course were considerable because of indiscipline, failure to make the grade and accidental death, the latter being a bit more common than many imagine, so Ponca City has a part of its cemetery that is forever Britain, where seven of the not so lucky remain. American cadets who died were buried in their own home towns.

WINGS

It follows that as we approached the end of the course we regarded ourselves as something like survivors, and we held our breath more and more as the final examinations and flying tests started. Are we really as near to those elusive wings as it appears? Surely nothing can go wrong at this stage! Oh no? what about Bloggs and what about Jones? – there were plenty of dismal jimmies who could wipe the smile off your face before it had started to appear, with dreadful tales about cadets who were chopped five minutes before the distribution of the flying badge!

My misery ended with the receipt of a letter dated 24 September 1943 from the Director of Flying Training with the Royal Air Force Delegation in Washington D C, congratulating me "... on obtaining the highest place with 80.3% in the recent 'Wings' examination. Not only were you top in your School, but in the whole Output numbering some 400 cadets..." Some twenty per cent of these were cadets from the USAAC. It was very hard to believe – that the junior clerk from a local government office in Ipswich was top boy at 'Wings' of the five RAF schools in the USA.

Congratulations came from far and wide, with the notable and remembered exception of the Station Commander. There must have been something about me that he did not like, because he must surely have realised that my success was a credit to the School. The Station Adjutant did and was warm indeed with his praise.

But there was worse to come. The School enjoyed a system of Cadet Officers under which selected cadets were given ranks from Cadet Pilot Officer to Cadet Wing Commander, and the other cadets were required at certain times to respect these 'officers' as if they were real. This was a bit of a joke because many of us were real non-commissioned officers with a lot of service experience and we had been deliberately left out of the scheme. We were accordingly mere cadets under the authority of chaps who had only recently joined the service.

That was acceptable – after all, you shouldn't have joined if you can't take a joke. But it was carried too far when, at the public parade on which the wings brevet was pinned on us one by one, all of these 'officers' had been dealt with before I was called as first in order of merit. The CO must have lacked any sense of justice and his ears must have burned afterwards when I could not get away from the well-wishers who were loud in their criticism of the silly man.

Worse perhaps was the fact that I was not included in the small number of cadets who were commissioned direct from the course – while the known 'duffer' on the course, who had even failed his pre-wings examination, became Pilot Officer. Regardless of the 'wings' result, I thought that something had been shown about me by the Vaudeville success and by my trouble-free recovery from the flying accident. Perhaps I should not have argued with Joe, the gateguard (page 62).

By way of an historical note, this latter disappointment was put right very quickly on my return to England. It was normal for aircrew

Sergeants to be promoted to Flight Sergeant after a minimum of one year of service in the rank, and it was not normally possible to be commissioned before reaching Flight Sergeant. My promotion was effective after only nine months, and this was followed quickly by a commissioning interview with the Air Officer Commanding the Group, who questioned me closely on my service career and particularly on the goings on at Ponca City. I was promoted to Pilot Officer, effective from the 8th of August 1944 – within ten months of 'Wings'.

But I rush ahead. The evening after the parade was a time of feverish activity by girl-friends sewing the coveted wings brevets on to tunics, and a fair amount of time was spent by the fledglings in admiring the sight in any available mirror or shop window. The celebrations, including the 'Wings' Dinner and Dance, went quickly by, and we were soon ready to get back to England and take our places in the war effort. I now had a total of 212 hours and 14 minutes flying time.

Chapter Four

GOODBYE USA

HEART-RENDING farewells, tears at the railway station, and suddenly we were away, again on the AT & SF express to Chicago – but now a smaller, older, wiser and perhaps happier bunch than we were when we travelled in the opposite direction only six months before, except that for me it was nine months. After the change in Chicago to the Canadian train we arrived in Moncton once more, this time to wait for a boat.

Again in the strictest security, we were hearded aboard another train some days later and eventually found ourselves on a ferryboat crossing a wide river at night. The equivalent of our WRVS served hot drinks and buns inside a huge shed before we were ordered to up-kitbags and file along and up an open staircase which led to a door high up in the side of the grey wall. It was only as we stepped through the hole in the wall that we realised that we were on a ship. The most delightful memory of this night was created when, as we followed in a crocodile through the passages in the ship, we came across a tall sailor wearing a white polo neck jumper with nothing on the front. One of the chaps close to me asked, "Is this the Queen Mary mate?" only to receive the reply, "I don't know, son." We understood then the true meaning of the word security.

The silly thing was that at first light on the following morning we were able to go out on deck where not only could we see the unmistakable lines of the Queen Mary all around us but just next door was the Queen Elizabeth and on the other side was the French Normandie, while the dockside of easily recognised New York City teemed with all of that with which docksides teem anywhere.

Steaming down the Hudson River past the New York skyline and the Statue of Liberty was made a little bit serious by the sight of the US Navy Airship which accompanied us until we were way out to sea. Then we were alone, the Queen Mary and some 17,000 troops of all nationalities – well, the allied ones anyway. The morning sing-songs with many hundreds assembled were quite remarkable if only for the wide range of verses from all over the world sung in response to the loudly chanted chorus – 'that was a cute little rhyme, sing us another one do.' It was quite an education to learn where some quite extraordinary ladies and men came from, and to hear of some of the things that they got up to.

My bedspace was one of a triple bunk bed erected on a wooden slatted floor under which there was another mass of triple bunk beds – so we were six deep in the main lounge of the ship. The beds were so close together that two bodies could not pass between them. I am not sure who had the worst time of it because those on the lower floor suffered a steady bombing with cigarette ends, matches, combs, coins, etc., which dropped through the slats, while the lads above lost many such valuable items never to be seen again.

We had the greatest admiration for the US troops who fed us, or at least those of us who were able to eat, twice a day with the most efficient cafeteria system by which they kept you jammed up against the next chap until the nosh was thrust into your hand, then you were allowed to sit down for just five minutes less than it took you to eat it. The toilet facilities should not be described, but you prayed for constipation, and you blessed those who felt not the need to wash or shave because they left a bit more room for the others.

This magnificent ship altered course about every ten minutes in order to fox any waiting U-boats – this at the high speed it was going gave us a taste of sea'obatics because she heeled over to an enormous angle. All thanks to the Royal and Merchant Navies, we arrived safely at Gourock where we were taken off the ship by tenders.

HELLO ENGLAND

We were then put on to trains to Harrogate where the RAF had taken over most of the Spa's hotels to accommodate people like us while they sorted everybody out and decided what to do with all these brand new pilots and navigators. We arrived on the 17th October 1943.

Can you imagine my feelings at this time? Throughout the years at school, then the short time as a clerk, followed by the years as ground staff in the RAF, I had dreamed of flying an aeroplane. Any pilot was a figure on a pedestal to me – even the pretty little Peggy Williamson who had got her 'A' licence with ten hours flying in a Hillson Praga at Ipswich Airport in 1939 – she aroused admiration, and envy, as someone who had attained what appeared to me to be the unobtainable.

Now here was I, a Sergeant in the Royal Air Force, with that beautiful brevet, those magnificent silver wings proudly displayed on my left breast! I was so conscious of these wings that, can you believe, I was happier walking out with an overcoat to cover them up! No doubt a psychologist could give a reasonable explanation of this peculiar attitude in wanting to hide something of which I was inordinately proud.

The most important thing at Harrogate was the selection board. Each one of us had to appear before a group of three officers who had our records, and we were asked what we would like to go on to – fighters, bombers, transport etc. It appeared to me that, having trained on single-engined aeroplanes and having proved what a bright boy I was, there could be no doubt that I would be given a Spitfire at once so that I could go up into the wide blue yonder, taking on the Hun and demonstrating to him that he was a little out of luck in having to face a most outstanding pilot of the RAF.

My request for SEDF (single engined day fighters) brought the response that this would be granted but, first, it would be necessary for me to do a tour as instructor. "By the end of that you will have over a thousand hours and be able to give a good account of yourself."

How were we to know that the RAF had a surplus of pilots at this stage of the war – I learned, much later, that it was something to do with expecting losses of ten per cent in Bomber Command whereas the actual figure fell to about six per cent – so we were, in the nicest sort of way, to be buggered about for a little while. Some of our chaps actually finished up as glider pilots, while others converted to four-engined Stirlings to tow them!

While waiting for posting to whatever our next stage was to be, many of us were packed off to flying stations to gain experience and pass the time away. So on the 19th November I found myself back at No.15 Elementary Flying Training School, Carlisle, where I had done my grading course over a year before. Now I was required to make myself useful as a duty pilot in the wooden control 'tower' keeping an eye on what was going on, and ever-ready to use the Verey pistol with a red flare if danger threatened from some wretched student pilot, or to ring the crash bell if worse occurred.

The Station Commander, one Wing Commander Homersham, liked to get into the air on occasions and he did not like the draughty rear seat of the Tiger Moth which had to be used when it was flown solo, so he had to take someone with him – guess who was chosen for that as soon as he arrived? He allowed me to take the controls, but after the Stearman and the AT6, the Tiger was a very different kettle of fish, and his pointed questions to me afterwards about where I had been trained and how many hours I had, left me in little doubt that he was not very impressed. He did however clear me for solo to do a bit of flying with among others, a fellow sufferer named Sgt Bennett, who in civvy street had been a Clerk in Holy Orders.

TO BE A FLYING INSTRUCTOR

My posting to No.10 Flying Instructors' School, RAF Woodley near Reading required me to report on Boxing Day of 1943, for attendance on a course of instruction leading to qualification as an Elementary Flying Instructor. Woodley was a former civil airfield which also housed the Miles Aircraft Company.

This course was quite absolutely first-class, with instructors who were the cream of the RAF. We flew mainly on DH Tiger Moths and Miles Magisters with a bit of experience on the Miles Master 1 which boasted a Rolls-Royce Kestrel engine and reminded us of the Spitfire, and the Miles Master 2 with its huge Bristol Mercury radial engine.

The latter aeroplane had a problem for the poor old instructor who in his position in the rear seat in tandem could not see anything forward on the approach to land – this was overcome by an ingenious device which turned the roof of the canopy just above him by 90 degrees so that it stood up, providing a windscreen, and he was able to pump his seat up to give him an eye level above the canopy. However in this configuration it was essential for the student to keep the airspeed below 120 mph otherwise the windscreen would be blown back to its position as the roof of the canopy, with dire consequences for the instructor's head immediately below.

We learned how to fly accurately, how to demonstrate air exercises, how to co-ordinate the patter with the demonstration, how to lecture, how to brief, and generally a lot about flying.

On March 22nd 1944, with another 101 hours 25 minutes and a few more aircraft types under my belt, I graduated from No.26 Course as one of two who made 'B' (average) category – newly trained instructors were normally categorised 'C' (below average) until they had gathered some instructing experience. The other graduate was a Flight Lieutenant who had already done an operational tour on fighters so I was in good company.

Here I was then with 326 hours flying training of probably the highest quality in the world, ready to start work as an elementary flying instructor, with no experience but with knowledge and ability enough to warrant an average category.

POSTING TO ELMDON

My first productive posting was to No.14 Elementary Flying Training School, RAF Elmdon (now Birmingham City International Airport), on the 29th March 1944 – just two weeks short of two years since I had been posted for flying training!

It all started with flight checks first by my Flight Commander and a few days later by the unit's Chief Flying Instructor. My instructing career started on Tiger Moths with brand new cadets on their twelve-hour grading courses which would help to select them into pilots, navigators or bomb aimers! I knew the feeling of being on the other end – suddenly it did not seem so long ago.

Fledgling instructors like me were closely watched by their flight commanders, and our students were checked by senior instructors or flight commanders to ensure that we were getting the right message across. Also, at intervals the unit was subjected to visits by the 'trappers' – a likely name for the Examining Flight from Central Flying School who checked everybody and everything on the unit and issued general reports on their findings, and individual reports on each instructor. Thus was the high standard of RAF flight training maintained.

Some of our time was spent working with qualified and experienced pilots whose flying had been confined to overseas areas. They generally needed to be familiarised with the problems of flying in this country with its weather, overcrowded maps, overcrowded skies, balloons and other little peculiarities like blacked-out night flying.

The joy of flying from Elmdon was not lost on me – I loved every minute of life on a unit with some 100 Tiger Moths of which probably 70 were flying on any one day. It is perhaps difficult for today's young pilots to appreciate that these open-cockpit two seaters had no radio communication and no radio navigation aids – instrumentation did not include artificial horizons or direction indicators but we did have good turn-and-balance indicators, the former being driven by suction from venturi fitted outside the aeroplane.

Intercom was by means of the Gosport speaking tube which had a mouthpiece in each cockpit and open ends into which tubes from the ear pieces in the leather helmets could be connected. Generally the training airfield was all grass although some, like Elmdon, had a single hard runway, in which case the edges were level with the grass so that aeroplanes taking off or landing in a different direction could run across it.

There was no air traffic control but a duty pilot in the watch office did have a Verey signal pistol with which he could fire a red in grave emergencies like an aeroplane approaching in the wrong direction. Takeoffs and landings were controlled by the use of one's eyes, always into wind as indicated by the windsocks but backed up by a landing 'T' in the signals area to forestall arguments. If the direction of the 'T' had to be changed while the circuit had traffic, which was almost always, a smoke signal was first set off in the signals area – this belched white smoke for four minutes during which takeoffs and landings were prohibited.

The Austin Motor Company's factory on the field was building the Short Stirling four-engined bomber so we were frequently entertained by production test flights, with the excellent Doug Cotton landing these monsters spot-on the turning circle of the single hard runway.

Another involuntary entertainer at this time was the great Alex Henshaw who was the chief test pilot on Spitfires and Lancasters from Castle Bromwich. Elmdon was between there and his home near Henley-in-Arden and he had a habit of diving a Lancaster down towards the homestead and pulling up into a chandelle back to base. I met this delightful man by arrangement many years later, in 1982, on a farm airstrip in Suffolk nearby where he then lived – his son frequently used the strip for visits. And that is how I got the signed copies of his 'Sigh For A Merlin' and 'The Flight Of The Mew Gull'.

On 'Graders' an instructor would normally have four students and it was not unusual to do seven or even eight flights in a day – with only twelve hours for each cadet, it followed that nearly all of the flying was dual and so we were kept fairly busy but my greed for flying resulted in my being always ready to volunteer to do a bit of flying with cadets of the Air Training Corps on Sundays.

It was at Elmdon that I committed the cardinal sin of mixing drinking and flying. Uncle Stan after whom I was named, had come up from Dartford to Meriden to visit his brother Walter, after whom I was also named and I might have been Walter Stanley if he had got to the Christening before Stan. That is a bit beside the point – the story follows the fact that Uncle Stan could not stay long enough for me to get across to Meriden to see him, and as I had not seen him for some years we arranged to meet at the Crown Inn which was on the Birmingham to Coventry road, between Elmdon and Meriden and a bit closer to Elmdon; we duly met in the bar, each having borrowed cycles for the journeys.

Uncle Stan had been a barman in his time, and outside of that he had spent a fair proportion on the other side of the bar. So he was something of a drinker, but then, as a member of the Sergeants' mess, so was I. It was not surprising therefore that during the short, animated lunchtime-break meeting, we consumed a considerable quantity of Mitchell & Butler's best bitter – and no lunch.

My flying programme was due to start at 1400 hours with a student in a Tiger Moth, and it seemed quite proper during our touching farewells to suggest that we might see each other again before his departure if I were to fly over the house at Meriden; in fact a challenge was issued that I could get to the airfield, install the cadet and myself in the cockpit, start up, get airborne and fly to the house before he got back.

I won! There he was, pushing his bike up the steep hill on the lane between the main road and the house, so I gave a short display for him and the household – flying in the way that had endeared me to the young lads living in this local authority home for difficult boys. Hill House was in the charge of my very caring Uncle and Aunt, and they must have cursed me on the odd occasions when my visit resulted in the boys dashing out of their classrooms to see it. Nevertheless they loved me for my personal visits without the aeroplane, when I came for a good meal, because it gave the boys the chance to see, touch and speak with a real live pilot – I was never slow to respond to hero adoration, and I am sure that there was some therapeutic value in these visits.

This is pure digression – what am I really on about? Oh yes, the booze! Well now, for some reason the wing-ding appeared to have been executed quite safely – perhaps the excitement of the chase had delayed the effect of the bitter – so I now handed the control of the aeroplane over to the delighted student, and gave the crisp instruction to climb straight ahead. This would allow me to sit back and relax for a few minutes after that scramble.

Oh dear! What is happening? The horizon is swaying about and I feel decidedly giddy. The student cannot be doing this, it is all too unreal. "Level off at 2000 feet" – but even in straight and level flight, my view of the world was very unstable, but it did not take long for the truth to dawn upon my befuddled brain – I was pickled – but not incapable, because the sheer irresponsibility of my behaviour came to me at once. It was not just that I had put our lives at risk, but the waste of time during his grading training might well lessen the student's chance of selection for pilot training.

"Turn left for base". It was getting worse, I might pass out just sitting there waiting for the student's necessarily ponderous positioning to land. "I've got her, sorry old chap but I will have to cancel this lesson: the time will not be counted against your twelve hours, so you've had an extra trip just for fun".

We got down without incident but I learned something from this – I had been really frightened in the air for perhaps the first time! Can you wonder then, that I gained a reputation as a flight instructor that all would not be well for anybody who approached me with a view to flying if they had a hint of alcohol about them.

There were occasions when we ran out of students because of some delay in posting in a new intake but such was the policy that at these times instructors were required to fly together for instructor's practice – this was all very fine for an hour or two of refresher flying but when it involved many hours during a week we suspected that someone must be benefiting from this waste of resources.

THE SALMESBURY INCIDENT

One of the perks of the job was that we could take a Tiger Moth away when we had a long weekend, for the modest charge of ten shillings (50p) to the Benevolent Fund. I had a common interest with Pilot Officer Holden-Hindley who was a friend on the same Flight, to go to Lancashire, and we did this a number of times, he to his stately home near Bolton and me to Preston where my wife lived. The procedure was to fly to RAF Salmesbury where the Communications Flight would look after and service the aeroplane. Departure would be after flying on the Friday for return on the Sunday afternoon.

On every trip we had a minor diversion to the Holden-Hindley mansion just a few miles to the east where a Tiger Moth at low level over the lawn at the back was the signal for the chauffeur to hasten to the airfield to transport the son to his family. My destination was to the west so I had to make do with the local bus service.

This worked all very well until the 11th of April 1944 when our return to Elmdon had been delayed by weather until the Tuesday morning. I remembered being quite impressed by the attention given to us by an airman who insisted on taking our bags to load into the luggage locker of the Tiger while we carried out the necessary pre-flight procedures in the flight office. Everything was in order and his assistance was available to help us into the aircraft and start us up, so we were very soon on our way. We would be a bit late for the morning details at Elmdon but we had cleared this with our Flight Commander.

One hour and fifty-five minutes later we taxied into the flight parking area, to be greeted by the Flight Commander! "Kindly check your luggage locker before you do anything else" – he did not sound any too pleased. "A Squadron Leader Taylor has been on the phone from Salmesbury, and he is a bit annoyed. He has to leave the station this afternoon and his grip is missing from the Comm Flight Office. The only aircraft to leave this morning was yours and he suspects that one of you idiots took it by mistake." It took only a moment to confirm that the Squadron Leader was only too right in reckoning that the grip was in our aeroplane.

"Ward, get that aircraft refuelled, have a pee and get right back to Salmesbury with that bag just as soon as you can because he sounds likely to raise hell."

After another one hour and fifty-five minutes flying I was back at Salmesbury, climbing out of the aircraft and bracing myself to receive the onslaught from this senior officer, when I was met by the airman who had been so helpful. "I'll get her refuelled straight away Sir." I was not a Sir – just a Sergeant but a little flattery does no harm. "But where is Squadron Leader Taylor? I must return his bag and apologise for the inconvenience I have caused." "That won't be necessary Sir, he is not here at the moment and he asked me to leave the bag in the office."

I took the bag into the office and had a cup of coffee while the aeroplane was being refuelled. As I went out of the door the airman approached me saying that he was now on leave and wanted to get to Wolverhampton, "Will you be going anywhere near there?" I would be passing Wolverhampton airfield but I was in enough trouble already without delaying my return anymore. "I am going to Elmdon, Birmingham" "That would suit me fine Sir, could you give me a lift?" Well, I did have an empty seat and it would be a bit mean to refuse an airman a lift home on leave. "I haven't got a parachute for you so you will be sitting a bit low in the cockpit, which is perhaps just as well because you won't have any flying clothing." He put his bag into the locker and I checked his strapping into the rear cockpit.

Another airman swung the propellor and we were away for another one hour fifty-five minutes flying to Elmdon which was enlivened by heavy rain – I thanked my lucky stars that I had chosen to fly in the front cockpit from which the view was a bit better and maps did not suffer so much downwash water flow from the upper wing. I was only a little sorry for my unprotected passenger but could not communicate this because with no helmet I had no speaking tube contact with him.

I do not remember how long it was before I realised that there was of course no Squadron Leader Taylor, but full marks to the bright airman who had worked out a way of getting a Tiger Moth back to Salmesbury with an empty seat to Birmingham.

THE AIRSPEED OXFORD INCIDENT

On June the 29th an Airspeed Oxford arrived at the flight in the hands of an instructor from an Advanced Flying School who was just paying a social call on one of our chaps, the same Pilot Officer Holden-Hindley. None of us had ever flown a twin-engined aeroplane and I considered myself lucky to be one of the two invited by the pilot to go along on what was just a joyride for his friend. The trainer Oxford had only two seats, each with a set of controls, and the engine levers were on a console in between. The instructor sat in the right hand seat. The other two of us had to sit just behind on the main spar of the wing which conveniently formed a bench where it passed through the cabin, but we all wore pilot-type seat parachutes so it was not too uncomfortable.

All went well and Holden-Hindley very decently suggested that he should change places with one of us in the back to give someone else a go. It appeared to be my turn so I was soon up there in the left hand seat flying this comparatively large aeroplane with great glee. We were at 5000 feet when the instructor asked me if I had ever done a stall turn in an Oxford. "I have never done anything in an Oxford, but I would love to see it." He immediately took over control and put the nose down to gain some speed.

Being used to teaching aerobatics in Tiger Moths, where we have the mandatory "checks before aerobatics", I naturally looked at his lap strap because he had not asked me to fasten mine when I had got into the seat – seeing that his was not fastened, I innocently assumed that the sort of thing he was going to show me would not require us to be strapped in – after all, the chaps behind didn't even have any straps!

That is how I learned a little more about flying. At some suitable speed he applied full power and pulled the nose up until we were pointing vertically upwards, then full left rudder went in and he closed the throttle on the left engine so that the aeroplane yawed sharply until we were pointing vertically downwards. The only snag was that we bodies accelerated faster than the aeroplane, with the result that we found ourselves propelled into the top front of the canopy. The pilot, with his hands on things, had managed to close the other throttle so we now had the accompaniment of the undercarriage warning horn to add to our discomfort.

It really was an extraordinary predicament with our heads forced painfully downwards by the slope of the canopy and both of us reaching down for the control column amid the dreadful noise of the horn and the increasing airspeed. I remember thinking 'Oh no, surely I am not to die on my first ride in an Oxford during an instructing tour".

But it was not to end like this because after what seemed an age but could only have been moments, the pilot pushed himself back from the canopy and with his hold on the control column managed to pull it back, the result of which was that we were immediately propelled downwards somewhere near our seats. A further gentle movement pulled the Oxford out of its dive to regain normal flight – we were at 1500 feet! I cannot repeat the remarks of the two chaps who had been sitting on the main spar.

OTHER (MINOR) INCIDENTS

I have every respect for London policemen and I never refer to their feet, but I did have an incident with a cadet who came from the force, and I will have to refer to his leg. Very early in his training I would involve a cadet in the takeoff, by giving him the rudder while I took care of the throttle and the stick, which controls the elevators and ailerons. He would be briefed that the rudder should be used as necessary and that he would find that more left rudder would be required to check the natural yaw to the right, and this would be greater at the start.

We were nicely lined up for takeoff and I advised him to use some feature at the far end of the airfield by which to keep straight. So off we went, slowly at first, zig-zagging a bit as was usual with a beginner, while I was lightly following with my feet near the rudder pedals. Then, suddenly, he pushed on full right rudder! I pleaded with him and tried desperately to get some left rudder in, but all without success – he had locked his knee. I had closed the throttle immediately but with no brakes, once a turn had developed it took some stopping. The Tiger hurtled on describing a beautiful wide circle to the right while I struggled – first to overcome his pressure but then having to give up on this and fight with the controls to keep the tail down and the wings level.

It seemed a very long time before we came to rest, having startled everyone in sight – including me. Then it was possible to realise how lucky we were that I had chosen to start the takeoff well over to the left of the airfield, and that there was nobody doing things like taking off or landing which would normally have been to the right of us.

There is an entry in my logbook at August 30th 1944 that I landed at RAF Penkridge during a navigation exercise with a Flying Officer George. A bit naughty this and it came about because word had got around that when the WVS tea van (now the Women's Royal Voluntary Service) called to dispense char and wads in the mornings, they also gave away cigarettes. The trip was therefore solely to get some free fags, and we had to hang around a bit overhead waiting for the van to arrive. Hardly the way to win a war.

But perhaps the funniest thing that happened to me while at Elmdon was on August the 18th when Flying Officer Phillips asked me if I would be good enough to fly him up to RAF Wolverhampton near to where he was staying for the weekend. It was a Friday afternoon and the weather was very hot so that I was wearing only a lightweight flying overall over a singlet and underpants. Visibility was extremely poor but I knew the country well and was able to mapread my way without any particular difficulty. Phillips was not a flying man so on arrival I had to stop the engine to go into the Watch Office to book in and out, so I said farewell to him at the aeroplane.

The Duty Pilot was not helpful, "All flying has been stopped." "But I have to get back to Elmdon." "Can't help that, we haven't been flying from here for a couple of hours because of the poor visibility and it is not likely to improve now." "But I only want to take-off." "Sorry, but you can't." This was getting me nowhere and Elmdon was a mere 25 minutes away.

You're in a jam mate, I told myself, fancy coming without even a hat – you can't even salute the Chief Flying Instructor if you decide to appeal to him, and he was known to be pretty hot about this sort of thing. This station and Elmdon would be closing very shortly – for the weekend – and I had only a thin flying suit which was not allowed in the Sergeants' Mess. Come to think of it I had no identification whatever, I could not even prove that I was Flight Sergeant, dammit I could not even prove that I was in the RAF, and what was more I had no money at all. Most of this could have been overcome by telephone to Elmdon but what a stink it would cause and what sort of trouble would I be in for getting myself into such a daft position.

"Could I speak to the Duty Officer please?" Reluctantly the Duty Pilot called him and I had to confess the whole of my sins, but I also explained that in my view the chimneys on the other side of the airfield were a bit clearer than they were when I arrived, that I was an instructor with considerable experience, that I knew this area like the back of my hand and that I was here because I had actually been doing a great favour for an Officer. He let me go.

I have clear evidence of how much our views can change as we get older – and no doubt I am not all that different from other folk when I suggest this. A notice appeared in Daily Routine Orders around this time to the effect that a new scheme to ensure that all pilots retain a high standard of physical fitness was to be introduced. To this end all pilots would assemble in the main hangar each morning at 0630 hours for physical training.

This was indeed a small disaster to the drinking classes who liked to cut things a bit fine in the mornings, so it was a slightly disgruntled bunch of pilots who reported to the Flight Office where we were met by a beaming Flight Lieutenant Hammond, our Flight Commander. What had he to be so pleased about? "Did you not read to the end of the notice" he asked, "where it says that pilots over the age of 35 are excused from this order, I'll be thinking of you as I turn over in bed."

It was not jealousy that shook me, it was the amazing revelation that he was over the age of 35 and still flying! I had earlier been slightly shaken by the sight of an instructor wearing glasses. Today I can look back on flying at the age of 71 (admittedly only in an advisory capacity after 61) and the fact that I wore glasses for 45 years of flying – and it didn't seem at all shocking.

HOW NOT TO BECOME AN OFFICER

Shortly after my promotion to Flight Sergeant which had come three months sooner than expected, the Adjutant advised me that the C O was considering me for commissioning and that I would be required to demonstrate my fitness for this by doing things like taking the morning parade which was normally done by an officer. Also, the C O would be expecting me to greet him and his party as they arrived on their duty visit to the Sergeants' Mess Dance in a few days time.

Neither of these tasks caused me any difficulty but my advancement would have been in some doubt if he had been advised of occurrences later in the evening after he had left the Dance. Sgt Timmis had become a bit more tiddley than some of us and he decided that he would become a flame-thrower by snipping off the end of a tube of cigarette lighter fluid and then squeezing it between his teeth. He thought that a light applied to the stream of fluid would throw a flame but in fact it burst in his face, burning off a lot of eyebrows and lashes and other hair, and severely singing his face.

Now Timmis was a farmer at Kidderminster, and somehow he had convinced the powers that control these things that he could run his farm while serving his country at Elmdon, if only they would give him some petrol coupons for his car. Thus Timmis became the only instructor running a car on the unit. Petrol so allowed came with a restriction, in his case confining the car's use to journeys between Elmdon and Kidderminster. The fact that Timmis had collected his girl friend from the other side of Birmingham and intended to take her back there after the Dance was a matter for Timmis alone – or would have been but for the unfortunate accident.

The last thing that Timmis did as he was carried off to the sickbay was to give me the keys to his car and seek from me a solemn promise that I would take his girl friend home.

It was singularly unfortunate that while I was doing this through the blacked-out streets of Birmingham under the guidance of the girl friend, I ventured the wrong way into a one-way street and unhappily came upon a Policeman who was beckoning me to stop. In a flash it occurred to me that this was no time to be discussing matters with a Policeman so I avoided him and continued on my way.

In the sober light of day, the next day, under the hangover, I tried to establish the position I would have been in if I had been identified. The charges at a rough guess would have included failure to stop, driving the wrong way along a one-way street, driving under the influence of drink, driving without a licence, driving without insurance, and using a car for purposes and on a route other than that permitted by the petrol regulations.

On this score I was clearly not suitable for commissioning but this was only 'might-have-been' and I was duly appointed with effect from the 8th of August 1944.

DIVERSIONS IN THE LIFE OF AN RAF FLYING INSTRUCTOR

The RAF was really very good to its flying instructors – we did work hard – flying Tiger Moths day after day especially when we were on 'Graders', suffering the monotony of repeatedly starting new students, and then flying them only for the exercises appropriate to the first twelve hours. So, little breaks were available – for example, when the Examining Flight came they brought a Hawker Hurricane which selected instructors were invited to fly – I was duly selected on one occasion but was denied the opportunity of breaking it, because someone else got there before me and damaged it severely on landing.

Another perk was the opportunity to fly as a supernumerary crew member on a bomber operation. Such trips may have been confined to instructors destined for future bomber command postings but I was never invited to go.

However in September 1944 as a Flight Sergeant I was detached for seven days to No.3 (Advanced) Flying Instructors' School at RAF

Lulsgate Bottom (now Bristol City Airport) for conversion to the twin-engined Oxford. This was quite super – the unit was full of ex-bomber types who had completed tours of operations and were on 'rest' – being trained for instructional duties. I flew with a number of them having been cleared to fly as pilot-in-charge after two dual trips, and I returned to Elmdon very pleased with myself.

COMMISSIONING

When thoughts of commissioning had started to arise I wondered about the financial side because there was a general feeling among non-commissioned officers that one really needed a private income to get by as a very junior officer, so I asked Holden-Hindley if he was managing on his pay and allowances. "I'm sorry Stan, but I really don't know. My pay goes into the bank with other money and I just do not keep account." Oh well, ask a silly question! It must be comfortable to be like that – as far as I was concerned I had so little that I could tell you the state of my wealth immediately, at any time. However, I presumed that I would manage – given the chance.

A funny little thing about money was that my rate of pay as a Pilot Officer would normally have been twelve shillings and sixpence (62.5p) per day plus two shillings (10p) servant allowance – but my pay as a Flight Sergeant was sixteen shillings and ninepence (83.75p). You cannot however get less pay on promotion so the difference was made up, and I managed comfortably on it.

It was easy enough to change part of my uniform to that of an Officer by simply buying a Warrant Officer's Glengarry (hat) from stores and getting the camp tailor to take off the crown and stripes, and stitch the thin blue ribbons on to the epaulettes of the battledress. The full gear had to await a visit to an approved tailor's shop, and was paid for later out of fairly generous allowances. I moved at once into the Officers' mess which was housed in what had been the Airport Hotel, and it cost me a fair number of halves of bitter to get my health well and truly drunk.

POSTING TO SCONE, PERTH, SCOTLAND

The policy in Training Command was to move a newly – commissioned officer to another unit, probably to get him away from his old mates in the Sergeants' mess, so my posting on the 27th of November

1945 was no surprise. This was to No.11 EFTS at RAF Perth in Scotland, as good an appointment as anyone could want, with a fly-fishing CO who regularly donated a few fresh salmon to the mess. It was a bit difficult to stay within the £5 limit on a junior officer's bar bill for alcohol, but we managed with help from the fine hotel bars in the fair city of Perth.

Our Chief Flying Instructor was a Squadron Leader Bennett popularly known as Hippo. He was a big chap, who had been awarded a Distinguished Flying Cross during the first world war – he had some humour and wasn't shy in claiming that he had been lost in a Sopwith Camel above cloud over the western front when a hole appeared in the cloud through which he could see the ground – he stuffed his nose down to vertical to get through the hole. At that moment a German Albatross happened to cruise along just below the cloud level and into his gunsight so he opened fire and shot it down – and that was how he got his DFC, at least that is what he told us!

For the first three months here the job was entirely to familiarise new pilots and navigators with flying in the UK, and nothing particularly exciting occurred except one incident which involved Arthur Wint, the Jamaican Olympic runner. A most delightful man, newly qualified overseas as a pilot and as keen as mustard. He stood head and shoulders above me and possessed a pair of very long legs. We were scheduled to carry out the exercise of spinning in the Tiger Moth in order to clear him for solo practice later on.

After a lengthy briefing before takeoff, we climbed to some 5000 feet which was the required height to ensure that recovery could "be effected with 3000 feet to spare", and I was demonstrating and talking through the method of entry to a spin to the left and the recovery, in order to freshen his memory and to show him how the Tiger behaved. A spin is a condition of stalled flight in which the aeroplane is rolling, pitching and yawing while falling at a high rate of descent. The recovery was taught as a safeguard against accidental spinning.

The first action in the recovery is to apply full rudder opposite to the direction of the spin, so while telling him what I was doing I tried to do just that. But it wouldn't go – I could get only partial rudder and however hard I pushed, it would not go any further. The Tiger continued spinning! Then a startled voice advised me, "My leg is jammed between the rudder pedal and the dashboard."

I could picture the problem – when the right rudder pedal is pushed forward, the left pedal comes back a similar distance, and if your foot is on it, this has to come back. During small movements the ankle can deal with it, but full rudder requires the leg to fold up a bit. In Arthur's case there was not enough room for it to retract far enough. It was now urgently necessary to get his foot off the pedal, so I had to change back to into-spin rudder. "Now take your feet off the rudder pedals Arthur", and thus was full recovery effected. If I had been a little sharper I would have felt that we did not get the full rudder movement on entry to the spin, but I didn't and it had entered okay.

Back on the ground we could see that when the pedal was fully back there was not room for his exceptionally long leg between the pedal and the underside of the dashboard. However, it was unlikely that he would fly Tigers anywhere else so he was excused spinning while he was with us and we had to hope either that he would not get into an accidental spin or that if he did he would remember to take his foot off the back-moving pedal. Anyway he survived the war and got back into running.

In February 1945 it appeared that the RAF had decided that the war could be nearing its end because we received our first full elementary course which had been recruited from the University Air Squadrons. Not only were they UAS cadets but they were potential permanent commission material who would go on to advanced training at no less an establishment than RAF College, Cranwell. Among this group were the sons of many Air Rank Officers including Chief of Air Staff, Sir John Slessor. It was clear that some of these cadets would form the backbone of the RAF of the future, and so it turned out – perhaps there is some satisfaction in the knowledge that my name appears on the early pages of the logbooks of many retired Air Marshals!

With full-course students life really brightened up as we were able to enjoy the teaching of aerobatics, formation, night and instrument flying.

Two lovely incidents come to mind from this period. One taught me the simple lesson that some things should not be rushed. After we were satisfied that students had learned enough during dual instruction, we were able to send them off to practice exercises solo – solo flying is after all a most vital part of flying training. The instructor is necessary to explain and teach the various elements of flying, but it is during solo work that the student learns about himself and builds up the confidence that is essential for a pilot.

For solo flying, the straps in the empty front cockpit of the Tiger Moth were fastened securely so that they could not flap about or become entangled with the flying controls, and to make sure about this, the joystick was removed and stowed in the luggage locker which was situated in the fuselage just behind the rear cockpit.

I flew with one of the Flights which operated from a large grass field called Whitefields, situated a few miles away from the main field at Scone, Perth. This satellite operation was necessary in order to reduce the number of aeroplanes operating from the main field, and it required that at the end of the day, all of the aeroplanes had to return to Scone. At this time, most of us were keen to get finished and go to tea or to do something even more exciting so the main field became something like a beehive at honey-making time, and it was not unusual to have as many as seven Tigers on the approach at the same time. It was all a matter of discipline – you always landed to the right of the one in front of you and you turned left after landing. If there was no more room to the right, you just started at the left again.

I had sent an early-hours student off during the last period of the day to practice something, with strict instructions to return at a particular time so that I could get back to the beehive, land and get away to somewhere. Of course he was late and I was fuming. I collected his gear from the students room and waited outside. As he taxied in, I indicated that he should keep the engine running, and I stowed his and my gear in the locker, leapt into the front cockpit and as I strapped myself in, shouted for him to taxi out and take-off.

It was as we entered the rat-race circuit at Scone that I realised with some horror that there was no stick in my cockpit. This meant that I would not be able to scream "I've got her" as we usually do when a small crisis arises, like imminent collision or a disastrous landing attempt. Now is the question, to tell him or not?

At his tender stage of training it might screw him up to know that I could not help, whereas leaving him to get on with it could give him a chance to show me the advanced state of his airmanship. I could always yell an instruction at him if the worst happened. My eyes were standing out like chapel hat-pegs looking for anything dangerous like other aircraft as he entered the circuit but in fact nothing came near enough to cause me any concern and he pulled off a beautiful landing! It would have been such a job trying to fly the thing by sticking my finger in the hole left by the absent stick.

The second incident concerned the locker as well. The lid was about two feet six inches wide, hinged near the top of the fuselage on the right side and secured at the bottom by a latch at each end. Cadet Poolman had climbed us to 5000 feet for some spinning practice but when I looked at him through my see-back mirror I could see that the locker door was wide open, standing vertically up. Oh misery! We could not spin the aeroplane like that. This would mean descending back to land and then that awful climb back up to this height, by which time most of the period would be lost.

Unless – "Poolman, someone did not do a very good job on his pre-flight checks – the locker door is open." "Sorry sir, I really am." "Now I reckon that you could do something about that, but it would mean unstrapping and getting half-way out of the cockpit to turn around. What do you think?" "No trouble at all sir." "Wait a minute then, and note carefully what I say. I will fly as slowly as possible keeping straight and level while you unhook your speaking tube first, then unstrap and turn around to kneel facing aft. In that position you will be able to lower the lid and reach the forward latch to do it up. Don't bother with the after latch."

I concentrated on careful straight and level, grateful that at this height the air was dead smooth. The happenings behind me were all revealed in my mirror showing that he was doing as he had been told, but then he started to wriggle aft until most of his torso was lying face down along the top of the fuselage – in that position he secured the rear latch. It took a little longer to get back into the cockpit, and I had to wait until he had reconnected his Gosport tubing before I could express my feelings about his idiocy in going for the rear latch with the clear possibility that he could have fallen off the aeroplane.

"I had a parachute so that was no problem." Oh no, no problem at all – except that I would have had to return to base flying a Tiger solo from the front cockpit and would no doubt have been required to explain what I had done with my student!

But Poolman was a good student and I had the satisfaction of learning later that he won the Sword of Honour on graduating from Cranwell.

In July 1945 two of us received notice to standby for posting to the Fighter Conversion Unit at RAF Ternhill giving us the opportunity to desecrate a popular song with our own words which we sang in the mess – I can remember only the lines "In a Typhoon over Rangoon" – but it never came to anything because 'VJ' Day on the 15th of August interfered with service procedures so that Ternhill was closed immediately and the posting was cancelled. We were extremely lucky in this because fellow instructors who had been posted one month before us ceased flying at once and were moved as required to take the place of adjutants, armament officers or supplies officers etc who were now being demobilised. Whereas we continued instructing until our own demobs came along very much later.

'VJ' DAY

Going back to "VJ" Day, I was Orderly Officer on the 7th and the duty carried through the flying programme that night to 0800 hours on the great day. Night flying had paused for a teabreak just before midnight and the night duty pilot had temporarily abandoned his watch office which was situated on the tarmac apron between the hangars. It was during that break that the radio announcement was made that the war was over with effect from midnight! Of course pandemonium is the only word for it – you would never believe how a bunch of normally responsible flying and ground staff can behave at such a time. People were running, jumping, shouting, screaming and generally going mad.

Even in my responsible position I was quietly enjoying all this until poomph, and then poomph again, as two Verey signal lights soared into the night sky from the vicinity of the Watch Office – the silly buggars had got hold of the two Verey signal pistols and who knows now many cartridges. I dashed across the tarmac and was able to catch two officer-students just after they had fired another salvo. It was not difficult to dis-arm them and collect the cartridges, but just as I entered the Watch Office the telephone rang.

It was the CO who had been wakened by the noise, and was now raging about the idiots who were endangering the aircraft and hangars, indeed the whole installation. I hastily advised him that I was Orderly Officer and had taken immediate action to retrieve the pistols and cartridges which I was about to secure in the Watch Office so all was now well and (I added under my breath) do you see what a bright boy I am? It was at that precise moment that a 28-star signal rocket burst overhead! Sometimes you just can't win.

But although he groused "I don't suppose that anyone here has done much to win the war against the Japanese", he directed that the officers' mess bar could open for an hour for drinks all round and said that he would be down in a few minutes. It was not long before the piano was moved outside and a jolly sing-song got under way about washing on the Siegfried Line and packing up your old kitbag and smiling.

PEACETIME

After 'VJ' most of us were looking forward to demobilisation to get back to civvy street and start a normal life – we also hoped that we could continue flying until that day arrived.

The numbers of aircraft in use were now being reduced to meet peacetime requirements and three of us were detailed to ferry three Tigers to RAF Little Rissington. The leader of the flight was to be Bob, a friend of mine and we will leave the name at that. We delayed a number of days because there was just not enough weather to get from

Perth in Scotland to Little Rissington in Gloucestershire in our aeroplanes with their limited equipment, but in the afternoon of the 25th July 1945 we set off in marginal weather for Carlisle to refuel before going on to Sealand near Chester for a night stop.

The next day the weather was worse but Bob, being a 'press-on' type, got us airborne again heading for my old stamping ground at Elmdon to refuel. It was now raining steadily, the cloud was quite low, Little Rissington was 730 feet above mean sea level in the Cotswold hills and there were some masts nearby. It is a bit difficult reading a map in an open cockpit when it is raining and I would have enjoyed a night stop with old friends.

But it was not to be – we must press on! So off we go although there is no flying going on at Elmdon. Close vee formation is now necessary in order to stay in sight of each other, so the navigation is necessarily entirely in the hands of the leader because you cannot safely read the map, look at the ground and stay close to him at the same time. After passing our estimated time of arrival it is clear that we do not know where we are. It is still raining and the ground is very close indeed as it has been for some time. I for one am very frightened and would willingly drop out and find myself a field to land in, but you cannot let a friend down like that. We can communicate with each other only by hand signals and even that is dangerous.

So we are darting about all over the place when suddenly we fly across a vast expanse of gleaming tarmac – an airfield! Thank heavens, it is all over. The leader is turning, scarcely above the station buildings, to line up with the approach, so we drop into line astern to do a stream landing – not all that easy, on tarmac with a tail-skid and no brakes, but the wind is kind and we have no problems. There is a manned box to the left along the runway and Bob leads us along to it. A man covered in camouflaged waterproofs comes out to discuss things with him against the wet propellor wash, after which – would you believe it – we get the signal to take-off.

Oh well, perhaps it is not so bad – obviously Bob has found out where we are and he knows where to go to get to Little Rissington. That happy thought was dispelled not all that long after take-off because once again we started darting about all over the place with Bob probably hoping for a miracle. I actually saw a mast higher that we were! This went on longer than I care to think about, when lo and behold there was another airfield, shaped like a letter 'T', with no aeroplanes in sight. We landed and taxied in towards the buildings, relieved to see Bob stop and shut down his engine.

As we got out of our aeroplanes, an airman appeared, "This is RAF

Chedworth. The station is closed, we only have a holding party here. I don't know if you can stop the night, I'll get the Sergeant". We were forty miles from Elmdon and it had taken us exactly two hours to get here. Although we were just ten miles west of Little Rissington, it was now too late to go any further, a fact that certainly pleased me and the other pilot. We learned then that the airfield at which we had landed before was Brize Norton, a huge United States Air Force base, just eight miles south-east of Little Rissington.

When the Sergeant appeared he had no doubt that we could be accommodated. The holding party consisted of a Squadron Leader in charge, plus a Sergeant and seven airmen looking after the place until the full closure. They had a squadron of Hawker Tempests before this but now there was no flying at all. We were concerned to tie our Tigers down in case of high winds, but he said that we could taxi them over to a blister hangar which was empty and dry.

No, there was nobody on the station qualified to swing the propellors of our Tigers so we would have to start them ourselves. We were parked in long grass in no particular order and there were no wheel chocks – I suggested to the other pilot that he should start me, then I would get out and start him and Bob. But I had barely got into my cockpit when there was the roar of an engine at full throttle just behind me. I leapt out in time to see Bob hanging on to the left lower wingtip of his Tiger while it was pivoting round him, but before anyone could do anything to help, the tail came up and the propeller screwed itself into the ground at maximum revolutions, smashing itself and the engine cowlings. The thing came to rest on its nose, looking very sorry for itself with two wingtips smashed and the upper mainplane hanging forward grotesquely.

Bob, in his best press-on manner, had decided that he need not wait to be started up properly with him in the cockpit, so he had just put the switches on and without even checking the position of the throttle, had swung the propeller. It was normal shutting-down procedure to open the throttle wide to stop the Gypsy Major engine cleanly after switching off, and then good airmanship required that the throttle should be closed again. Bob had left the throttle fully open and it was his bad luck that the engine had fired in this state.

By this time more airmen had appeared, so with their help we pulled the tail down and man handled all three Tigers into the hangar. The CO was not on the station so there was nothing more we could do that night and we were shown to a nissen hut formerly occupied by the Women's RAF where we chose beds surrounded by pin-ups of Clark Gable and Cary Grant. A fry-up was provided in the one-officer mess but we had to go to the village pub for alcoholic sustenance, where a likely tale was cooked up for our explanation to higher authority tomorrow as to how the accident had happened.

We saw the CO early the next morning and found that his main concern was that he had not known of our arrival the previous evening and consequently he had missed the opportunity of having three officers to drink with in his normally lonely mess bar. He reported the accident to his parent station a few miles away, and a small board of enquiry was sent to investigate and report on the matter. No one was terribly worried about damage to a Tiger Moth which was on its way to undoubted demolition, and the story was readily accepted that, after being started-up, Bob had used too much power when his wheels were stuck in the long grass, with the result that the tail came up etc., etc.

However, the weather was brighter that day and by afternoon the two remaining Tigers were on their way to Little Rissington – mine had a passenger. He was later awarded a red 'bad show' endorsement in his logbook and we never knew whether or not our story was believed nor if anyone was worried about it. I merely advised him that if he ever said 'press-on' again in my presence I would hit him. However, he was duly demobilised in due course and went on to a full and satisfying career in civil aviation.

At Little Rissington, only the runways were clear – the remainder of the airfield was covered in a mass of aeroplanes of all types packed wingtip to fuselage in every available space. We had to leave ours to be manhandled into the mass.

Talk of permanent commissions was frequent, but after four years of married life in the service, I had had enough. I felt also that with the armed forces essentially in decline after the war, and with the intakes of university graduates on permanent commissions, there would not be much going for the likes of me with no operational experience and the modest rank then of Flying Officer.

UNIVERSITY AIR SQUADRONS

I was recommended as a suitable officer to fill an instructor vacancy at Liverpool University Air Squadron, and I duly moved there in October of 1945. We were a group of three instructors with a Squadron Leader commanding officer and a civilian lady secretary/driver, and our job was to teach undergraduates to fly during any periods that they could get away from their other studies. The squadron headquarters was one of a terrace of five-storey houses overlooking Abercrombie Square, many miles from our airfields on the other side of the river Mersey.

Initially we flew from an otherwise disused station at RAF Hooton Park where the main activity appeared to be the destruction of brand new Lancaster and Halifax bombers which flew in to join a line on the grass where they progressively dropped bits like engines, gun turrets, instruments and so on to the end which was a shining heap of cut-up sheet metal.

A fellow instructor was given to making models of autogiros out of balsa wood and tissue paper – these he dropped out of the top floor window and we watched as they flew with varying degrees of success into the grass square below. He and I frequently went out at the same time to fly cadets and we occasionally took the opportunity to perfect our loop-in-formation over the airfield. Alan Bramson, for it was he, went on after release from the service to become one of our foremost pilots in general aviation, the co-author of an excellent series of books on flying training, a prominent member of the instructors' panel of examiners, an appreciation test pilot and reporter on hundreds of different types of aircraft, and the author of many authoritative volumes on aviation.

Hooton Park closed at the end of April 1946 and our aeroplanes were moved to RAF Sealand near Chester, still reachable through the Mersey tunnel by our Humber staff car; this was a rather more used airfield, occupied also by an active Maintenance Unit.

My return to civil life to the job held for me as a junior clerk in the office of the County Architect with the East Suffolk County Council was delayed on the suggestion by my CO that if my demobilisation could be deferred for six months, this would be very convenient for the squadron. The Council approved, but even before the normal date for me to go, orders came that Liverpool University Air Squadron was to be closed on the 30th of June, and my service was to be continued as an instructor to Leeds University Air Squadron with effect from the 1st July 1946.

The headquarters was in University Road and its aeroplanes were based at RAF Church Fenton, the station on which I had manned a ground gun in 1940!

While I was at Liverpool the chief flying instructor gave me a check ride after which he recommended that I should be given the opportunity to go for the A2, above-average, category as a flying instructor. These things take a lot of time so it was not until July the 10th that I took a Tiger Moth from Church Fenton to the Empire

Central Flying School at RAF Hullavington, via Derby for refuelling. The tests were carried out the next day and I was awarded the higher category with effect from that date.

Practical demobilisation came on the 9th of October 1946 with an official date of the 14th December – the difference being demob leave. On reporting to RAF Uxbridge for demob I had my first taste of the rackets of civil life when the nice officer was offered a better suit than the normal issue, in return for a consideration of ten shillings (50p). I paid up and was immediately shown to a rack behind the others, but of course the suits were exactly similar – it was a trap for the greedy and I had fallen for it.

Chapter Five

POST-WAR FLYING

AT THIS time I noted that I had 1313 hours of flying in my logbooks and a civil 'A' (Private Pilot) Licence from the 1st July 1946, with a flying instructor's endorsement, but my hopes of a flying career were dashed at the demob medical examination when it appeared that my eyesight had deteriorated and was then below the standard required for the issue of a Commercial Pilot's Licence.

Under the law as it was then, I could earn a living as an instructor with an 'A' licence for which the eyesight standards were lower, but such work would be confined within a flying club using club aircraft and teaching members only. This was no basis for a career because I would be constantly under the threat of a further deterioration which could lose even that licence, and also there was already talk of withdrawing the privilege of instructing for reward on an 'A' licence.

My job in local government was guaranteed on return from war service, so I reluctantly returned to a desk, and incidentally to a drop in income to one quarter of what I had enjoyed in the RAF, but I harboured a determination to fly whenever the opportunity arose.

During my demob leave at the end of 1946 Dorothy and I with our three-year old son Robin were playing at nothing in particular in a park which was not too far from Ipswich Airport, when we heard a light aeroplane engine, and spotted a small high-wing monoplane climbing out. My suggestion that we might go to see what was going on at the airport was met with some enthusiasm, so we caught a bus.

The aeroplane was in fact a Taylorcraft Plus D two-seater, with a 90 hp engine and the registration G-AHUA and this, with its sister G-AHNG, was being operated by the West Suffolk Aero Club. Mr Eugene Prentice, a name very well known in local aviation circles and the motor business, was on the field and showed some pleasure in welcoming this ex-RAF instructor.

After a quick 'whip round' with him, to show that I could be trusted with an aeroplane, I became airborne with Dorothy by my side and

Robin on her lap. They were having their first flight ever while I was experiencing, apart from the check-ride, my first flight in a civil aircraft, my first flight with the smell of scent in the cockpit and, incidentally, my first flight without a parachute! The parachute was a must on every RAF flight I had made, so although the need to use one had Arisen on only one occasion it was hardly surprising that I was a little aghast at the thought of flying without it – now, some thousands of flying hours later, mostly without, I suppose that I am getting used to it.

I could not afford to pay for flying, even at the comparatively low cost at that time, but I did manage to get some by persuading one or two less impecunious people to fly with me at their expense – all a bit illegal.

Early in 1947 I was invited to become instructor to the club with a salary of £7 per week plus five shillings (25p) for each hour flown by me. I might have accepted this even with all the problems involved if I could have had the security of a contract for say two years, but the continued operation of the club could not be guaranteed for even two weeks. To have given up what was considered to be a promising career in local government for such a shaky place in the flying world would have been a bit selfish at this uncertain time so soon after the war. The club closed just a few weeks after this.

THE POST-WAR RAFVR

In June 1947 I learned that the RAF Volunteer Reserve had been re-formed as a post-war organisation, and that there was a unit at Cambridge. My big worry was of course the eyesight test, and it was from this time that I developed an extraordinary skill in memorising test charts.

So it was, that I started flying with No 22 Reserve Centre RAFVR at Marshall's Aerodrome Cambridge on the 13th of September 1947 as a weekend pilot and reservist instructor until the unit closed in 1954.

During that time I flew some 550 hours on Tiger Moths and Chipmunks and, I believe, proved that the spectacles I had worn for some time were no handicap to a pilot because I became a frequent winner of some of the flying competitions which were organised as three-cornered battles with the Cambridge University Air Squadron and Marshall's civil flying school.

I thought for some time that I had hidden the fact that I wore glasses whenever I flew with the Reserve, by not wearing them until after taxiing away from the flight line and by taking them off before reaching the line on return. But the day had to come when chief flying instructor Gordon Hubbard said, "Ward, I'd like you to take Jones and introduce him to formation flying – Smith will take Baker and I will take the third aircraft with Leary – briefing will be at eleven o'clock."

I could hardly take a student on formation flying without wearing my glasses but this would mean that the chief instructor, in close formation, would be able to see me quite clearly and the truth would be out! Oh well, it had to be. However, the only time this was ever mentioned was during a party some time afterwards when Gordon merely commented that he had known for some time that I wore glasses. Although he did not approve of glasses for RAF pilots, he did not in fact do anything about me. I believe that, even in peacetime, corrective goggles were permitted by the RAF, and no doubt it was mere vanity which was forcing me to cheat.

This covering up was later proved to be unnecessary, because the time came when instead of being checked at local medical examinations, all reservists had to submit to an RAF Medical Board in London, where five specialists had a go at five different parts of each of us. At the end of it all I was seen by the President of the Board who actually said, "From this report on your eyes, it looks as if you're a bit past it old chap!" To this day I do not know if it was my tears or my experience which did it, but I was kept on and my engagement was renewed for a third term of five years.

In my early days with the Reserve Flying School I had no private means of transport so I travelled to Cambridge for weekend service by scrounging lifts on a Friday evening or Saturday morning with a fellow reservist, returning on the Sunday afternoon, or I would travel by train. In the latter case I was often able to organise a flying lift back to Ipswich to land at the airport which was deserted at that time.

Authority to do this was required but this did not cause too much difficulty because I was an instructor and the trip would be a cross-country training flight or I might give some instrument flying instruction on the way to the pilot who was flying me home, and he would get some solo time in returning the aeroplane to Cambridge. On arrival at Ipswich we would taxi to one end of the field where I would get out, observe his takeoff and then climb over the barbed wired gate to catch a bus home.

This scheme went along beautifully until the day when the reply to my usual request to Gordon Hubbard was that he would come with me today. "Oh no sir, I really wouldn't want to inconvenience you to that extent, you must have many things more important to do, and Pilot Officer Simmonds could do with some instrument flying." " Not a bit of it Stanley, Simmonds will have to do his instrument flying some other day because this will be an opportunity to check your aerobatics for the forthcoming competitions, and anyway I would like to see Ipswich Airport again and I would enjoy the solo flight back."

There was no answer to that and so it was that on the afternoon of Sunday August the 21st 1949 I climbed into the front cockpit of Tiger Moth N9276 for my last flight home to Ipswich after a weekend of reserve service at Cambridge, because when the Chief Flying Instructor observed the skill with which I put the aeroplane down between the gorse bushes, bedsteads, old bicycle frames and other bits of assorted junk, he was somewhat impressed, a little frightened and utterly determined that never again would he endanger one of His Majesty's aircraft by authorising Flight Lieutenant Ward to be flown home to Ipswich.

There was a good social side to the Reserve Centre at Cambridge which included frequent 'open days' involving competitions of skill with the other two units on the field – Cambridge University Air Squadron and Marshall's civil flying school. These days included a flying display in the afternoons to which the public were welcomed – it was on the one of these that most of us were amazed by our first sight of three aeroplanes flying at incredible speeds without a single propeller among them! They were Gloster Meteors from RAF Waterbeach.

The evenings afterwards saw us in the RAFVR club on the airport contributing to a massive party. One of the highlights of these was the ceremony of the drinking of the Rosebowl. This quite beautiful silver bowl was presented at the end of the afternoon to the unit judged to be the overall winners, and during the party this unit was required to nominate two members of the winning team to drink the contents of the bowl – one gallon of best bitter – against the stop watch in an attempt to beat the record time.

I enjoyed the privilege of taking a half share in this competition on no less than three occasions with partners Ison, 5 minutes 10 seconds, Nurney, far too long (partner retired sick!), and Pointer, 2 minutes 25 seconds. The last time was never beaten before the Reserve Centre closed, and therefore Pointer and I remain the champions for all time.

The bout with Ison had beaten the best time previously set up, by drinkers from the University Air Squadron. Sadly the two chaps involved were killed in an air accident shortly afterwards. It was typical of the service attitude to this sort of distress that Ison and I were subjected to mass comment assuring us that our turn was sure to come if we ever had to fly together. We could not tolerate this threat hanging over us – after all we might be detailed to fly together at any time, so on the 12th of December 1948 with due ceremony we deliberately climbed aboard Tiger Moth DE773 and flew together for 50 minutes – my logbook records that the flight duty was 'to shatter the bogey'.

In the competition flying, I was not always as clever as I may have implied – the weather of one 'Open Day' was quite appalling with low cloud and poor visibility, so that it was not possible to send off the usual crush of pilots wanting to do the aerial treasure hunt. This exercise involved a sealed envelope containing a small section of the local area map and a sheet of instructions, for example, to fly a track of X degrees for Y miles to locate something on the ground which was countable – like the number of arches under a bridge or the number of hangars on a disused airfield.

Using that number you had to add, subtract, multiply or divide by something to ascertain the bearing or distance to the next turning point, and so on. All of the figures had to be entered on the sheet. The pencil for this was the only tool permitted so there was no protractor and no measuring rule.

It was decided that three aeroplanes (Chipmunks) could go, one from each unit, and each competitor would be accompanied by a staff member to act as safety pilot, who was to take no part unless the safety of the aircraft was endangered. My record in this competition was considered such that it was agreed that I should be the representative of the Reserve Centre. The error of this decision was to be seen later that morning when after more than an hour of flying without finding a single turning point, I advised my safety pilot that I was returning to base.

The other two had got round without any difficulty! It was only during the debriefing that I realised that instead of giving us a section of the half-million scale map normally in use, the organisers had popped in a piece of a quarter-inch map and I had failed to recognise it. It followed that when I estimated 14 miles to some chimneys, the distance was actually nearer 7 miles and I had flown over the three chimneys that were the target, to arrive at the London Brick Company's works where I counted and recounted no less than thirty chimneys – very closely because we were a bit low and some of them were quite tall. Multiplying this by 90 as instructed gave something quite different from the 270 degree track that was intended and I had finally convinced myself that there had been an error in the typing!

In addition to the flying that qualified instructors did at Reserve Flying Centres, we were frequently required by the RAF to help out at Summer Camps. University Air Squadrons did fifteen days of concentrated flying in their own aircraft at an RAF Station but their normal staffing of instructors was adequate only for the casual type of flying done during term-time, so there was a demand during summer for additional instructors.

As well as this, there were one-week camps for Squadrons of the Air Training Corps, during which every cadet was expected to get at least one air experience flight. They did not have any aircraft and did not necessarily require an instructor because their flights were often just rides in whatever aircraft the RAF Station operated. But where such

Cadets of 188 (Ipswich) Squadron Air Training Corps enjoy a flight in an EAFC Auster with their C.O., 1957.

In the RAFVR we flew the old Harvard (AT 6) and the new piston Provost at South Cerney, September 1954.

rides were not possible because of the type of aircraft or the workload of the unit, then suitable aircraft were moved in and reservists like me were called for.

My holiday allowance was five weeks plus two more for normal annual training at reserve summer camps so because we could afford only a week of holiday each year, I was able to spend six weeks with the RAF on full pay and allowances at rates which adequately covered the full costs of the almost essential gin and bitter consumption, with some to spare for family expenses. And so I enjoyed many attachments to various RAF Stations throughout the country flying Tiger Moths, Chipmunks, Harvards and Provosts.

In 1950, after I had completed studies for the external Diploma in Public Administration in connection with the earning of my real living as an administrative officer with the former East Suffolk County Council, I was invited to become a civilian instructor in aircrew subjects with No 188 (Ipswich) Squadron of the Air Training Corps, and sometime later I was commissioned in the training branch of the Volunteer Reserve with the rank of Flying Officer. I was a Flight Lieutenant in the general duties (flying) branch at the same time and there was no problem while the two jobs were kept separate, but the time had to come when I was on the same RAF Station as an F/O with the Squadron at summer camp and as a Flt/Lt giving the same cadets their air experience flights. It certainly puzzled some of them in the mess. The difficulty, if it can be called that, was cleared up in 1955 when I became Officer Commanding the Squadron, because that carried the rank of Flight Lieutenant.

As 1954 approached the Air Ministry decided that aeroplanes in the RAF were becoming so complicated that flying them was a bit too much for the weekend pilot, and that flying in Chipmunks was keeping our hands-in to nothing, so the Volunteer Reserve was gradually run down, at least as far as pilots were concerned. I forget the order in which we were chopped, but it depended on our previous experience, remembering that as wartime pilots we had all by now lost that first flush of youth which makes the dashing fighter pilot – so they were the first to go, followed by bomber boys, coastal, transport and, lastly, instructors.

They closed down seven of the twenty-eight reserve flying schools at a time and Cambridge was in the last seven – it was all very sad because we had some marvellous boozy evenings and had done some magnificent flying. The school at Cambridge closed in March 1954, and those of us who were qualified instructors were kept on as reservists, without the weekend commitment, but we had to go back into the RAF for two weeks each year to refresh on instructing techniques. The joy of this was that we were attached to units which had aeroplanes a little more sophisticated than the Chipmunk, so I was able to fly the Harvard again until it was succeeded by the piston-engined Provost, introducing us to the side-by-side seating arrangement where you can actually see the frightened expression on the student's face.

EAFS LTD AT IPSWICH AIRPORT

By an extraordinary coincidence it happened that a company called East Anglian Flying Services Ltd which operated passenger services from Southend Airport, re-opened Ipswich Airport at Easter in 1954, just as the Cambridge Reserve Flying School closed. Their lease required that they should provide facilities for flying training at the Airport so I did not waste too much time in notifying my availability, and I was duly appointed instructor, but more of that later.

The company had taken over the lease in 1953 from Ipswich County Borough Council who were the owners. The place was quite derelict by then and a considerable amount of work was required in getting it up to the standard required for a passenger terminal and for licensing as a public aerodrome. This task was in the hands of Dan Burgess, a man with an undisclosed number of operational tours in Bomber Command during the war, as well as considerable experience as a commercial pilot in general aviation and on scheduled passenger services to say nothing of a stint of flying Halifax ex-bombers on the Berlin Airlift.

One of nature's gentlemen and one of the calmest men I ever met, Danny directed and worked as leading hand in demolishing, re-building, concreting, joinering, re-wiring, plumbing, painting and decorating, pulling out hundreds of gorse bushes, ploughing and sowing, to say nothing of the enormous administrative task in getting an airport operational for scheduled passenger services. Even then if there was a shortage of pilots on the airline, Danny would drive off to the base at Southend to take an airliner full of passengers to the Channel Islands.

After the re-opening and the start of services, Dan remained as manager and airline pilot with which he combined a task he loved, of farmer to the 160 acres put down to the production of corn, sugar beet and potatoes, all of which helped to make Ipswich one of the few financially viable airports at that time. I have frequently seen waiting passengers and friends in a packed lobby, move out of the way of a filthy driver who had come off a farm tractor parked just outside the airfield entrance doors. Little did they realise that this man was the pilot of the aeroplane some of them were about to board, and that he had come in with just enough time to have a shower and change into his immaculate blue uniform with its four gold rings at the cuff – and thus he would appear minutes later to pass through the same crowd in the opposite direction. Similarly, on the arrival flight to night-stop ready for the first flight outbound next day, the resplendent Captain would within minutes be in his working clothes doing a bit of weeding to the garden area in front of the terminal building.

East Anglian Flying Services Ltd., started operations to and from Ipswich with four De Havilland Rapides, fabric covered, twin-engined biplanes, seating eight passengers in four seats on each side of a central gangway leading from the door at the rear to the nose of the aircraft where there was a single seat for the pilot – the total crew. At this time Ipswich had no radio facilities nor approach aids although the aeroplanes were fitted with radio communication and primitive navigation aids. It followed that in really bad weather they could not get any nearer than Southend, which was the company's base.

There was no such luxury as a loo or in-flight refreshments, indeed they did not even carry an hostess. The normal procedure was that the ground hostess at Ipswich would check the tickets, weigh the luggage, lead the passengers out to the aeroplane, put them into the seats, fix their lap straps, and then get out and wait by the door. Then, and only then, the pilot would stroll out, climb aboard, and pausing only to check that the hostess had closed the door from outside, he would walk up the gangway to take his seat.

The story goes that on one occasion, Captain Frank was on his way between the fully occupied lines of seats, four on each side, when he was hailed by a male passenger, who was an acquaintance, with a "Hello Frank" to which he offered a courtesy "Hello", hoping thus to end the conversation in the interests of the time keeping. But it was not to be because the fellow continued, "Nice to see you again Frank. Are you better now? Feeling quite well? No more fits?" The effect on the other passengers who were not in the jesting mode, is not recorded.

It was not long however before Ipswich had ground-to-air radio on a fixed company frequency, to provide two-way communication with approaching and departing airliners, so that the office could be advised by the pilot that he would be there in five minutes or so. He could also ask for an unofficial weather report and suggest what he could do with a sandwich, or "Be quick with getting the passengers off and on – things are getting a bit fraught timewise." Later on, direction finding equipment was installed, the airport obtained a public radio frequency, and a licensed air traffic controller was appointed to provide homing and descent facilities with full radio-telephony communication – big stuff!

The first real improvement in aircraft into Ipswich was the purchase in 1956 of six De Havilland Doves – very modern looking, low-wing, twin-engined, ten-seater monoplanes with nose-wheel undercarriage which was, wait for it, retractable! Chatting to the Chairman's wife shortly after this, I was amazed to hear her say that she was not as happy in these because she always feared that the wheels might not come down when required.

THE 'HONEYMOON EXPRESS'

I don't suppose that I will ever forget the day when we had no less than three happy couples waiting for the 'Honeymoon Express' which was the 1830 flight, a Dove, on a Saturday to Jersey. At that time the flying club shared an office off the lobby with the ground hostess or receptionist, so I was on the spot.

The lobby was packed with the jolly parties from the receptions who had arrived an hour before the scheduled time of take-off, many were a bit pickled, all were very happy and boisterous. Ominously, no aeroplane had arrived by 1800 hours, but Maureen, the ground hostess, had no great difficulty in parrying the many queries. At 1830 she had to announce that there was a slight delay, and fortunately their good humour enabled most of them to find a joke in it. At 1900 hours we had to telephone Southend operations only to learn that the Channel Islands were 'closed in' and they had problems, but would get an aeroplane to Ipswich as soon as they could.

Maureen announced another half-hour delay and then explained to me that she had a date, so would I mind holding the fort for her? It was not my job, but I had to be there anyway because I had club aeroplanes flying until dusk. By 1945 hours the passengers and their guests were becoming a bit restless, some were clearly suffering from hangovers caused by earlier consumption and long abstention. Demands were made for me to telephone somebody, but I knew that this was useless – I could by now make up the stories to explain non-arrival as well as the people at Southend could – "There has been fog all day in Jersey and no aeroplanes have been able to get in until late so there is a big backlog of passengers at Southend from earlier flights who had to be got away first – your turn will come. We cannot help the weather and we don't have blind landing facilities yet."

At 2030 hours I could not hold them off any longer, but the call to Southend brought the anticipated comments with the continued assurance that the aeroplane would be coming, and a gentle reprimand about the cost of telephone calls to Southend. I badly needed a pee but dare not run the gauntlet of the hostile mob between the office and the loo.

It must have been nine o'clock when the dreaded telephone call came from Southend – "Regret no flight tonight into Ipswich. Advise passengers that they will be accommodated on an aeroplane at 0900 hours tomorrow." How do you gather enough courage to face all these people with such news after their wait since 5.30, with six of them at the start of their honeymoon. The company were no fools – if the passengers had been moved to Southend they would have commenced their journey and the company would have had to find them accommodation for the night, but these people had not started so they had no claim. And I was the unfortunate, really only a bystander, who now had to explain it all.

There was no other course, so here we go – a brief announcement, with apology and regret, then a quick return to the haven of the office. A good theory, but you do not get away that easily – you are followed by unhappy bridegrooms, weeping brides, disappointed friends, but most violently, the best men determined to prove their worth in those appointments. Some actually beat me on the chest with their clenched fists and I remember mentally thanking my protector that I had refused to allow them to use the non-public club bar because their tempers might have been even more inflamed by the additional alcohol.

Nobody got hurt, physically anyway, but I was saddened by the whole affair as much as any of those more directly involved. And these included an elderly couple with the tearful lady pleading "What are we going to do? I threw out the last of the bread and milk just before we left home." It was really nobody's fault, except perhaps that 'they' should have abandoned much earlier the attempts to get an aeroplane to Ipswich – in trying to avoid disappointment they had increased the distress.

I was able to do a bit more to help on Saturday the 9th of August 1958 when the morning flight, a Dove from Southend scheduled to return to Southend, failed to appear. Two passengers, Mr & Mrs Paul Walter, were relying on this to connect with their midday flight to Bergen, Norway, by Lapair. A telephone call to Channel Airways at Southend revealed that in the chaos caused by the previous day's bad weather, they had no aeroplane to send up.

The agony of all this was explained to me by Maureen, the ground hostess, asking if there was anything I could do to help them. There was not enough time to get them there by any other means than flying, and all I had was a non-radio Auster with no self-starter, no baggage space, and a third seat which required the passenger to sit across the aeroplane behind the two front seats! But that was nothing compared with the legal difficulties in view of the fact that I, with no commercial licence, would be carrying scheduled service passengers who had paid their fares. I thought that I should not do this without higher authority, so I rang the boss and explained the problem, but this was a wasted phone call because he just did not want to know anything about it. I was on my own, with the passengers who were now in real danger of losing their holiday flight to Norway.

Southend air traffic control cleared me by telephone, to follow the usual procedure of circling a point to the north of the airfield until they gave me a green Aldis lamp signal which would be permission to land. There was some difficulty in getting the suitcases into the rear cockpit and then getting the lady into her seat just in front of them – I did not dare to do a weight and balance calculation because I knew that this would show us to be outside both weight and balance limits. This may appear a little irresponsible, but it wasn't really because I knew my Auster well enough to be able to tell before we got airborne whether or not it would be controllable.

We taxied on to the apron at Southend just as the passengers were boarding the Lapair flight. Mr Walter leapt out and ran across to speak to the loading staff – and their holiday was saved. My face must have had a slightly worried expression as I unloaded Mrs Walter and their suitcases, because this was all happening just below the windows of the control tower, and I still had to book in and out.

But nothing untoward happened, and I received a letter dated 10th August from Paul Walters at the Victoria Hotel, Bergen saying that no words could express his thanks for my kindness and service, and he waxed a little lyrical as follows:-

There was a good fellow named Ward
From Ipswich to Southend he soared
To enable a stranger to board
Another plane bound for the Nord.

Well its nice to be appreciated!

Ipswich was however looking up as an Airport. The Doves were followed in 1957 by the Bristol Freighter, a monster converted to carry 40 passengers, in 1960 by the Douglas DC3 (Dakota) and in 1965 by the

HS748, a really modern propjet with good short takeoff and landing capability. We were in good company because the 748 came into service with the Queen's Flight of the RAF as the Andover.

In 1962 East Anglian Flying Services Ltd had become Channel Airways Ltd and Ipswich was providing feeder flights to Southend to meet their scheduled services to Rochester, Portsmouth, Ostend, Rotterdam, Jersey and Guernsey. Other aircraft owned and operated by Channel Airways from Southend and later, Stansted, included Vikings, Viscounts, a DC4, a BAC One-eleven and an HS Trident. By 1971 the fleet totalled 21 airliners and Channel was concentrating a lot of its capacity on inclusive holidays to Malta, Majorca, Barcelona and Rimini.

THE EAST ANGLIAN FLYING CLUB

As I said earlier, one of the conditions of the lease required the company to provide facilities for flying training, and one of the pilots on the airline had an instructor's rating attached to his licence, so he was appointed to the post of Chief Flying Instructor to the newly formed East Anglian Flying Club. The snag was that he was required rather extensively to fly on the airline, so nothing happened until I volunteered my services as a part-time instructor.

Although my offer to serve had been snapped up by Jack Jones, the Managing Director, he proved to be a hard bargainer while I was a softy, easily convinced that he was really doing me a favour by allowing me to do the flying that I loved so much: he did not actually suggest that I should pay for the privilege because he offered me five shillings (25p) for every hour of dual instruction that I flew. Sometime later I calculated that although I was only a part-timer, my hours at the airport in summer exceeded the 38 hour week required by my employment with the County Council. I am no longer convinced that the 7 or 8 hours that I sometimes flew in one day indicated nothing but my love of flying – and it certainly wasn't for the money. It was, I have to admit, just that I couldn't say no to anyone who wanted to fly – even to the student who arrived at sunset. As the acting CFI from the start, my appointment quickly followed as a Royal Aero Club Observer in which capacity I was authorised to conduct the examinations for the issue and renewal of Private Pilot's Licences. It was not long before my position as CFI was confirmed and, in view of my record and experience, the Guild of Air Pilots and Navigators of the British Empire authorised me to train assistant flying instructors.

Flying duly commenced at the club on August the 14th 1954 in Auster J1N Autocrat G-AGXP, and on that day I flew four trips with students. That was after two flights to familiarise myself with the aeroplane – the first of these being with my ten year old son Robin.

Generally speaking I was able to work only on Saturdays and Sundays except that in summer I could fly also in the evenings. Every Tuesday evening was devoted to ground school from 7.30 to 10 pm, and one of the reasons I did not become a rich man was because I never thought of charging for this service.

The club remained open throughout the week so that licensed pilots could fly – the manager, Dan Burgess, or the chief engineer, Jack Squirrel, could authorise such flights. If there was any doubt about the weather or the pilot's ability they would telephone me at my office. After 1965, when instructor Peter Collier joined us, he was able to come in one day initially, and later, two days per week to provide more instructional time.

The Auster G-ACXP which was the club's first aeroplane had started life at Ipswich in 1947 when ten local businessmen each contributed £100 to buy the £700 aeroplane, new, for their own use. It was still flying as a group aircraft when Jack Jones made an offer to buy it in 1954 to operate it from Ipswich as a club machine.

XP was a high-wing monoplane with two seats in the front of an enclosed cockpit, and a single seat in the rear which was positioned crossways so that the passenger's weight, acting through the bottom, could be kept forward, nearer to the centre of gravity of the aeroplane. The front seats were side by side with dual controls, and the advantage that lady students (and men for that matter) could hold the instructor's hand if they became frightened – the student's, not the instructor's.

The aeroplane had a 100 hp Blackburn Cirrus engine, it climbed and descended at 65 mph and cruised at 80. It boasted none of the modern frills like cabin-heating, self-starter, radio, navigation aids, auto-pilot or blind flying instruments, and it was a bastard to taxi and to land – but for all that, it was a fine training aeroplane as long as the instructor was prepared to work hard. There were no short cuts in this thing, and it took time and application to teach people to fly it properly, but few would dispute the claim that if you could land an Auster, you could land most light aeroplanes.

It was much later that this Auster was modified to clear it for spinning and limited aerobatics by the fitting of strengthened seats, so the company obtained a Tiger Moth G-ANKG to enable us to meet the spinning requirement of the course, and we started flying this on October the 2nd.

The Tiger was for the more hardy. Apart from having to fly this for spinning in the early days, students could elect to learn on it. Most RAF pilots pre-1950 had flown or had received their elementary training on the Tiger. It had two open cockpits in tandem each with a set of controls and instruments, the power was provided by a DH Gypsy Major engine of 125 hp and she enjoyed climb and descent at 65 mph with a cruise at 80. It therefore had the same speeds as the Auster but fewer of the comforts because it had no cabin, no flaps and no wheel-brakes.

The Tiger's landing characteristics were not all that different from the Auster's and it has been described, correctly I believe, as the easiest aeroplane to fly safely and the most difficult to fly accurately – that must make for a good training machine.

In addition to the club machines, it became my lot to do odd bits of flying with people who owned their own aircraft or who belonged to other flying organisations, and there are one or two tales to tell about these.

Close to Ipswich there were two air bases, Woodbridge and Bentwaters, which were occupied by the USAF. A group of airmen were operating a two-seat Taylorcraft G-AFWM under the adopted title of the Bentwood Flying Club, and they came across to me in March of 1955 asking if they could base the aeroplane at Ipswich with me as their instructor.

There appeared to be no difficulty at that time so Dan, the company manager, agreed that I could do this as long as they realised that I had to give priority to the East Anglian Flying Club. I cannot remember what arrangements were made about maintaining the Taylorcraft but things went along quite happily until the 1st of May 1955, when Tom Atkins, who had come to us as resident engineer, took a close look at it.

"You will be careful not to fly that thing under a thunderstorm, won't you Stan. If you get caught in hail or a heavy rainstorm, you'll find yourself flying a skeleton – that covering is completely rotten." That of course grounded the aeroplane and they could not afford a re-covering so the aeroplane was sold to someone who could, but it left Ipswich.

It was followed in November 1955, by Tiger Moth G-AOEL operating under the same arrangements, and I flew this with many American airmen and a lot of pleasure until a most of them were posted back to the USA in November 1956, when the aeroplane had to be sold. It went to somebody on another airfield, so it too left Ipswich. The chaps were happy to receive the sum of £350 for a Tiger Moth in full flying condition with a valid Certificate of Airworthiness!

After this, the USAF agreed that the joint bases should have their own flying club at Bentwaters, using American aircraft with a full-time manager/instructor.

Most club members wanted to have a fly in the Tiger at sometime, and many liked it because it was more or less fully aerobatic, but only a few wanted to do their basic training on it – the result was that compared with over 500 hours per year utilisation on the Auster, we achieved only 150 on the Tiger, and this was barely viable. It was however unfortunately written off in 1958 by a visitor from New Zealand when he was flying solo. With 15 hours flying time, he decided to do a climbing turn immediately after take-off instead of carrying out the proper circuit exercise that instructor Frank had briefed him to do. Frank had just taken off on the scheduled morning passenger service to Southend, so our friend from down-under probably saw his opportunity to show himself how good he was – he was not hurt but the cost to us in his proving that he was not as good as he had thought, was an aeroplane.

But the Auster was more popular with most of the students probably because they could fly this in everyday clothing, while in the Tiger they needed protective clothing with a helmet and goggles. Messages from the instructor came via "Gosport" tubes into the helmet, while the

EAFC's Auster HZ banks over its base at Ipswich Airport.

screams going the other way went through a speaking tube whose mouthpiece was fixed just under the crash-pad in the front of the cockpit.

Our fleet was increased each winter by another Auster, G-ANHZ, which was a Mark 5 fitted with two rear seats and a 125 hp American Lycoming engine. It offered the luxury of a self-starter, an artificial horizon (now called an attitude indicator), a direction indicator, navigation lights and a manual carburettor heat control. But it had no generator so the battery had to go on charge before "away" flights, night flying or whenever it showed signs of flagging. In the early years we lost HZ in summer for more profitable use in "joy" flying at Portsmouth, but the demand for instrument flying training, night flying and long distance trips resulted in its full-time transfer to us. Unfortunately the engine had no silencers – they were expensive and burned out too quickly – so instructional patter was not given in the full-power climb when even a parade-ground bellow could not be heard!

One of the joys of this aeroplane was the happy hour or so that could be spent swinging the propellor to start the engine if the battery happened to be too low to turn it over adequately. If properly primed, the engine would start easily, provided that it was cold or very hot, but woe betide you if it was in between these two extremes – there was a socket for an external battery and we had one at Ipswich, but these were not available on most airfields. At 80 knots (92 mph) she cruised a little faster than XP and was a very stable aeroplane, so with its direction indicator and artificial horizon it was popular for cross-country flying. It carried only 15 gallons of fuel and burned 6 per hour, so its still-air safe range was only 180 miles but nevertheless it achieved some remarkable long-distance expeditions.

Two more Auster Autocrats. G-AJUE and G-AIZY, joined the fleet during 1964 and we were really on our way – with four Austers.

*

It may be that my standards were too high but the occasion arose while I was still authorised to train instructors, that a pilot came to me from another flying club, asking for a course as quickly and cheaply as I could manage. He had something like 150 hours total flying time which indicated quite a bit of flying since his licence at about 30 hours. After a lot of questioning I said that it would be necessary for me to fly with him before I could make any decision about taking him on.

At the end of the de-briefing after the flight, I summed it all up by saying "Far from taking you on as a potential flying instructor I have to tell you that if that had been a test for the issue of the Private Pilot's Licence, I would have failed you". The sequel to this was that after what seemed only a short time, a DC3 airliner landed at Ipswich with its load of passengers and – guess who was the second pilot resplendent in his uniform with two gold bars on the sleeves?

*

There is a dreadful tendency for some students and pilots with low hours to want to show off their prowess to the folks at home and, while those from the town would hesitate to expose themselves over the town, their country cousins would consider it safe to ignore my strict instructions against the sort of showmanship which in the RAF had so frequently ended in a demonstration of, "Look at me as I so cleverly write this aircraft off and kill myself." The method of detecting many culprits at my club evolved in an interesting way.

I was not averse to publicity for the flying club, and in those days the local newspapers were always ready to publish anything faintly novel about civilian flying. Combine this with my tendency towards exhibitionism and we have the fact that my part-time adventures received a lot of publicity. It followed that I was well known at the headquarters of the County Council where I was employed. Many of my fellow employees lived outside the town in the lovely villages of Suffolk, and whenever their attention was drawn to an aeroplane near to their homes they assumed that I was in it and would delight in telling me that they had seen me: they would then either praise or criticise me according to what 'I' was doing and according to their attitude towards me and flying.

In order to ensure that the flight was one that involved me I would explain that I must ask where this was, what time it happened, did they get the registration, what did the aeroplane look like and what was I doing? With whatever answers were given, I would not always admit to being the pilot involved, but with the information obtained I could generally decide whether or not the aeroplane was one of 'mine', and if it were, I could easily identify the pilot from the flight records. If he should not have been in that area and/or if he was doing something he shouldn't have been doing, he learned of the wrath of Ward. Is it surprising that one culprit voiced the amazement of club members when he commented, "You don't seem to miss much of what is going on around here – have you got eyes everywhere?"

The instructor team at EAFC May 1966 – Jack Pickrell, author and Peter Collier.

*

Jack Pickrell, a former Spitfire pilot in the RAF, came to me for his instructor's course in 1958 and, after qualifying, he drove up from Southend most weekends to make a very useful contribution to the job of teaching. One or two of my own students became assistant instructors and returned to help me out with the increasing task at East Anglian.

*

Student Peter Collier started his course with me in September 1960 and qualified for his PPL without any trouble at all, becoming one of those pilots whose sense of responsibility makes a chief instructor's lot a happy one. After he had gained a lot of experience he suggested that he was going to take the assistant instructor's course at Cambridge, and I was happy to assure him that there would be some instructing work for him with East Anglian when he completed.

He duly qualified and spent many years with the club – as I said earlier, instruction then became available during the week instead of just at weekends. Peter became a very sound instructor so it was not surprising that he should have been offered the post of full-time chief flying instructor to the newly opened Ipswich School of Flying in 1971. After a successful period there, he opened his own Suffolk Aero Club in

(Above) Cessna 152 Aerobat G-BGAF of the Suffolk Aero Club taxies out at Ipswich piloted by Enid Bishop, c.1982. (Below) EAFC instructor Bill Wells in his Tipsy Nipper.

1976, which rapidly became a top class training establishment with the highest standards of maintenance and management.

*

Christopher Crowther from Leiston in Suffolk, a keen cadet of the Air Training Corps, came to me in 1961 to get his PPL and he did a lot of flying with us before obtaining his instructor's rating elsewhere. He began his instructing at Biggin Hill, then came to us at East Anglian for a time before becoming Manager and Chief Instructor to the Bentwaters Flying Club on the USAF base. He then went to helicopters, qualified for commercial work and spent many years surviving the rigours of working the off-shore oil rigs in Nigeria – the last tally I have of his flying was that his total hours had reached 18,000 of which about 11,000 were on helicopters.

*

Bill Wells came to learn to fly with the background of an ex-pilot father and an enormous ambition to follow suit. He was not the best student I had ever had but he was probably the most enthusiastic – this would not be evident to the casual observer and is something he would probably deny to this day. He duly got his PPL in 1967, and built up a great deal of experience.

Bill was the pilot in one of the incidents which live in my memory as a CFI. The weather forecast on the 15th of February 1969 warned of isolated snow storms, and I had passed this to Bill who wanted to get airborne in Auster G-ANHZ with a friend – my advice was that as the storms were to be isolated, he would be able to fly around any that appeared. He taxied out ahead of about three other aeroplanes and duly took off, only to disappear a few moments later into a huge snowstorm. The others turned about and taxied back in.

Bill was however now faced with the problem of getting back to the airfield in conditions of practically no visibility, with no radio communication and no radio-navigation aids. But he did have nearly 200 flying hours which included about 7 hours of instrument-flying training. At first he enjoyed some faith in the forecast that it was an isolated storm, so he turned hoping to fly out of it, and found himself over the centre of Ipswich. It was now evident that this isolated storm was of immeasurably large dimension, and he had come into what was just a small clearing. This was a nasty position to be in, and back in the office I was not amused to see that the airfield had disappeared even to ground observers.

I won't agonise on this too much because he got back; he flew a heading which he estimated would take him along the line of the river Orwell where he could descend to low level without sight of the surface, with only a modest chance of hitting anything, in the hope that something would turn up. The something that did turn up was the river bank, which he followed until he saw the caravan site beside the airfield – then it was easy.

Some folk get all the excitement, because it was on the 12th of April 1970 that a much more experienced Bill took off on his own at 0750 in Auster G-AIZY to go to Seething where the airfield was being defended against all-comers by their small fleet of aeroplanes. This was called a breakfast patrol and the idea was that you tried to get in to land without being spotted by the defenders – success being rewarded with a free breakfast.

Full of well-earned bacon, egg and beans he took off at 0930 to return to Ipswich. At Ipswich however, I had decided that the weather precluded any useful flying training and I was busy answering the telephone to that effect. Except that one call was from someone at Rushmere golf course asking if it was one of our aeroplanes that had just flown over at very low level. Within seconds of this, at 1010, ZY loomed out of the fog and landed. He admits to being more frightened of my wrath than of the flying – recalling that I went over to meet him as he got out of the aircraft; but evidently I was so relieved to see him and the aeroplane in one piece that I had remained 'moderately calm'.

He reported that he had flown into reducing visibility around Woodbridge and had decided to fly a bit to the left hoping to hit the river and then follow it back to the airfield. But to keep in contact with the ground he had to fly lower and lower; to this day I think of Bill whenever I pass a mast on the old Felixstowe road just outside Ipswich. He had confessed that on his way in he had passed alongside that mast – it must be all of 120 feet above the ground!

Bill went for and got his Instructor's Rating in 1969, and came back to become one of my most reliable instructors. Then after the traumas that followed the end of Channel Airways, he instructed part-time with both the Ipswich School of Flying and the Suffolk Aero Club, and did a bit of freelance work. He also packed in a lot of flying in various aeroplanes of the Tiger Club and in Typsy Nipper G-AVXC of which he was a part-owner. He even flew into Ipswich in the Tiger Club's DH Fox Moth G-ACEJ on one occasion, in order to give me a flight in the tiny passenger cabin of that aeroplane.

He worked hard and at his own expense for the Commercial Pilot's

Licence which he obtained in 1977. He then worked through intermingled periods of instructing, joy flying, unemployment and First Officer work on passenger-carrying Twin Otters, Bandeirantes and Short 360s before becoming an airline Captain.

*

It is said that you cannot win them all, but this is probably just an excuse for a failure somewhere along the line, and certainly I suffered such a failure, caused by my own error of judgement in the appointment of an assistant flying instructor. This man had learned to fly with us in 1964, obtained his assistant instructor's rating somewhere, and by some hynotic achievement had got into instructing with me.

It was only gradually that I became aware that students were less than keen to fly with him, the reason being that that is just what they had to do – fly with him. He spent their costly time showing them what a clever pilot he was, and the student rarely got to fly the aeroplane. I have no excuse – it was simply a matter of my accepting him without too much question – but I do claim that the harm was minimised by quick action as soon as I became aware, so that the harm done was small.

*

Arthur, a well-known local coach operator and County Councillor, came to me in 1966 asking what he had to do to get a Private Pilot's Licence, in view of his flying as a pilot before and during the war. "Not a lot" I assured him. "When did you last fly as pilot?" "1945" "What were you flying?" "A P51 Mustang" "Well we'd better have a look at you".

Now, apart from the 21-year gap, the Mustang, a WW2 fighter, is a bit different from the Auster – for example, their weights at 11,600 lbs against 1850, and maximum speeds at 437 mph against 160. It is I believe always more difficult to move from a heavy aeroplane to a light one because of the need for a much more gentle touch, but the number of knobs and switches is far less in the Auster, and there are not so many handling figures to remember. So the pre-flight briefing was not too extensive, and Arthur noted on his knee-pad the vital things like speeds for the climb, cruise and descent, together with engine speeds, temperature and pressure.

It did not take long to get the Auster started and we taxied out to the pre-takeoff position for the usual checks. "She's all yours Arthur – just show me a takeoff, circuit and landing". And he did, without my having to say another word, except to comment that it was all very safe, if not elegant. He got his licence after doing the minimum requirement of flying and tests, and he enjoyed many more years of flying.

I must have done something very similar with Wing Commander Jack Meadows DFC AFC AE who described in an article in Aeroplane Monthly of June 1990 how he came to me in 1971 with a little under 4000 hours and 50 different types from elementary to fighters, twins, four-engines, jets, and a bit of gliding! He had confessed to me that his last flight had been eighteen years before, and his article described our next conversation as "Well, let's have a go shall we?" and as we walked over the grass towards the Auster, "What did you last fly?" "Meteors" (jet fighter). "Ever flown an Auster?" "Yes, but not for about 26 years" "Oh well!"

He described the flight in detail, described me as 'a good man', and noted that during the 45-minute flight my hands never moved from my lap. The report of my comments copied that of Arthur's almost exactly with its reference to elegance and safety. But it wasn't until I read his article in June 1990 that I learned that he had previously held a RAF Flying Instructor's A1 category! It was interesting also to note that when I sent him off solo, he remembered his first solo, 34 years earlier almost to the day, in a BA Swallow, from a little hut at the far corner of the same airfield in 1937.

*

I referred earlier to the authority vested in me by the Guild of Air Pilots and Navigators to teach flying instructors, but the Guild was later to evolve a scheme whereby this personal authority was removed in favour of granting the authority to the flying training organisations, and then only to those which reached certain laid down standards – one of which was the employment of a full-time commercially licensed chief flying instructor. I did not reach these standards, so even after my appeal, conducted in London by a Court of the Guild which reminded me of descriptions of the Star Chamber, I lost this facility.

Apart from the slap in the face, I was not unduly put-out by this because I had trained a few instructors and found that the task was too time-consuming for me, largely because of the extensive and specialised ground-schooling required. After this, whenever a pilot suggested that he wanted an assistant instructor's course, I boosted my status in my own mind by suggesting that he should go to the school of his choice and obtain his instructor's certificate, then if he came back to me I would teach him how to instruct.

Auster ZY crazy flying by the author in a "stolen" aircraft at Ipswich.

Chapter Six

DISPLAY FLYING

IT WAS in 1959 that I started giving aerobatic and crazy flying displays at both civil and RAF shows, variously called 'At Homes' 'Galas' 'Open Days' 'Fetes' or 'Battle of Britain Days'.

Our Auster G-AGXP was by now semi-aerobatic, which means that although it was a standard Autocrat, it was fitted with strengthened seats and was thus authorised to do loops, stall turns, steep turns and spins. Using a bit of artistic licence I was able to turn this into a reasonably entertaining display which, when operated from an airfield, would include some slapstick humour on the ground before the flying started.

The show took two forms – depending on whether the site was an airfield or overhead a school or village fete or somewhere that could not include the take-off. In the latter, it was largely a matter of formal aerobatics with a bit of crazy cavorting, all carried out within a very small radius and at quite low level so that the crowd could enjoy a close-up view of this comparatively quiet and definitely slow aeroplane.

From airfields, it took the form of a comedy act in which, under one disguise or another, I 'stole' an aeroplane and then demonstrated how I was unable to fly it. Few pilots watching this act for the first time would have believed that an Auster was capable of doing what they were seeing – one CFI wrote to me suggesting that this was even more robust than Ranald Porteus demonstrating the aerobatic Auster – and Ranald was Auster's chief test pilot. But I suggested that what I was showing were merely demonstrations of what some students do to long-suffering instructors.

An item like this soon catches on in the flying world, and I found myself in demand for flying displays in all parts of the country. Obviously I could not run a flying club in my spare time while spending every weekend somewhere else, so I had to restrict this sort of thing mainly to the local area, but even then the frequency soon rose to some 12 to 15 shows per season.

Being a bit of an exhibitionist, I enjoyed the whole thing very much

– the disguises included a French peasant onion seller, a Russion VIP, a patient in the flying doctor service, and even a prisoner escaped from a local prison; all of these sweating under a long black beard and a black beret or a black Grecian lambskin hat.

The format involved a very good friend, Roy Wilks, who was in each case announced as the pilot of the aeroplane. He might for example be taxiing out to do a demonstration flight, when he would stop somewhere in front of the crowd and, with a display of very bad airmanship, would leave the engine running while he got out to inspect the tail wheel for some supposed fault – as the commentator would explain. Meanwhile, what looked like a French onion seller because he had a black beard, wore a beret and had a string of onions hanging from the handlebars of his bicycle, would pedal on to the runway and around the aeroplane. When I was an escaped prisoner the act was similar except that the dress would be prison garb complete with arrow heads.

In either case, the commentator would demand that the interloper be restrained immediately – but not before I had time to fall off the cycle and get into the aeroplane on the passenger's side. For the flying doctor service, Roy would taxi the aeroplane out in front of the crowd while two ambulancemen came through the crowd carrying a stretcher with a drip feeding into my arm from a bottle of gin. They had some difficulty in getting me into the right hand seat, so the pilot would similarly get out, this time to help to load the passenger, and the aeroplane would move off as he was returning via the tail to his seat. The routine was the same with the Russian VIP except that it all started with the blackbearded visitor being paraded in an open car before the crowd, prior to his having to be helped by the pilot.

The various introductions always led to the same thing while the tension was being worked up with varying degrees of competence by the commentators. In each case, the aeroplane would move off before the pilot could get back to his seat – generally he was just by the tail so the only thing he could do was to go down full-length and grab the tail-wheel, and Roy, bless him, made it all look so realistic by hanging on to be dragged along grass, mud or even tarmac until he had seemingly done all he could to stop the runaway aeroplane.

The take-off involved many of the blunders student-pilots have faced me with as an instructor, plus a few that I had thought up to make it a bit more exciting. Anyway the commentator would be stirring it up by advising the crowd that this untrained person would never be able to land it.

The show would continue with the aeroplane cavorting all around the airfield including specialities like the very slow fly into wind – even going backwards on some occasions when the wind was strong enough – and a heavily ruddered flat turn downwind over the crowd, giving them the impression that the aeroplane was travelling sideways. Rolling around would continue with the Auster gradually gaining height to fifteen hundred feet where it would do one or two clumsy aerobatics before it fell off the top of an excruciatingly bad loop and dropped into a spin from which the recovery was made along the runway, and clearing the ground with only a few feet to spare. No real danger here because the apparent recovery could be delayed deliberately for a short time after it is effective.

After that, up to five attempts would be made to land, including down-wind and flapless, a high hold-off with a late recovery at the stall, an enormous bounce with recovery about thirty feet up, and a wheel-landing with the aeroplane rocking violently from one wheel to the other, and wingtips only a few inches from the ground. The final one would generally be from a full-flap, steep, side-slipping approach turn to land on one wheel while still in the turn, and, if the wind were not too strong, we would end up with a controlled ground-loop.

I did these shows all over the place including twenty-one consecutive years at Seething near Bungay, and inevitably there were some funny incidents. I once asked a Policeman who was on duty at a show, if he would be good enough to 'arrest' me after landing, only to get a forceful explanation as to what his duties were – and these did not include "playing bloody games". On another occasion Anglia Television showed a bit of this hair-raising flying in their news programme and blamed Roy Legge for it, while ignoring his excellent, more formal, aerobatic display at the show. Bill Wix who was the delightful and unflappable officer in charge of the crash truck, once commented that the crew enjoyed my contribution, and he claimed that my display was clearly the most exciting, "As a matter of fact" he said, "we always start the engine as you come on"!

At Sleap in Shropshire, we had some difficulty with a nitwit of a commentator. I had tried unsuccessfully to brief him before the show (alas, he knew it all), but he did have a written description of the act. So imagine my amazement as I heard him tell the 45,000 crowd, just as Roy was taxiing out, that someone had stolen an aeroplane: I was in fact still hiding behind a shed with my beard and bicycle waiting for the aeroplane to get into a suitable position for my entry!

At Seething I had one of the two real scares of my life as a stunt pilot when, after a gliding stall-turn in an Auster, I found myself pointing vertically down at 500 feet with no airspeed, and a joystick that felt like a piece of wet spaghetti. At that moment it seemed that nothing would alter the attitude of the aeroplane, or its flightpath towards the ground. Afterwards, I could not remember whether or not I had opened the throttle – but somehow, the aeroplane had rounded out before reaching the ground, and the show went on.

I was a bit naughty on one occasion at Ipswich in that during the display, I added an item which seemed to offer a bit of heart-stopping excitement for the crowd – quite contrary to my normally highly-disciplined procedure, and it was outrageously impolite to the commentator. This was at a time before the building of the bridge over the river Orwell, and perhaps before I had learned of the danger of departing from your own set programme. With the Airport having an elevation of 128 feet above sea level, and the river close by, there was a fairly steep escarpment that I could disappear behind.

If the throttle is closed sharply, the engine produces a loud bang through the exhaust, so I employed this at about 200 feet along runway 32, in front of the crowd, thereby creating the impression that the engine had blown up. From there I was able to glide down to the left towards the river which was on the other side of the airfield below the crowd's line of sight – and that is where the aeroplane disappeared from their view. As soon as I was below the level of the cliff I opened the throttle again and turned the Auster left down-river, and then left again across the shore-line keeping low, out of sight and hearing, until I was in line with the trees on the threshold of runway 32.

Meanwhile, poor old Ron was left stranded – being the good commentator that he was, he kept going, deliberately building up the tension that something awful had happened to me, except that now he was not sure that this was still make-believe. Then, just as he was considering alerting somebody, the Auster appeared over the trees – it could only have taken me four minutes to get round to that position at low level, but it was a very long four minutes to Ron and the crowd. I never did that again.

It was at Seething at such an air show in 1968 that I stopped smoking – actually at 15.30 on Sunday the 30th of June, since when I have been able to look smugly down on, and express my sympathy for, those who still have to smoke – there can be nobody worse than the ex-smoker – but it was really all very simple.

Having just finished my display I parked the Auster and walked over to join club members who were watching from the privileged position of a special enclosure. Friend John was standing there so I picked on him to scrounge a cigarette from. As he lit it for me, his dishy blonde girl friend, Penny, looked across with what I hoped was a warm admiring gaze and said quite innocently, "I should think you need a cigarette after that".

I don't know what it was, maybe I took it as an insult to my manhood or an implication that I needed a fix or something, but my reaction was simply that if it appeared that I had to have a cigarette to help me recover after a display flight then it was time that I gave one of them up. So I threw the cigarette away, and continued showing off in aeroplanes for many more years.

Another amusing incident at Seething followed my 21st show there. A young lad who perhaps should not have been in the area of the 'display aircraft', came up to me as I was fiddling with the Auster after my display and said, "You know Mr Ward, you ought to think about altering your disguise: you have used that beard so often here that the people don't believe that the aeroplane has been stolen, because they know it is you!" Such is fame.

As a civilian pilot I took part in a number of "Battle of Britain" displays at RAF Stations, but without doubt the funniest one was at Coltishall in 1969. George Black, former leader of Treble-one Squadron with its famous 16 Lightning formation team, was Wing Commander Flying at this Operational Conversion Unit, and he wrote asking me if I would like to consider doing my stolen Auster show at their display on the 20th of September.

A show-off like me was being given the chance to display in front of about 100,000 people – would I just? A change of format for this occasion seemed reasonable to me so details of this were submitted by letter and telephone to George, along with a request for the co-operation of their commentator. Both were approved with no difficulty.

Don Peacock was happy that I should use his home-built Luton Minor at any time – this was a tiny, single seat, monoplane with a modified Volkswagon engine. The idea was that announcements would be made over the Tannoy that this aeroplane was so easy to fly that, later in the day, volunteers from the crowd would be invited to come forward and fly it, even if they had never flown before. If the selected person made a success of this, he or she would be invited to fly an Auster, and if this were satisfactory then the next offer would be the opportunity to fly a Lightning jet fighter.

The RAF commentator entered fully into the spirit of the thing, working up a great interest in the item by his many advance references to it, so that when the time came to invite volunteers to come forward, I was nearly killed in the rush! The officials had some difficulty in selecting a black-bearded gentleman.

There followed an immaculate display of flying in this lovely little aeroplane, including some low level work close-in along the line of the huge crowd, so that everyone had to agree that I should be given the opportunity to fly the Auster.

It was in fact a Taylorcraft Plus D owned by Eric Stephenson of Colchester, substituting for the club Auster because my employers were unwilling to provide the insurance cover required by the RAF. You could hardly blame the Company – they were after all in the business of selling flying to passengers of their airliners, or to students who were learning to fly. The top men in the Company did not get to know too much about the shows that did not require the extra insurance, but they had to be approached about the RAF requirement, and not surprisingly they did not think that a slightly crazy flying act in one of their aeroplanes would be the best advertisement for their services, especially if it were to have an accident at such a public event.

Anyway we were quickly settled into the Taylorcraft which was, up to this moment, definitely classified as a non-aerobatic aeroplane: the antics which followed departed from this if one accepts the official description of an aerobatic as 'any sudden change of speed or direction', because there were a few of those.

However, my slightly alarming standard display was much enjoyed, but nobody could have been surprised when the commentator stated with regret that it had been decided that the pilot would not be invited to fly the Lightning.

What most of the people except George, did not know, was that with his 16 Lightnings steaming away at the end of the runway waiting to take-off, I muffed the last crazy approach to land, and had to go around again before landing – 20 seconds behind schedule!

Earlier, I described one of the two scares of my stunt-flying career when I misjudged things a bit at Seething. The other happened at Felixstowe during a Battle of Britain fly-past and display when I was slotted in between an RAF Comet transport and a Phantom – both fairly big irons, one before and one after the little civilian non-radio Auster. I had four minutes to entertain the large crowd collected on the beach and the promenade south of the pier. Clearly, time was important – I had to be around waiting for the Comet to do his stuff while keeping well out of his way, but not far enough to allow the crowd to get bored while I struggled to get into position at 80 mph. Any time lost would have to come out of my four minutes before the Phantom would take over at about 500 mph.

Now all of this is very tricky – without radio you had to watch your watch, watch the Comet in case he over-ran or under-ran his time, watch where you are, then watch your watch and look out for the

Phantom while you are tearing the guts out of the aeroplane and yourself in front of the crowd and at low level over the sea.

Being ultra careful, I normally flew all such shows solo so that the aeroplane was as lightweight as possible, and I did not have to worry about anyone throwing-up over me, falling on me or otherwise distracting me, but on this occasion it seemed that to have an assistant with a watch and a pair of eyes would be a positive asset. Bernard Daniel had a feeling for aerobatics and he could count numbers, so he was the partner I selected, and he jumped at the opportunity.

So off we went near to the appointed time heading towards Felixstowe, with four eyes searching the sky trying to spot the Comet in, as they say, good time: the timing was perfect – it was the flying that caused the trouble, and then only to the two of us. Once again it was the low level stall turn that caused it – not a gliding one this time, at least it was not intended to be a gliding one because I went into it from sea level with full power and lots of speed, but I had misjudged the extra weight of Bernard normally my aeroplane was very light because there was only me and only just enough fuel to do the show, which often started and finished on an airfield.

But here we were, a bit heavy with Bernard and extra fuel for the return flight and a possible hang-around, so that we lost speed a little more rapidly than usual in the vertically upwards part, with the result that when I ruddered into the yaw which should have put us vertically downwards, we were going very slowly. So slowly that the change of attitude from upwards to downwards was delayed enough to starve the engine of fuel from the gravity-fed system. That was a pity because the propellor was now slowing down, and I knew that it would not get any encouragement to go faster until either the aeroplane speeded up in the dive or the fuel started flowing again with the change of attitude.

This probably sounds all very technical and unexciting, but it wasn't to us because as the propellor slowed to the point that we could see the individual blades, we were faced with the possibility that it might stop. If we had a self-starter it would have been only a small problem at 500 feet, and the fact that we did not have a self-starter would have been no problem at all if we had been over an airfield, even at 500 feet. But we were over the sea, and the beach and promenade were well covered with people – beyond them was a row of hotels and funfairs. If we had to come down, it followed that we had only the sea.

Of course, it didn't happen: don't ask me why not – we hadn't time to pray. Somehow the nose of the aeroplane went down far enough for our speed to increase sufficiently to keep the propellor windmilling until the fuel started to flow again as we pulled out of the dive, and we were back in business. The dry mouths, shaking hands and white faces were not visible to the crowd as we completed our four minutes without further incident.

Generally speaking, display flying is not really dangerous provided that the pilot maintains a firm personal discipline, keeps well in practice, and never does anything that he has not tried out before. Many an item can be made to look dangerous for the effect – for example, the recovery from a spin can be made to look as if there was only a few feet left at the bottom of the recovery dive by delaying the moment and rate of the pull-out.

Personal discipline is required to resist the temptation to add something that has not been thoroughly practised at high level where an accurate assessment of height loss can be made: a sudden desire to add something to an old routine, in the belief that because you are bored with it the crowd will also be finding it dull, can lead to excessively exciting additions that had not been intended.

THE BROTHERS

They came to me at about the same time in 1955, both wanting to learn to fly. I realised that brothers are sometimes very competitive – how true this could be I was about to find out. Jason, the elder, was a former Lieutenant-Commander, Royal Navy, who had served on destroyers – that should have warned me – but he was a nice guy, as long as I did not call him that. Shortish, round, face a bit pock-marked, he tended to look down even on those who were taller than he. He was clever enough to realise that in the country, working wives were ever-willing to get out of picking peas and strawberries, so he set up a small factory in a disused barn at the bottom of the garden of his house situated out in the wilds of Suffolk – wherever were the planning boys!

Timothy, his brother, was tall, lean and less boisterous. He ran a real engineering business in Colchester because being younger he had missed the war and had been able to take a degree and do things at a higher level. Because of that he was not so superior, and did not mind getting his hands dirty.

The flying club was at that time operating an Auster and a Tiger Moth. The brothers each duly took trial lessons after which Timothy elected to train on the Auster with a cabin like a motor car, while Jason went for the Tiger with open cockpits, head out in the wind, helmets and goggles with scarves and all that.

Within a couple of lessons I was closely questioned by each in turn as to how the other was progressing, and it soon became clear that here was a continuing contest to see who would get to the next exercise first, to say nothing of the battle for leadership in such delicate areas as first solo, cross-countries and eventually the licence itself – and I was piggy in the middle. I explained that flying instructors have a professional code which precludes any discussion concerning one student with another, but it was not possible to hide everything.

Jason frequently booked the first slot on Saturday mornings – unfortunately, as I soon realised, Saturday breakfast was not the most peaceful time in the Jason household, and he would arrive boiling over after some terrible domestic occurrence, and this took up about eighty per cent of his available powers of concentration, leaving me with only a small part of his brain to work on. Without this problem I am sure that he would have progressed as steadily as his brother, but he did fall behind, and if he had been aware of this it is certain that matters would have got worse.

So what do you do? I hate to confess this but I did deliberately slow down on Timothy in the early stages so as to keep their progress as even as possible – yes, a bit unfair on Timothy, but he was a brother and I was not doing it for profit. In that way we got them both solo within a lesson of each other – after that, progress in the advanced stage was fairly even. It all seemed reasonable to me because after the trauma of the first solo, it is normal for students to go steadily along at about the same pace, regardless of any pre-solo problems.

But poor Jason over-cooked it. I first detected a slightly superior ability during engine-assisted approaches, and then again during practice forced-landings without the engine. He not only handled things far too well during the exercises but was ahead of me during pre-flight discussions in a way which indicated some practical experience.

The truth slowly started getting through to me. A call to the nearest flying school using Tiger Moths resulted in my being informed that they had a student of the same name taking dual instruction!

This is no crime – in fact it could even be applauded as a student really keen to get to know all about it from two independent sources. I did not tax him with it – I had enough problems already.

They reached the licence test at about the same time in 1966, and it was here that my struggle to keep them together ended when Jason twice fell into a spin from his demonstration of stall recoveries. He was a bit put out at having failed, and generously accused me of feeding in rudder just as he was recovering, but I don't think that he meant it, and after a little more dual stalling, he passed with no further trouble. After that we enjoyed a long friendship.

A STUDENT CROSS-COUNTRY

Alan was Managing-Director of a small manufacturing company; a very pleasant fellow aged about 40, with a ready smile and a well developed sense of humour – so we got along together in fine style from the time he came to me in 1959 to learn to fly. He had been an observer in the RAF during the war – observer was an aircrew position which has been superseded by the navigator; the brevet was a half-wing attached to an 'O' – a combination which had long ago earned it a slightly indelicate nick-name. It indicated that he was quite an old sweat, but he was not very keen to talk of his experiences on bomber operations, although I did learn that he had suffered a flaming crash in a Wellington bomber.

He did not however try to hide the fact that he was a former alcoholic who had been dried out the very hard way – so hard that it was a nightmare for him even to think of the treatment. For that reason, while he would readily join in the odd drinking session at the club, he would take only soft drinks because the smallest amount of alcohol would result in his immediate return to the craving.

He created a minor incident during his training, when he was on a short solo cross-country flight which should have taken about an hour. My philosophy when sending early students off on cross-country exercises in non-radio aircraft was that once the decision had been taken to send him or her off, then the thing to do was to forget about it – because after the take-off there is not a darned thing you can do about the flight, so you may as well relax instead of worrying yourself into an early grave.

But Alan stretched my resolve a bit when after three hours Jack, our engineer, appeared out of the darkness to call through the window, "Do you think I might close the hangar doors – don't think he'll be coming in now". I agreed, in fact, my prayer was almost audible – please don't let him be heard overhead an unlighted airfield with no night experience as pilot! "Yes, thank you Jack, close it up".

I carried on with my normal writing up of the day's activities and students' notes, feeling just a squeak of concern. He must be down somewhere because his fuel is exhausted by now, so why hasn't he telephoned? If the worst has happened, surely the police would have identified the aircraft from the flameproof plate in the cockpit. Nonsense – Alan was too clued-up to continue flying after dark, even if he was lost.

"Hello Stan, Alan here, sorry about all this." "Where the devil are you?" He was in the Kings Head Hotel in Beccles, safe and sound and the aeroplane was undamaged, standing out somewhere on a disused airfield at Ellough. "Not tied down?" How could he, without any picketing stakes? "Stay there, keep sober, and I'll get to you as soon as possible."

Later that evening, he told me that after turning overhead Sudbury to return to Ipswich, he had set course on what must have been a few degrees in error to the left with the result that instead of passing Ipswich slightly to his left, he had passed it out of sight to his right. When the town failed to show up, he decided that it would be best to continue on course because he must meet the coast eventually, and he would then be able to pin-point his position accurately.

Eventually was the right word, because he hit the coast just north of Lowestoft, forty miles away. After circling for a while, he realised that he was nowhere near where he had expected to be, and he did not know which way to turn but, probably from his navigater's training in the RAF, he was aware that you cannot hold back the sun which was already sinking a bit low in the west.

The awful realisation that he was unlikely to get back to Ipswich before dark brought to his memory the fact that he had passed over a large airfield before reaching the coast, so he turned on to a reverse heading, found the disused airfield at Ellough, and landed. To collect his thoughts and probably to relieve himself, he switched the engine off, forgetting that with no self-starter and nobody to swing the propellor for him, it would be impossible to re-start even to taxi the aeroplane to a more sociable and sheltered spot.

There was not a sign of life on this huge airfield: the whole thing looked pretty bleak from his position in the middle of a runway, with the gathering dusk and without the slightest idea of which way to go. There was not much that he could do about the aeroplane except to check the brakes and secure the controls as best he could, so with this done he set off hoping to find a road. After a very long walk he found one but then a great deal of time was spent before he had any success in thumbing a lift from the few cars that used it. That was the reason for the delay in calling me.

After his call, budding-pilot John drove me to Beccles in the airport car, where we met Alan, found the aeroplane and tied it down for the night with stakes and ropes. Alan then treated us to a very fine meal in the King's Head before we drove back home. Good old Alan, he enjoyed the ribbing on the fact that as an observer in the RAF he was a navigator!

Fortunately, the next morning was fair so that we were able to fly up very early in another aeroplane: I briefed him for the return flight and thus he completed his first solo cross-country without further incident, and I flew back in time to get the Sunday programme started at 0900.

Alan went on to complete the course without any difficulty, and qualified for the Private Pilots Licence. He continued to take dual trips with me so as to further his knowledge and experience. During this time he made the startling observation that Le Touquet across the Channel was nearer to us than Brighton – and thus it was that it was he who started the club on cross-channel flying on the 1st of July 1960, when we visited Lympne (later Ashford, now closed), Le Touquet, Lympne and Sandown in one day, without radio, at 80 knots! On the 3rd of August 1960 we did Ipswich, Lympne, Lille, Rotterdam, Ostend, Lydd, Ipswich, in the same conditions and again, in one day.

AUSTER TO ROME

"How about Rome in HZ?" This was Alan again, early in 1961. "Good idea, I'll check your flight plan, hope you have a good time." "No, you idiot, I mean you and me." There was probably nothing I would rather do than go on such a trip but things were getting busy at the club, and I was well aware of the enormous amount of administrative work involved in planning a flight like this.

"I would love the trip Alan, but you know that I am the only instructor with the club, so it would have to be done between Monday and Friday and you would have to do all the flight planning, with clearances and things." So we planned for June with the longest daylight, and we agreed the route to be followed: it would be necessary to land at international airports for customs clearance out of England, into and out of France outbound and on return, and into and out of Italy – we would need written authority to use these airports in a small aeroplane without radio. That was not the only problem – it would be necessary for us to land for fuel after about every 160 miles, because the HZ carried only 15 gallons and burned 6 per hour, during which she would fly 80 nautical miles in still air.

It was a credit to Alan's administrative flair – and to his firm's secretarial and telephone services – that these problems were solved, and there was no difficulty in agreeing his final flight plan.

HZ was a more popular aeroplane for cross-country work than the modest Autocrat, largely because she cruised at 80 knots against 80 mph (i.e. 12 mph faster) and she had those 'modern' gyro-driven blind-flying instruments – the artificial horizon and direction indicator. She also sported a self-starter – the only one among the EAF Club's fleet; but here was another snag – the starter relied on a twelve-volt battery, and the aeroplane had no generator. All would be well with a newly-charged battery, but if we suffered one difficult start, we would be left with nothing for the future – the beautiful Lycoming engine could spoil your whole day in a propeller swinging marathon if it was other than cold or very hot – but this had to be accepted.

To get a little more time for the trip, we left Ipswich shortly after lunch on the Sunday, which was the 4th of June: customs was cleared at Lympne and we arrived comfortably at Beauvais to stay the night. Sadly we awoke to low cloud and drizzle so it was late morning before we got airborne in very marginal conditions, aiming for Chalons-sur-Saone. We groped along at about 1000 feet until roughly half-way where we met higher ground which was 'in it', and after some flying along below the ridge searching fruitlessly for a break, we realised that we had no alternative but to land somewhere.

The map showed an airfield at Pont-sur-Yonne which was not too far away, and lower than the high ground; we were however not well enough equipped with information to know that with no flying on Mondays, sheep were allowed on to the field to cut the grass! But after a couple of runs along our selected landing path, we were pleased to see the sheep indicating their willingness to move aside and allow us to land.

The place was deserted so our arrival excited no interest whatever, unless you count the sheep. It was obvious that we were not going anywhere by air for some little while, so we waited by a bus-stop on the adjoining road, and found some lunch in the small town of Sens. We had flown for one hour twenty-five minutes which meant that we had to get some fuel before going any further, so it was with some relief on return to the airfield, that we found a gentleman who was quite co-operative and understanding of our problem. He provided us with some fuel and a bit of weather information which assured us that the weather would not get any worse.

We could now see a gap between the ridge of the high ground and the cloud base, so we got into the air again on our new heading to Chalons. Unhappily, all was woodland, and we could get only 200 feet above the tree-tops: there were no pinpoints of navigation to be seen, so we were unable to check our track over the ground. With no radio or radio-navigation aids we just had to maintain our compass heading, and hope. As navigator I was not too unhappy as long as we had the gap between trees and cloud, because we were flying towards the river Saone which crossed our intended track at roughly a right angle, so it was reasonable to believe that we must hit it somewhere.

We did just this after 55 minutes of slightly hair-raising tree-skimming, but I had not been bright enough to deliberately aim to one side or other of Chalons, so when we reached the river we did not know whether we were north or south of the airfield. We made a guess to fly north, only to find after a few miles that Murphy's law had prevailed, because the airfield we found had the name Beaune painted on the roof of its hangar; that saved us from making a silly landing, so we turned 180 degrees to the south and got to Chalons with no further trouble.

Our plan now was a quick refuel then down the rivers Saone and Rhone to Avignon, but the controller at Chalons told us that this was not possible because we were entering a defence area and would therefore have to land at Valence for clearance. After a short argument he made a telephone call to someone to seek a way out of this but we were advised that this was the law: So we were now really in a hurry, because the going down of the sun cannot be slowed. All very vexing especially when we landed at Valence where the controller more or less said what are you doing here if you are going to Avignon? We did not hang around, and that was how we set off on one of those flights that you wish you had never started.

There is I believe little worse than finding yourself on a flight which has passed the point of no return and you are not sure that you can get to the destination – especially in a foreign country. Airfields that are new to you are not always easy to find even if you are a perfect map-reader and it is in reasonable daylight. As we ploughed along it became clear, if that is the word, that it was going to be mighty duskish when we got there.

We got there after 55 minutes from Valence, or 2 hours 20 minutes from Chalons, or 5 hours 20 minutes for that day from Beauvais – 5.20 of constant concern about weather, fuel and daylight! I was tired, but fortunately we had no difficulty in finding Avignon, and landing before everyone had gone home. A gentleman whom we named Long John Silver because he humped himself around on a single much-too-long crutch, went well beyond the call of duty to get us tied down, booked in and transported into town for our night-stop.

Tuesday gave us no weather problems so we set off in high spirits, reasonably satisfied that we would make Rome that day. High across the mountains to Cannes (Mandelieau) for customs out of France – I was reminded of Alan's pre-start assurance that we would stay only at the best hotel available, for any night-stop, planned or otherwise, with the exception of Cannes, but it looked as if the question would not arise.

We landed after one hour twenty minutes, refuelled and got airborne without delay heading for Albenga, which had been planned as the Monday night-stop but the delays had altered the plans; the stop was necessary however in order to clear customs into Italy, and to pick up fuel. Albenga nestles in the foothills, enjoying a single runway with its threshold very close to a goodly-sized mountain, so that landings were made towards the high ground and take-offs were made away from it.

What was that ominous rumble? It sounded like thunder. The time was 1300 hours local. "Across the Gulf (of Genoa)? Not today my friends. Such flights in small aeroplanes have to be made in the mornings – by afternoon, the moist breeze from the sea sweeps in, gets lifted by the mountains, water condenses into cloud and up it goes into thunderstorms." Pilots of the Italian Air Force were available in numbers to contribute their confirmatory stories about the weather in the Gulf, enough to convince us that we had a half-day to ourselves in nearby Alassio – and a great afternoon and night we did have at this delightful seaside resort.

Then it was Wednesday, a fine day with a bit of wind. Swift calculations indicated that we would be tight on fuel by Rome so a landing would have to be made at Genoa a little more than half an hour away, to top-up for the long haul down the leg of Italy. So we filed a Flight Plan to Genoa. Can you imagine today a small non-radio aeroplane landing at Genoa to pick up about four gallons of fuel? But at that time Genoa did not have its huge runway which runs parallel with the coast – the runway then was the little stub which connects today's runway with the land, except that since then it has been considerably improved. Once again we had the situation where it was safer to land towards the mountains and take-off the other way.

With refuelling completed we rechecked our calculations for the new Flight Plan to Rome! Horror upon horrors, with the updated wind forecast we would still be unable to reach Rome with sufficient reserve of fuel. There could be no messing about, we would have to land again somewhere for a further top-up. Someone kindly offered Sarzana, explaining that it was a small grass field just inland from Spezia – this was about an hour's flying to us and therefore just right for our fuel requirement. A telephone call confirmed their willingness to accept us and supply fuel, so our Flight Plan was adjusted to include the stop at Sarzana.

There was a small snag on this leg! Spezia boasted an Italian Naval Base, and to protect it from sneak bombers or spies in the sky – even in an Auster – they had a ten-mile radius exclusion zone. We were informed with all due severity that we must not under any circumstances enter this zone because the Navy had a habit of shooting first and asking questions afterwards. No problem for us, it merely meant that instead of flying down just off-shore to Spezia and turning left inland to Sarzana, we would have to climb about 2000 feet over the Ligurian Apennine Mountains bordering the west coast, and fly down the valley.

So off we go, full equally of fuel and confidence. Except that a few minutes later, Alan put out the mock-horror statement, "Oh dear, look Stan, the mountain tops are in cloud". "I had noticed, but we have a good distance to go, perhaps we'll find a break before Spezia". This wishful thinking did not help one little bit because the tops remained solidly in cloud even as we approached the boundary of the exclusion zone.

Decision time was upon us – we could go out to sea and fly around this ten-mile zone back to the coast and then northwards to Sarzana, but this did not appeal to us because with no radio and no navigation aids, the avoidance of the zone over the sea would have to be entirely by dead reckoning. It was the 'dead' that worried us – we were both ex-RAF aircrew and it appeared to us that the Italian Air Force may well have the courage to take on a heavily-armed Auster which could end up under the water.

The only immediate alternative was to do a 180 degree turn back to Genoa; and this we did, but our eyes remained to the right on the line of the cloud-base where it met the hills, in the hope that we might get a sight of the mountain ridge. In the meantime we were reading the map to find that the ridge which was in cloud fell away on the other side as steeply as it rose on this side, so that once we had crossed the ridge, we could let down into the valley beyond and continue to Sarzana without any difficulty.

Then a shaky cloud-flecked ridge appeared – we looked at each other. "Shall we have a go?" Violent nodding gave approval. We reckoned that 2200 feet would clear the ridge with safety; we were below the cloud at 1800 feet and we estimated that this small climb could be achieved by aiming directly at the gap. We were soon in cloud! This was very vexing – many years ago I had promised myself that I would never fly in cloud in the vicinity of hills because so many of them have hard centres.

As we passed 2000 feet without hitting anything, we knew that our climb calculation was good, and comfort was regained. Yes, but when do we let down on the other side? A good question and one answered by Alan who, while I maintained immaculate instrument flight, calculated the minimum time to clear the ridge without getting mixed up with high ground further inland. Based on this we duly descended; I wonder how many readers of this have ever had to let-down in this way, and how many have experienced the funny sensation in the part you are sitting on, that, at any moment now, you are going to feel the aeroplane scraping along the ground. But it didn't happen – soon we were below the cloud, and there was the valley with hills on both sides, dead ahead.

So we gaily proceeded towards Sarzana – or so we thought. But after a short time, we became aware that the valley floor was rising, so with the hills on both sides being locked in cloud we were flying into a dead end where the valley floor also disappeared into cloud. In the meantime, we were low flying relative to the ground and the ground was getting nearer.

Nasty! But why had it happened? The valley should be lowering towards the river which went out to the sea at Spezia. A glance at our compass heading revealed it all – with a heading of 130 degrees we must be in the wrong valley; the valley we wanted was nearer due south. In our excitement at having cleared the ridge, we had been daft enough to go for the valley that appeared dead ahead, without bothering to check its direction.

Experience gained in stunt flying near the ground does have some value as I found now in having to complete a 180 degree turn below the cloud and within the walls of the valley, but apart from frightening a few farm animals and perhaps one of two Italian farmers, this went well, and after a bit of back-tracking then a turn left down the valley required, we reached Sarzana.

There was not a lot going on at this little airfield, and we had taxied in, parked and shut down before anyone appeared. Then it was a couple who gesticulated wildly towards a small building. They did not have a word of English and we were without any Italian, but their manner indicated that all was not well, and that this was not going to be the simple matter of re-fuel and away, that we had hoped for.

After some discussion between them, one dashed off, to return very quickly with a middle-aged lady who explained that she was an English school-teacher, married to an Italian and living nearby. She was able and willing to act as interpreter and soon explained that we were required to contact Pisa Air Traffic Control on our arrival at Sarzana. She made the telephone contact and I took over to be advised that Rome had refused our Flight Plan because of inclement weather forecasted for the estimated time of our arrival.

So that was that – tomorrow was Thursday and I had to be back to run a flying club on Saturday morning so our attempt on Rome was now finished. Because of the usual weather in the Gulf it was too late to start the return journey that day, so we must stay the night here. I wanted to refuel in readiness for an early start the next day but no, we could not refuel the aeroplane today because the Commandant was no longer here; he had received the message that we could not go on, and had expected that we would try again tomorrow, so he had pushed off.

However, all was not gloom because we obtained a promise that our interpreter would be present at 0800 in the morning, and she called a taxi to take us to the best hotel in Spezia. My clear recollection of this journey was of high speed around hairpin bends with mountain on one side and sheer drops on the other, and of frantic overtaking on the drop side of blind corners; Alan and I took to looking at each other and shaking hands in farewell at each of these hazardous moments.

The Spezia Hilton Hotel made it all worthwhile – not frantically busy, they provided no less than four waiters in attendance on us at dinner, and I will swear that when my napkin fell from my lap, one of them caught it before it reached the floor.

After a good night's rest we were ready for the hazardous ride back to the airfield, but not for what greeted us there. The commandant was obviously a former local fascist boss, now having to satisfy his authoritarianism in the tiny role of boss of this tiny grass airfield, where refuelling meant pouring in from jerrycans!

He played us up until we could have burst, by inspecting every piece of paper that we had, and then asking through the interpreter for more documents, although it was clear that he could not understand those that he already had. For example, it is normal to enter the word 'self' in your own logbook in the column headed 'Captain' when you are flying in that capacity – he questioned Alan very searchingly as to who this Mr Self was.

It ended when he saw that we just had nothing else to show him, by his picking out a sheet of paper with hand-written details of the flight times of the aeroplane which we were keeping to enable our engineer to make up the aircraft and engine logbooks on our return: "This is what I wanted" he said; in better times we might have started laughing.

Refuelling could now proceed from five gallon tins as I looked fearfully at the cloud already forming at the top of the hills that had caused some of our problems the day before. So I went back into the office with the interpreter and asked the boss man if we could now takeoff for the return to Albenga. "You may not take off for one hour", I was told. "But cloud is already forming on the hills and very soon the tops will be completely in cloud, and we have to get over to the other side. We are ready for immediate departure, and we could cross the hills in the clear if we left now". I might as well have saved my breath, he was adamant – no departure for one hour.

As I walked back to the aeroplane with the teacher, I told her that I intended to start up on the pretext of taxiing away from the fuel store, but then we would takeoff and get away. "Don't do that" she advised, "he would call Albenga, and you will be arrested and thrown in jail as soon as you land". And so we waited for exactly one hour with no explanation why – an hour during which I had watched the cloud thicken and lower, until the whole of the ridge was blanketed.

As we had anticipated this, Alan had been working out our track up the valley to ensure that we could safely enter cloud and climb to 2200 feet before we came anywhere near high ground. Then it would be a simple matter to allow enough time to get north of the exclusion zone before turning left. We would then fly for long enough to clear the mountains, and we could be generous about the timing here, because we would be letting down over the sea.

And that is what we did, then we kept well clear of Genoa by staying out at sea, and duly landed at Albenga to clear customs, one hour and thirty minutes after take-off. Albenga to Cannes for customs into France took one hour and five minutes with a quick refuel and push-on for the two hours twenty minutes to Chalons-sur-Saone. And that was enough for Thursday the 8th of June. Weather permitting, Ipswich was on the cards for Friday to start work on the Saturday – except that Alan spent some of the evening convincing me that we could ease some of our disappointment over Rome by dropping in to Paris for Friday night; a nice early start on Saturday morning would have me back at the club only a little bit late. His persuading took all of twenty seconds.

There would be no problem at Paris – I had been to Toussus-le-Noble many times; it was an airport for general aviation – they required no notice of arrival, were happy with non-radio aircraft and had customs for our clearance next morning.

So after a night in Chalons, we set off direct to Toussus which was about twenty miles to the south-east of the city. As we approached Paris the clock indicated that we were eating into our reserves of fuel but the gauge kept us confident that we had nothing to worry about. A pity really because as we flew down-wind in the circuit, just after pre-landing checks had shown sufficient fuel to go around again if necessary, the engine stopped!

Alan swore that I had taken over control and turned in towards the runway before he realised that we had lost the engine, but I had been around a long time in single-engined aeroplanes and had become acutely aware of the value of that noise. It was unfortunate for the French twin who was in the late stages of his approach to land, because I had no option but to cut across in front of him, so forcing him to go around. The runway was of goodly length so it was not difficult to judge this dead-stick approach, and we landed with no problem, using our momentum to roll off to the left between the landing lights and on to the grass.

I expected at least a crash wagon to race to us with immediate assistance, because the tower must have seen that our propeller had stopped during the landing. Or they might have sent an official to demand an explanation of our dreadful airmanship which had caused a French aircraft to abort his landing. But I have had to conclude that on noting the British registration, they put it all down to the potty English who are best left to their own devices. Unhappily for us this meant that we had to push our aeroplane across a lot of grass and concrete to a parking place on the apron, where we could tie it down. We reported to Air Traffic Control who confirmed my conclusion about their opinion of the English, because they did not even refer to our obvious difficulty.

However, Alan was good to his word and after a taxi ride to the city, we booked into the Hotel Windsor-Etoile in the Rue Beaujon and had a most enjoyable evening in Paris.

Two hours to Lympne the next morning, a phone call, and fifty minutes to Ipswich, enabled me to do no less than five instructional trips during that afternoon. We used to work in those days!

And that was how Jack, our engineer, learned that the fuel gauge of HZ indicated two gallons when in fact the tank was down to the unusable. This was adjusted on our return, but that was no excuse for me – instead of believing that the rate of consumption was low when it showed two gallons after two and a half hours flying, I should have accepted that the gauge was lying.

TO GERMANY

This trip was a classic example of the idea that many major accidents are the result of the coming together of a number of more minor incidents. The chapter could have been written to demonstrate the truth of that doctrine, but every incident did actually happen on that flight – in fact, I have used the details in a number of flight safety lectures.

It all started with an invitation to Bert Quinton to visit an hotel in Rheine, Germany, by the German owner who had enjoyed some hospitality from Bert during a visit to one of the flying club's rallies in 1965, and I was invited along to accompany him.

So we planned to depart on Tuesday the 31st of August 1965 and return on Thursday the 2nd of September, to fly in Bert's Cessna 175 G-ARMN. We were sure that the aeroplane would be fit because I had taken it over to Cranfield for servicing on the previous Thursday, and I had flown it to Le Touquet and back on the Friday.

It was based at RAF Wattisham so we were able to obtain a weather forecast for the period of our flight direct from the met-office, and this was good. MN had been refuelled at Ipswich on the previous evening so, as we pushed her out of the hangar, an early start was on the cards. The pre-flight inspection showed all to be well, Bert started the engine – and there, gleaming on the dashboard, was the generator warning light, indicating that something was amiss in that department.

It continued to shine at us throughout the warming-up and the running-up, so we decided without hesitation to fly the aeroplane back to Cranfield to get it fixed before departure for Germany – a sound decision. At Cranfield, a number of engineers descended upon the engine with spanners and screwdrivers, and in a short time pronounced that all was well.

We set off for Southend for flight-plan filing and customs clearing, and were soon airborne to overfly France, Belgium and Holland en route to Nordhorn for customs into Germany – our ultimate destination was Rheine but that small airfield had no customs facility.

It was at mid-channel that the generator warning light came on again. We considered turning back – out of the question: land at Calais – what, and suffer all the problems of getting the French to look at it? Our conclusion was, "Sod that – our electricity demand is quite small and we'll cut down the use of radio to the bare minimum, so let us press on".

There was no need even to talk to anyone so we switched off the radio and continued navigating by map-reading with watch and compass, enjoying the detail of the low countries in quite good visibility. Then a slight trauma was felt at the sight of a line of blackish looking cloud ahead and to the right – yes, the met-man did say that there was some weather moving towards our track later in the day but not before our estimated time of arrival – the unpleasant thought was that we were now at least two hours behind our scheduled time.

Things looked nastier as we got nearer to the cloud, very black and reaching down to the ground – so there was no question of getting underneath it. And this is where I became the meteorological adviser, suggesting that as this looked like a cold front, it may be quite narrow. We would not be foolhardy about it, but would continue into the cloud, maintaining our heading for fifteen minutes – if we did not fly into clear air in that time, we would turn 180 degrees and come out of it.

That sounds reasonable doesn't it? It got rough even before we entered cloud, then it became really lively. In my peculiar way (I have improved since then) I rather enjoyed the battle with the elements – having taken over control by now – and we duly pressed on in the clag. Reasonable control was maintained although there was a bit of violent upping and downing about which nothing much could be done.

Disappointed after the fifteen minutes with no lightening skies to indicate that we were getting through the weather, we turned back and hoped to fly out of it in about the same time. There is no harm in hoping, but after 30 minutes we were still in it. After satisfying ourselves that we must be over the Netherlands, we deemed it safe and wise to descend to 800 feet in the hope that we would be able to see the ground. And the mist-shrouded ground did come into sight – just.

It did not however take us long to find that this was just a hole in the cloud, and we could stay in the clear only by circling in this area. I began now to look at our situation – and came to the conclusion that things were getting nasty. Not surprising considering my idiocy. Fuel was getting a bit low because I had not bothered to re-fuel at Southend after the trip to Cranfield. Now we were in a position that would require continuous use of the radio – with the generator warning light glowing brightly. And we were in weather that we might have learned about if we had taken the trouble to update the weather forecast after the two-hour delay in going to Cranfield.

By now a request for a bit of assistance did seem to be necessary, so we switched the radio on and selected the frequency of Hanover Control which was our planned call to get into Nordhorn. Repeated transmissions brought no response from Hanover, but a high-flying airliner called us to say that Hanover were not receiving us, and suggested that we call Amsterdam.

I changed frequency and did that, explaining our situation and asking if I might be allowed to make a precautionary landing in a suitable field in this area. My plea of thirty minutes fuel remaining and the problem of the warning light cut no ice – we wished then that I had gone ahead and landed instead of asking, although I must admit that the poor visibility would have made a landing approach on to an unknown surface, a bit hazardous.

We were then directed to climb to 2000 feet on a heading to steer for Twente, which was a NATO airfield just inside the Dutch border with Germany. This involved going back into the cloud, and just as we left the clear area that we had been in, we were startled nearly out of our wits by the sight of a huge mast-like edifice just a few feet below us – we learned later that this was a communications tower near Markelo in the Netherlands.

We now had to contact Twente Approach Control, and came up against as near a refusal to land as they could muster. This was a NATO airfield under strict military security, and was not available to civil aircraft. The airfield was closed-in by the most dreadful weather conditions. Our landing there would create considerable administrative difficulties for everybody concerned and it would be much better if we went away and landed somewhere else.

Being violently tossed about in cloud, and battered by torrential rain, we were becoming – to put it mildly – deeply concerned about our future, so it was not too difficult to declare an emergency on the grounds of the generator situation and our fuel state. From then on we received a series of headings to steer to reach Twente, but we were well aware that if the battery became drained by our use of the radio, we would be left with no communication and therefore no radio aids, and we would then be in real trouble. We did not discuss this throughout what seemed an age during which we received and acknowledged heading changes until we were eventually handed over to the GCA (ground controlled approach) Director who, with the use of radar, gave us headings and descent instructions down to the runway.

The final approach was completely blind so that my first sight of the runway was after we had crossed the threshold and were within fifty feet of the surface. Visibility in the heavy rain was such that, after landing, we had to be steered with radio instructions to the apron which we reached just three hours and five minutes after leaving Southend – but it was then that the trouble started.

We were escorted into the control tower which was a massive ominous-looking building in the German style. There were not a lot of laughs nor jolly greetings for us, and we got the distinct impression that we were where we should not have been. An extensive grilling started and went on and on – this was not actually the Gestapo, but it must have been very similar to it, albeit without the fear of the concentration camp to follow. Why had we landed there? where had we been going? why? why were we flying an American aeroplane? (it was American built but British registered) did we not know about the weather before we set off? why did we not ask Amsterdam to send us somewhere else?

Just as the questioning appeared to be getting more gentle and the atmosphere was becoming easier, we were asked to produce our passports. Bert's was okay but mine had details of a three-week stay in communist East Germany during February and March of that year – the result was that we immediately found ourselves to be back to square one, with a heavy show of deep suspicion. It was at least two hours before we were accepted as friendly, if unwanted, visitors.

By now it was well into the evening, and we were thankful that one of the Officers offered to give us a lift to an hotel in the nearby town of Enschede, which we gladly accepted after ensuring that our aeroplane had been safely housed for the night. The hotel had an international feel about it, and therein lay the seeds of the next incident.

After a good meal, we made our way to the basement which housed an enormous U-shaped bar around which were assembled a virtual United Nations of representatives of NATO, almost all of whom were engaged in boisterous non-stop talking and drinking. Unfortunately I enjoy this sort of thing so it was not long before we were embroiled in both activities, except that Bert was much more sensible about the drinking part than I was. Inevitably I got on to the one-swallow way of drinking Dutch gin and that is where I went seriously wrong.

The next morning was indeed the morning after, but I will spare myself from having to go over the dreadful details – suffice it to say that it was after midday before I was able even to get on my feet.

The only aircraft that we saw at Twente was an F86 Sabre fixed on a plinth at the entrance, but I cannot believe that the fear of our getting a sight of that was the reason they were so unhappy about our landing there on the previous day. There was no fuel available for us, but a visual check of our tanks indicated that we had enough at least to reach Nordhorn. The folk in authority were now quite friendly, and they did not question my fitness to fly, so we obtained clearance into Nordhorn and set off on the fifteen minute flight, carefully avoiding the bombing range nearby, which was in actual use by NATO aircraft.

A further fifteen minute flight had us safely on the ground at Rheine where we enjoyed the hospitality for only one night instead of the planned two. No problems on the return flight via Nordhorn, Ostende for lunch, and Southend again.

So let this be a lesson. The generator loss by itself may have been acceptable with the normal minimum use required – the fact that we had burned off some of our fuel still left sufficient for the trip including some reserve – and the weather by itself was not fatally dangerous. But the three things coming together provided the ingredients for a very nasty accident. The moral is clear – if something goes wrong, for safety's sake get it sorted before anything else gets added to it.

Chapter Seven

BILL

BILL CAME to us in 1966. Short, strong and stocky, with a shock of white hair, he was a coal merchant who had worked as a coalman throughout his earlier years, and who continued as a deliverer after he inherited the business from his father and until he handed it over to his younger brother on retirement.

He is one of nature's gentlemen, proud of his cockney roots and of his RAF service as an airframe rigger; a man of the world who could recognise a rogue from quite a number of paces. The two great loves of his life were horses and flying, probably in that order. He enjoyed the gift of a great sense of humour and a laugh which survived the tribulations of twelve months in the Army 'Glasshouse' at Colchester.

Bill quickly became an established part of the East Anglian Flying Club. He enjoyed the challenge of learning to fly and loved his time at the club, so that he spent the whole of every Sunday with us. During this time he would be ready to help anybody with anything, and among other tasks he became a great help to me by voluntarily taking on the job of swinging the propellers to start up the Austers' engines.

His tangle with authority could perhaps be described as a kindness to his fellow airmen, in assisting them to spend more time with their families. This was achieved by his early acquisition of a few pads of Form 295 (the leave pass) and an orderly-room rubber stamp, together with the simple ability as a Leading Aircraftsman to sign the said forms as Squadron Leader Agnew.

With this facility, the groundcrew team to which he belonged, reckoned that they could maintain their aircraft with only three of the four fitters and riggers. They had to work a bit harder, but there were no complaints about this because they knew that the reward would be their own extra leave periods in turn. This scheme evidently continued for well over two years before it came unstuck when all hands were suddenly required in the urgency at the time of the Normandy invasion.

At the resulting Court Martial he was sentenced to eighteen months detention – I can only assume that the RAF were not able to accommodate Bill at that time because he ended up with the Army. The very word 'Glasshouse' gives the shivers to any man with wartime RAF service but Colchester enjoyed a hardship reputation second to none, and it was here that he learned what is meant by 'roughing it' and 'hard labour'. However, he was a good boy there (I suspect that there was little alternative) and he was released after one year – for good behaviour.

That does not alter the fact that Bill had a heart of gold. He would not claim to have been the world's best student-pilot but he certainly did not lack keenness. His practical work was good but his mental arithmetic in the air left a lot to be desired, and this became a real problem as we got into navigation. Like most cockneys, he was pretty hot stuff at handling money but my suggestion that he should imagine that he was counting pounds whenever he had problems with degrees and miles got us nowhere.

When involved in assessing a student's ability, and his right, to hold a private pilot's licence, I used to feel it necessary occasionally to wander away from the fixed standards that had to be laid down by authority.

Bill Town – one of nature's gentlemen with Auster G-ANHZ.

People differ a great deal – for example, what I require of an over-confident young man with a tendency to show off can often be quite a bit different from what I expect from a quiet, elderly man who is achieving a long-held ambition to fly an aeroplane, and whose experience of life has taught him to appreciate his limitations.

With Bill, I had soon become aware that he was not one who would be dashing off to fly all over the continent. He had early shown his love of aerobatics or indeed anything that exercised his aim to handle an aeroplane with skill – quite the opposite to flying careful straight-lines for hours on end. If he wanted any of that he could, after getting his licence, always take another pilot along to do the navigating for him.

But we still had to get him a licence, and the syllabus required the completion of a number of solo navigation exercises including the test cross-country which required a triangular trip involving two 'away' landings, one of which had to be at least 50 nautical miles from base. The 'local' cross-country flights did not present too much of a problem – he could fly very accurately, his map-reading was quite sound and the trips lasted little more than an hour. So even if things went wrong he could easily fly to the coast and read his way home. In fact all went well on these so we were now faced with the solo test exercise which involved flying to Cambridge and landing, then to Luton for landing and refuel, then back to Ipswich.

Repeated dual trips during which we practised going off the planned track, and then calculating the necessary corrections to get back on track and to maintain it, merely proved that there was no way that Bill was going to be able to do such sums on his own. I had no intention of cooking the books to overcome this problem – that is not my style. But it did occur to me that because of Bill's ability to fly headings and airspeeds with such accuracy, the trip could be done without the need for these calculations.

All we needed was a windless day! We spent a lot of time practising getting into position overhead the airfield, at the correct altitude, with the correct airspeed on the correct heading for the next destination. We practised overhead Ipswich, setting off for Cambridge, we simulated overhead Cambridge, setting off for Luton and we simulated overhead Luton, setting off for Ipswich, until these were perfect. Then all we needed was nil wind – with that he could go off on his own, setting heading over the field as practised and holding this for 29 minutes by which time he would be overhead Cambridge. Repeating this from Cambridge for 21 minutes would get him to Luton and from Luton for 43.5 minutes to Ipswich.

After the exercise of some patience, the day arrived and following briefing as above, off he went. We usually reckoned that this exercise would keep a student away for about four hours. Without radio, we were – fortunately I believe – not able to communicate with them, and only on very rare occasions would we go to the expense of a long-distance telephone call.

So when Bill's time had exceeded four hours, the doom boys who had learned of his problem, started suggesting that he should never have gone, and comments as to what could have happened to him ranged from burning wrecks to landings in France. I was even asked if I ever worried after sending a student off on such a trip – my reply had to be that when there is nothing you can do after the departure, there is little point in worrying about it.

Bill duly appeared a little later, having had a most enjoyable day, and he had no intention of spoiling it by rushing anything.

And that is how it was done! Bill got his licence in June of 1969. He went on to aerobatic flying – limited in the Auster, but full in a privately-owned Chipmunk which we were able to borrow, and he became a master of it. He did a lot of flying and never let me down in any way – finally having to give up when his heart ended both flying and driving.

One of the more delightful stories of Bill concerned the deposit of a lump of coal weighing at least half a hundredweight on the rear seat of the Auster that I was about to fly with a student. My well-known standard patter covering the internal checks of an aeroplane before flight, was – left, front, right, centre, floor, ceiling, rear, and that final item included the comment, "check that nobody has dumped a sack of coal in the rear".

Bill had planned things while I was flying, so that to the joy of all the bystanders, he loaded this coal while I was in the office between flights. My face might have been red if I had not spotted it, but there really was no fear of that. It was however, a jolly good laugh made louder when I quickly arranged for someone to remove it and lock it in the boot of my car! In those days of coal fires and near poverty, half a hundredweight of coal was not to be sneezed at.

PETER

Peter was a Yorkshireman from Leeds. It was 1966 when he came to us in the East Anglian Flying Club as a licensed private pilot wanting to do some flying during his two-weeks holiday from work. I believe that at that time he repaired televisions and other domestic electrical equipment. Anyway, he was duly checked to ensure that he was safe enough to be allowed to fly one of our lovely Austers – he had not done any flying since his annual holiday the year before, but it was not long before he demonstrated his ability, and he was cleared to fly locally.

A most pleasant character, he mooned about the club, occasionally flying and occasionally getting into calm and quiet conversation with other members. His manner was always even and unruffleable, and he was very easy to get along with if you were interested, but if you were not, he would leave you alone.

Peter stayed with a landlady in seaside accommodation at Felixstowe, probably on a bed and breakfast basis because he would always snap up an opportunity to go out with members for an evening meal or to come and have a meal with us at home. Clearly he wished to do enough flying to renew his licence, which meant doing time as pilot-in-charge, but he was also keen to further his pilotage ability and accordingly he frequently wanted to do some dual flying with me. We did various things like instrument flying, aerobatics and low flying, and in these new joys he was not slow to learn.

He did not appear keen to go away anywhere by air although he would drive to RAF and American bases to watch the flying – he was especially fond of Mildenhall where he could see the enormous USAF transport aeroplanes. One day, I suggested that he might like to do a cross-country flight, and he readily accepted the idea but asked that I should go along with him. I left the flight planning to him and asked only that he advise me where we were intending to go, so that I could monitor our progress – and this I would do without any interference unless things went very wrong.

He elected to go to Skegness, by the long way around rather than across the Wash. I noted that he had not prepared any written flight plan nor did he even have line drawn across his map – this surprised me a bit, but he was a licensed pilot and there was nothing in the Air Navigation Act that said everybody had to do things my way, so off we went.

The aeroplane took up a heading which did not look to me to be the most accurate for our destination, but it was towards the north-west so I kept quiet. After a few minutes the heading changed but not to one that I had hoped for – however there was no need for concern because we were still going roughly that way. Headings continued to be changed at long or short intervals with no calculations being made nor jottings on bits of paper. It was some time before the penny dropped and I became aware that airfields, mostly disused but some still active, were clearly a part of the scheme – we did not always pass over them but one was always in sight whenever we changed heading.

It was thus that I experienced a new method of air navigation. In discussion on the ground Peter confirmed that he preferred to set off on a heading which would take him towards the nearest airfield in the direction that he wanted to go – in East Anglia, Lincolnshire or Yorkshire, you do not have to go far before it appears. You then continue towards it until the next one roughly in the direction required comes into view, then you change heading towards that and so on. It worked – after all we were discussing this at Skegness!

The compass and watch on which I based all of my navigation teaching did not come into the problem. Compass errors – what are they? Drift – well I lay off a bit if the wind is blowing. Straight lines – what do they matter? Visibility – well yes, you have to have a bit of visibility, but I don't want to fly else.

Up to now Peter had been to a different club each year to do his annual flying – he had no strings and so could please himself. But from then on he came to Ipswich while I was there, and he followed me to Monewden in 1973 and continued long after I lost my licence, until 1990, when a gammy leg forced him to give up.

But here was a man who was able to come along twelve months after he had last been in an aeroplane, get in, with me to monitor, and then fly it as if he had been flying only yesterday – and all without the slightest bit of bull.

THE WILLS FLYING TRAINING SCHEME

Early in 1968, Group Captain "Skipper" Allen of the British Light Aviation Centre in London, telephoned me to ask if I would like to enter the East Anglian Flying Club in the Wills National Flying Training Competition to find the best-trained private pilot in the United Kingdom.

In the full knowledge that my club was one of a very few still equipped with rather old-fashioned tail-draggers, and that we were able to teach only on a part-time basis, I had no great confidence that we had even a faint chance. It is difficult to know what standard you are instructing to but from my contact with the product of other schools during check-outs, I had no reason to be ashamed, and we had never been behind in having a go, so I said that we would be glad to enter the fray.

This was the third year of the competition sponsored by W D & H O Wills Ltd., the tobacco people. Initially, the scheme was advertised in the national press and the public were invited to seek the opportunity to

Triumphal arrival at Ipswich from Oxford with the Piper Cherokee G-AWBG won by student John Slater in 1968. On the wing are Slater and the author.

train for a Private Pilot's Licence at no cost to themselves, with the chance of winning a brand new Piper Cherokee 140, plus insurance and cash to run it for the first year.

Some 45,000 would-be pilots, who had never before received any flying instruction, completed a psychological test – simple questions set by a pilot-selection genius. Put into a computer, the answers would give away secrets that even the candidates were not aware of, and eventually the most promising 120 were selected, and in groups of six their names were sent to the 20 participating clubs or schools.

On the 6th of April, the six had to report to the various airfields where they sat a simple ground examination invigilated by an independent local citizen – in our case this was Wing Commander H E J Acfield OBE RAF (Ret'd), a very fine gentleman. After this test I, as chief flying instructor, had to give each one, first a fifteen minute air experience flight, followed by a forty minute instructional trip. Helped by the results of the written test, I then had to select three who in my opinion would be most suitable for the full course of training.

My six, five gentlemen and one lady, indicated that the psychological pre-selection had been fairly good because all six showed some aptitude. The task of choosing the three was not easy however, because past experience had shown me that ability indicated in the early stages was not necessarily sustained throughout the course. Anyhow, the selection had to be made, and regrettably I was not able to include the lady.

Training could be started at once and had to be completed by about mid-July on the standard Private Pilot's Licence syllabus, covering 40 hours flying to include at least 10 hours of dual instruction and at least 10 hours of solo flying which had to include at least 3 hours of solo cross-country, which in turn had to include a three-leg trip with two away landings, one of which had to be at least 50 miles from base.

At sometime during the course I had to nominate one of the three candidates to represent the club in the final tests, and I duly selected a John Slater who lived in Woodbridge, for no better reason than that I thought he had the best chance in most respects.

The flying test had to be carried out at the candidate's base airfield using the type of aeroplane on which he or she had trained. The summer of 1968 was such that the country south-east of a line from Newcastle to Land End suffered under low cloud for much of the time, while to the north-west they enjoyed the sunshine. As a consequence many schools fell behind the time-table, so it was early in August that an examiner from the Royal Air Force Central Flying School arrived and the test was completed. This same examiner went to each of the participating clubs and schools – twenty in all from England, Ireland, Scotland and Wales – so he had quite a busy summer.

In the first week in September, candidates with their instructors had to present themselves at Kidlington Airfield, Oxford on the Wednesday for ground examinations, written and oral, and for interviews on the Thursday and Friday. The final interviews were conducted by a high-powered panel of aviation experts, who had before them the results of the various examinations and tests – the five members of this panel were Marshal of the Royal Air Force Sir Dermot Boyle, Group Captain Douglas Bader, Air Commodore I G Broome (then Commandant of the RAF Central Flying School, later Air Marshall Sir Ivor), and the two Training Captains of the then British Overseas Airways and British European Airways – a knowing bunch if ever there was one.

A public display of flying was scheduled for the afternoon but before this there was a luncheon in a huge marquee on the airfield, for the candidates, their instructors and all the VIPs, at which the results were to be announced. All of this, our accommodation in a nearby motel since the Wednesday and all the food was provided at the expense of Wills.

We learned of the first three in reverse order, like a beauty contest, so that Mr Last of the Achilles School of Flying had not won the aeroplane because he was third. Mr Vint of the Ulster Flying Club was runner-up. So who was the winner? The tension mounts and could be felt. The first clue told us quite clearly because the Chairman announced that it was the entry from the East Anglian Flying Club – then he named Mr John Slater! Whatever can you say in this first minute? We had done it! Oh dear, I should not have had that gin and tonic before lunch, nor the wine with it – for how am I going to fly this lovely new Cherokee back to Ipswich. John was not even licensed nor converted to type. But I figured that as long as I didn't drink any more alcohol, I would be quite safe by the end of the afternoon.

But the post lunch period was truly intoxicating! It was something never to be forgotten by me. It was a great moment for John Slater – he had won an aeroplane worth £7000 (at 1968 prices) plus £1000 to cover the first year's operation. But I had proved that we could match, nay beat, the best, and I enjoyed an afternoon of congratulations from men whom I admired for being at the top of the flying profession, as well as from many colleagues in the flying world, and people that I knew, and didn't know, who were assembled there.

After the lunch party had broken up we were introduced to the aeroplane which was displayed on a high platform in front of the vast crowd – shining new, in blue and white with the registration G-AWBG. Back at home club member Bill Town claimed that this had to stand for All Ward, Bloody Good.

The afternoon's display of civil and service flying was very good, but we were a bit occupied in dealing with the paperwork in the handing over of the aeroplane by Rex Smith, the boss of CSE Aviation Ltd., who had organised things at Kidlington and who had supplied the Cherokee as Piper Agent. Rex was at that time also Chairman of the British Light Aviation Centre.

We telephoned the club at Ipswich and told them to expect us at 1830 hours, so after the end of the display, with John proudly in the pilot's seat, I started up this beautiful machine and took our place in the queue of aircraft waiting to take-off. Our radio clearance included the final congratulations and good luck wishes from the Air Traffic Controller. You can imagine the pride with which I did a low level run over the terminal building on our arrival at Ipswich where a sizeable crowd had collected to welcome us as the conquering heroes.

It was an exciting day, and even now in quiet moments I am guilty of a little smugness when I recall the examiner's comments that the standard of competitors in this the third of these competitions was infinitely higher than that of the previous two. We, the little club with old fashioned aeroplanes, with instruction on a part-time basis, with a part-time non-commercially licensed chief flying instructor and assistants, had shown that when all the bull is swept away, the enthusiasts' flying school as distinct from the highly commercial and professional flying organisations, could train private pilots to the highest standards.

If my slip is showing, it is because I had recently fought and won against a proposal that the product of the smaller outfits should be examined by the CFIs of their bigger brothers – in the interests of raising standards!

It was to the credit of all associated with the competition that the truth had been displayed of an early remark of mine to Dan Burgess, manager of Ipswich Airport, that "If it is run fairly and above-board, we will win".

PARACHUTING

Auster HZ had doors that could be jettisoned. It was not expected that we as civilians would ever need to jettison the doors – we did not carry parachutes – but when HZ was in the RAF during the war, aircrew wore parachutes and you couldn't get out of an Auster in flight unless you could get rid of the door.

I am telling you all this because one day in 1959 along came David Hall, a keen parachutist and instructor in parachuting. At first, all that he wanted was an aeroplane to jump out of, and HZ filled the bill. That appeared to be quite reasonable except that my licence did not have an endorsement allowing me to drop parachutists. To obtain this I had to fly for three drops under the supervision of a duly authorised observer, and David was an authorised observer so the EAFC got into the para dropping business.

David did a number of drops over the airfield much to the joy and excitement of spectators, but occasionally I had to drop him at public displays of one sort or another. It was at one such at Martlesham Heath that I had the nasty shock of seeing a failure – one shroud line had become caught above the canopy causing what is called a split periphery, and the canopy blossomed in two mounds.

This causes a higher rate of descent, but the real danger is that the line might burn through the canopy with fatal results. There was some fear that opening the chest-mounted reserve parachute could cause a tangle with the main, but it had to be done. Fortunately it opened clear, and he came down quite safely on the reserve chute with the main hanging down below him.

It was not long before other parachutists came along, and following this, even quite sane folk wanted to have a go. With HZ it was possible to carry two droppers if they were authorised to operate without supervision – one would sit on the down-folded seat-back to my right beside the door-hole, while the other would be in the rear ready to take the first one's place as soon as he had gone. This was quite satisfactory except that our well-loved engineer, Jack Squirrel, complained bitterly about the damage being done by the parachute packs chafing the door surround during the departures.

Student jumpers could only be flown one at a time, because David in the rear seat would have to act as Jumpmaster directing me where to go and supervising the student as he positioned himself outside the aircraft on the entry step. He would have to give the dreaded order to GO. In those days even the first drop was in 'free-fall' with the student having to open the parachute by pulling the rip-cord – whereas today such drops use a static line which automatically pulls the cord as the parachutist leaves the aircraft. After the drop I would turn the aeroplane sharply to the right so that David could observe the opening and the subsequent behaviour of the student. Then generally, David would re-position me for his own jump; parachutists appear to hate to land in an aeroplane although I suspect that the real reason is that it would be foolish to waste the opportunity to parachute, by coming down in an aeroplane.

I had been teaching son Robert to fly, largely facilitated by the generosity of Frank Waller who donated his aeroplane for the purpose. But the parachuting bug got him and he transferred to that. The minimum age was 17 so after all the ground training with David, Rob had to wait for his birthday, the 26th August 1960, when a large company, including the press, assembled to witness the event. Of course, I had to fly the aeroplane with David as Jumpmaster, and a happy time was had by all except his Mother who had a hanky-screwing time until the lad had landed safely. The whole thing attracted extensive press coverage, fortunately not including the party which followed in the club bar.

Rob continued parachuting and reached the level when he could do exhibition drops at air shows, and it was unfortunate that we had to give a fine demonstration of the sudden action of the 'sea breeze' effect at Ipswich airport. It was on the 28th of May 1961 during the flying display at a public 'At Home' at Ipswich; I had taken off with Rob from runway 32 towards the north-west. He acted as his own Jumpmaster and we duly dropped a marker from which he was able to observe the wind effect, and from that work out the best position to leave the aeroplane in order to land in front of the crowd.

I repositioned for the run-up, and he jumped at the selected point. As I circled overhead to observe his descent it became clear that he was not going to land in front of the crowd, in fact, he was not going to land on the airfield. Unfortunately this side of the airfield is bounded by a large housing estate which could be nasty with its two-storey roofs and cables on poles. So it was a relief to see him land in the roadway between two rows of houses, and he had got to his feet before I lost sight of him in the mass of people who had suddenly appeared.

My experience of the winds that blow at Ipswich Airport told me at once what had happened – the 'sea breeze' had arrived and had given us a change of wind speed and direction. This was soon confirmed by the wind-sock which was now indicating a brisk breeze from the south-east. It follows that I landed on runway 14 – in exactly the opposite direction from my take-off! The simple fact is that on sunny days early in the year, the surface of the land warms up faster that the surface of the sea – this causes the air warmed by contact with the land to rise, and

Author congratulates son Robert after his first solo flight in 1960.

cold air in contact with the water to flow in over the land to replace it. Unless the prevailing wind at the time is similar to the direction of this 'sea breeze', there will be a sudden change in the wind speed and direction over the land near to the coast.

I was acutely aware of these changes at Ipswich Airport when considering sending students off on early solo flights because the time of its happening could not be forecast with any accuracy, and with our aeroplanes being non-radio, it was not possible to advise the student of a wind change after take-off. It follows that I was vexed that I had overlooked this possible change during the para flight, but fortunately, apart from some gravel rash, Rob was not hurt and no damage had been done. He did another jump later in the afternoon to show that he had not been frightened off. When I went to view the scene of the landing the next day, I found (i) that with the maze of cables around these houses he had been perhaps more than lucky to miss them all, and (ii) that the children in the street had adopted a craze of parachuting with knotted handkerchiefs attached to all sorts of loads being thrown into the air.

ODD BITS OF FLYING

Occasionally there was a sad tale – "Can you come and do a local trip with me on Thursday evening?" was the sort of call that I might receive while I was 'at work', and if it was at all possible I would say yes. This one was in a privately-owned small two-seater, and I went along to find the owner armed with the most enormous pair of binoculars you ever saw – it was doubtful that he could manoeuvre them in the cramped cockpit, but he did. "I want you to take-off but to keep as low as you can. We'll go to a number of places nearby – I'll tell you where – then at each place, I'd like you to turn to the left as steeply as you can.

That was quite straight forward although there was no advice as to what is was all about. So off we went and found the first point quite easily, whereupon he opened the window on his side, stuck the binoculars through it and peered down at the countryside below. This went on at two others sites where he did the same thing, by which time it had occurred to me that they had one thing in common – they were all 'snogging' spots, the sort of place that you would take a popsie if you had ideas of doing something naughty in the fresh air. Was he I wondered, an aerial peeping-Tom?

The answer came a short time after. His wife was a former beauty queen and he had suspected her of some infidelity – the search was successful, he found her, and the paramour was a coloured gentleman. The world then crashed around my friend, and shortly afterwards he suffered a serious nervous breakdown.

*

I suppose that many pilots would love to have a landing at Croydon in their logbooks, so when the opportunity came to fly there with Frank Waller in August of 1958, I did not hesitate although I had been there once before. His aeroplane was a Taylorcraft G-ANHG, the one I had flown on my first civil flight in 1946! But its small Cirrus engine had caused Frank a bit of concern with its modest oil pressure which hovered very near to the minimum of 30 psi.

However we went quite happily on our way to the pre-war home of the great biplane airliners of Imperial Airways, until at about halfway the oil pressure crept low enough for me to decide on a diversion for an immediate landing at Stapleford. This was the home of Thurston Aviation, and we were lucky enough to see the great Eric Thurston in the hangar, nearby where we had parked. "What's your trouble son?" said he as I approached – I do believe that he remembered meeting me from some odd occasion before. "Oil pressure – we were on our way from Ipswich to Croydon, but it looks a bit low to me, so I wonder if you could do something for us."

"What are you in?" he asked, "A Taylorcraft Plus D", "How much have you got?" "Only 15 lbs", "15 lbs?" he cried in a startled manner, "you had better get out of here fast. There's a number of people here with Taylorcrafts who would like to have 15 lbs and they'll be after some of yours if you hang about."

We continued our flight to Croydon with our 15 lbs intact, and as far as I know, NG never did have any trouble with her engine!

*

Another Frank was a professional photographer who had got his licence with me during 1957. He and his lady Valerie who had also taken flying lessons with me, asked in 1959 if I would consider flying with them around the coast of southern England. The requirement was for me to fly from the left seat with Frank on the right by an open window through which he could use his cameras – Valerie would sit in the rear making records of what was being photographed, loading cameras etc.

What was being photographed was every seaside holiday camp and permanent caravan park – this for a friend who was in the postcard business. The postcards would be on sale on the sites so that holiday makers could send a picture with an X marking the chalet or caravan that they were occupying. We were to cover from the north Kent coast clockwise around, including the circumnavigation of the Isle of Wight, to Lands End and up the Bristol Channel to Weston Super Mare.

Quite a trip, and all a bit illegal because there was more commercial photography than flying instruction, and my licence allowed me to do the latter but not the former. But it was an attractive trip and I agreed to go. Not all of the shots were perfect so parts of the trip had to be repeated, and we did it all again in 1960 to get them up to date. The first took four days with numerous re-fuelling stops and night stops at Sandown (I of W) and Plymouth – where we were grounded for a day because of weather.

There were two interesting events. As we flew northwards along the north Devon coast towards Hartland Point at 500 feet above the sea, I could clearly see that the Army was deployed along the cliff top with a lot of guns pointing towards us and a lot of brown jobs collected around each one. This was very interesting and it occupied a lot of my attention until my eye caught sight of something on my left. It was a DH Mosquito rapidly overtaking us, at which time the awful truth dawned upon me – Mosquitoes were then used for target towing.

We did not have to wait long for the target drogue to appear and for us to realise that we were directly between that and the guns! Some say that there is a very real danger of being hit when they are not actually aiming at you, but the drogue was soon past us and it was evident that the guns had not fired at it. There now started a long period of quiet worry for me that they had got our registration and would be complaining to high authority about this gross breach of a notified danger area – but nothing was heard.

The other frightening experience was on the later occasion when we had come up from Lands End in the morning with the Bristol Channel completely covered under sea fog – that was not too bad because the cliff tops were in the clear at first. Then they disappeared as low cloud covered them, so that we were now flying in a narrow gap, a band of air between sea fog below and cloud above. Remember, we had no radio, no navigation aids and only a simple turn and balance indicator to fly by. But I continued for a time in the hope that the gap would increase as we got further inland – but it didn't, it got narrower.

I hate being uncomfortable in an aeroplane, but I certainly was at that time, with the possibility of soon finding myself in cloud with only one way to go and that was upwards with the cliffs so close on my right. And then where would I go – above cloud with high ground all around and no way of fixing my position for the descent that must come eventually.

Well, I am still here so something must have happened – and fortunately it happened before I had to show my terror to my passengers. The sea fog thinned so I was able to see the water and at very low level it was possible to find and get into Weston Super Mare airfield. The cloud then broke up and our problems were over. You learn a bit more about flying from incidents like that.

*

On August 25th 1963, Peter Branwhite and I were flown down to Lympne by a club member in Auster HZ, to collect and fly back to Ipswich, a Cygnet 2 which Peter had purchased from a lady owner. The aeroplane was a pre-war two-seater, all-metal and built like a battleship by General Aircraft Ltd with a 150 hp Blackburn Cirrus Major engine. It was perhaps one of the first nose-wheel types, but only a small number were built and these were used by the RAF during the war as light communications aircraft and in some instances as training aircraft to accustom pilots to the tricycle undercarriage.

Anyway, there it stood, looking very forlorn with its faded camouflage and general filthy tattiness. But Peter was full of enthusiasm – he was a garage owner, and had his ideas of going to work on this beauty and turning it into something to delight the eye, particularly of the owner. I had not flown one before and there were no handbooks available, so I suggested to the lady that she should come with me on a familiarising circuit to give me some of the essential operating figures – she agreed.

Early on it was clear that she thought that she had a very early student pilot on her hands and so I was given the full patronising treatment. As she took off and climbed, I realised that here was a subject on which I could spend many happy hours in teaching the elements of pilotage. When I took over to 'get the feel', her hands were never more than a fraction of an inch away from the stick. It was on the approach that she indicated that my handling had proved to her that her early thoughts were entirely correct, because she attempted to take-over control for the landing.

I resisted this quite firmly, trying to assure her that I had to get the feel of this aeroplane on landing and that I needed to do this landing with her to supervise and tell me if I was getting it wrong. She went along with this very reluctantly with her hand hovering beside the stick throughout the approach and landing.

While Peter was completing the deal I went up to the Tower to book-out for the flight to Ipswich. The Air Traffic Controller was shaking his head, "Did you do that landing?" he asked, I nodded yes, and his eyes lit up with what must have been admiration, "I'm glad I didn't miss it – I have watched that lady abusing that aeroplane for so many years, and now at last I have seen it landed properly. I had begun to think it wasn't possible." That was no real credit to me with my considerable experience, but it did show that Controllers do have hearts.

Peter did indeed do a great job on this aeroplane with the men and facilities of his garage, and we were proud to have this gleamimg silver monster on the airfield. It was a pleasure for me and other instructors to introduce it to club members and many of them enjoyed being checked-out in it and flying it as a special treat.

WE GO ACROSS THE CHANNEL

"You know Stan, it is nearer to fly to Le Touquet than to Shoreham, (Brighton)" – this was a comment in 1960 by Alan Long, who is referred to earlier in this story. Alan had come to me to learn to fly in August of 1959 and qualified in 1960, but he was determined to learn a lot more about the art of flying and he continued taking dual with me into advanced flying. And so it was that we began cross-channel flying in club aircraft. It started quite a craze, but I laid down strict rules governing such flights. No club pilot was authorised to fly across the channel without the necessary know-how. I had by now seen enough of the idiocy of half-trained people in charge of aeroplanes in this country, without developing any wish to export it, so I insisted upon the attainment of proficiency in blind flying on the 'limited flying panel' as well as a dual cross-channel flight, to ensure that our pilots had mastered the art of flying over water and of completing the paper work.

It was not long before we had a number of pilots trained in this happy exercise. We soon saw flights to almost every country in Europe, in little single-engined aeroplanes with no radio, no navigation aids, limited blind flying instruments and fuel for ranges of only 180 to 200 statute miles, with the need to use international airports for customs facilities for the last takeoff and first landings in every country visited.

It was a credit to common sense as well as to the competence of the crews. Today I am amazed and saddened at the change in so many things connected with club and school flying, and I have to smile when I am advised that it is forbidden to fly without radio into or out of some piddling little airfield, or that licensed pilots are unable to navigate without thousands of pounds worth of radio-navigation aids on board!

THE SPIN

This chapter is about Alan again – unhappily, the last chapter about him. The 24th of June 1961 was a clear day when he appeared at the club and suggested that we should go spinning in Auster XP – he wanted to see for himself that once the aeroplane is in a spin, it will stay in a spin even if you take your hands and feet off the controls.

A spin is a condition of stalled flight in which the aeroplane is rolling, pitching and yawing; in this stabilised state it is descending rather like a sycamore seed, and generally at a fairly high rate. I do not propose to go into a lengthy explanation of the principles of flight concerning this, so suffice it to say that in normal circumstances most aeroplanes will recover readily after the correct sequence of control movements, which are carved on stone in an instructor's memory as 'full opposite rudder, pause, stick forward until the spinning stops, then centralise the rudder and ease out of the dive'.

I thought that seven thousand feet might be a safe height at which to enter this exercise, bearing in mind that in an Auster a two-turn spin loses over six hundred feet, and the rules require that sufficient height be allowed to effect recovery with at least three thousand feet to spare.

Checks-before-spinning duly completed we entered a spin to the left by closing the throttle, holding the nose up and, just before the stall, feeding in full left rudder and pulling the stick right back. After allowing two turns for the spin to stabilise, we placed our feet flat on the floor and folded our arms; the spin continued, round and round, down and down. We looked at each other, and I felt it reasonable to smile, slightly smugly, with a there-you-are expression.

This was really quite pleasant – one could almost become hypnotised into allowing it to continue, but then Alan commented, "You know, this would be an easy way to go – you just sit here and very soon there is a bang, and its all over". I am sure that a frightened expression appeared in my voice during the immediate reply, "I do agree, but not during this trip please. Would you mind recovering now". And he did – with full opposite rudder, etc.

Within four months of this trip Alan, who was separated from his wife and family, gassed himself at his home – this was October 1961.

This was a dreadful blow, but there was worse to come. Alan had formed a liaison with Brenda, a student-pilot, who was understandably terribly distressed. When the arrangements were known, she asked me if I would drive her in her car to the funeral service in Sudbury because she could not possibly drive herself. On the way she became so upset that I had to stop the car to give her time to recover. Alan's Mother knew her, and after the service they invited us to go to the crematorium in Ipswich for the committal. I drove her there but after the service she asked me to leave the car at her flat because she was staying for a while with the family.

It was a Tuesday, my normal evening for ground school, so I suggested that she should come to the club that evening where she would be among friends. She did not appear – she was found in her office the next morning, dead by gassing.

To be faced with one suicide is a terrible happening, with the misgivings and the guilty feeling that there must have been something you could have done that would have avoided such a tragedy – but two within one week, and both were friends, with the close understanding that grows out of the flying instructor-student relationship, and which places so much responsibility on the instructor. It follows that I suffered a great deal for a long time after this.

GOOD AND BAD FLYING

I can, and do, claim the introduction of one or two novelties into the field of flying training – one in particular which strangely enough has not, to my knowledge, been copied elsewhere, perhaps because it was unpaid flying or maybe others did not get to hear about it or perhaps more simply it was not considered by others to be as good as I thought it was – however you can judge for yourself.

It was called 'Good & Bad Flying', and was generally arranged on one evening each year during summer; all students were instructed to attend – members and friends were invited. They were all collected on the manoeuvring area at the side of runway 14/32 where they could be addressed by an instructor, usually Peter Collier, who was armed with a brief, drawing attention to points which I considered particularly important in the demonstrations that I was giving in an Auster Autocrat, solo from the right-hand seat.

It started off with 13 items showing how various bits of higher level work should be done e.g."STALL WITHOUT FLAP (a) recovery without power – note loss of height," then "(b) recovery with full power

Typical advertising poster by John Castle for "Good and Bad Flying".

– note loss of height," or "STALL WITH FULL FLAP – note lower speed, more rapid deceleration, recovery with full power – note slow acceleration because of the drag of the flaps – nose held down longer than flapless although speed requirement is less (45-50), note low nose attitude in climb away" etc.

That part also included the loop, stall turn, barrel roll and spin – all well within the view of spectators, indeed, my knee-pad notes are marked 500 feet for turns and stalling, 1500 feet for aerobatics and 2000 feet for the spinning which incidentally demonstrated a 'show-off' precision recovery along the runway.

The notes on the approach and landing are interesting for their description of the glide approach to a 3-point landing, viz – "1. Round out to level flight attitude – pause for sink. 2. Nose just above the horizon – pause for sink. 3. Landing attitude – sink to ground, stick coming fully back on final sink to ground – then stick held back, keeping straight with rudder." Is it any surprise that one wag cartooned me as Stanislav von Pausensinque?

With the commentary drawing attention to the errors, and detailing the causes, the bad flying part largely involved take-offs, climbs, approaches and landings, with all the delights of excessive rudder use, violent pitching, wing-down climbs and approaches, high and low flares, high and low hold-offs, premature touch-downs, kangarooing, dangerous going-around etc.

Then came the correct flying with ten items indicating good airmanship and handling, and also drawing attention to the real connection between theory and practice in flying. These included short and soft field take-offs – three point, short field, and wheel landings, together with flapless, glide and engine-assisted approaches.

Comments by beginners and experienced pilots left little doubt that this unique demonstration was considered to be of some value in the understanding of what a student normally sees only from the cockpit.

CAREER CHANGE IN 1965

It was 1964 when suddenly – bang! I went sick with a bad case of over-work and my Doctor sent me away from everybody for two weeks. Nobody is indispensable but it was not possible to replace me for such a short period, so I was soon back in full swing – perhaps a little too soon, because I became severely depressed, partly because of general dissatisfaction with my job in local government. I had for some time felt that there was no place there for my particular talents and that accordingly I ought to get out before it was too late. The love of flying had stopped me from taking the plunge for far too long.

It was about this time that a club member who was managing director of a London-based company saw in me the end of his search for an export manager. The offer he made was too good to refuse so I resigned my local government appointment, and left the club to join him in December 1964.

As luck would have it, we had earlier that year been visited by a Wing Commander 'Pic' Pickford who had retired to Eye in Suffolk from instructing in the Channel Islands. When the job on the same part-time basis as I had been working was offered to him he was very happy to take over from me so that the club suffered no loss of a CFI.

My move proved to be a disaster for me – there was no satisfaction in commuting to London and chasing ticket-machine buyers all over Europe. The glamour of expense-account gin and tonics, lunches, hotels, flights by 707, Comet or Caravelle soon wore off and life in local government with the sanity-preserving flying with the club now appeared to be eminently desirable. By May of 1965 I was going downhill quite rapidly, so although I had nothing to go to, there was no alternative to resignation. Perhaps I never was meant to be a salesman.

But being out of work was a new and not very pleasant experience at the age of 44; however, I was fortunate in having a great friend in Bert Quinton who took me under his wing and gave me a job as a clerk in his building business. As I have noted in earlier chapters, we had done some flying together in earlier days and he owned a Cessna 175 which was based at RAF Wattisham. During this employment I did a lot of flying, and indeed some very interesting flying including many trips to the continent, some of these accompanied by our wives. During such trips we were required to give them an estimate of our time of arrival at wherever we were going, and we would know when we were within ten minutes of that because the aeroplane would fill with the scent of the pre-public appearance touching-up of faces. On the longer flights it was quite a luxury to have flying picnics with refreshments being served from the rear seats.

This sort of flying was a welcome change from the many years of essentially local flying in training students mostly from the ab initio stage. It was quite something to be able to take Bert through night work and actual instrument flying. The experience of working with the London firm had lowered my morale considerably, and there was a time when I had seriously doubted that I would ever regain the self-confidence so essential to a flying instructor. But I had not allowed for the effect of real friendship, and that is what I enjoyed with Bert Quinton and his wife, Mae.

During this period I made a number of applications for jobs in all sorts of places because there was a limit to the extent that I could sponge on Bert's Company, but it was from my former employers that I received an invitation to go back, and so, from August 1965 I was once again a local government officer with the East Suffolk County Council.

In addition to Bert's 175, I did quite a lot of flying during that year with various aeroplane owners including my first flight on a first test flight of an aeroplane – from Ipswich in a tiny, single seat, Luton Minor, built by Don Peacock at his home in Colchester.

IF YOU'RE NOT GOING TO FRANCE

Fourteen year old son Chris had, by July 1965, done a lot of flying with me on ferrying trips as well as with club pilots who were kind enough to invite him to take up an empty seat when they went flying, but the most impressive for a schoolboy telling tales to his mates must have been after I had met him as he came out of school on the 13th. It was all very simple really and came about because Freddy Gales had been forced by bad weather to abandon his Cessna 172 in Le Touquet over the previous weekend, and he had come home by a passenger service airline.

He arranged for Bert Quinton to fly me over in Bert's Cessna 175 to bring it back. When Bert suggested this to me during the Tuesday afternoon I decided that with empty seats in both four-seater aeroplanes, Chris could come with us. So I met him as he came out of his school which was nearby Ipswich Airport where Bert was to meet me with his aeroplane – we duly set course at 1705 local time for Southend to clear Customs and we landed at Le Touquet at 1850 by our time.

My logbook shows that it took me exactly one hour to file flight plans, find and check the aeroplane, pay the dues and get started up with Chris now in the pilot's seat ready to receive dual instruction on the flight back home. He did all the flying with just a little occasional help to get us back to Southend again at 2045 for customs, and into RAF Wattisham at 2140. Bert's aeroplane was based there and therefore his car was there, and as it was getting a bit duskish I left Fred's there for him to pick up next day – his farm strip was less than five miles away.

The funny sequel to this, for a young lad, was the fact that Chris's school friend had called for him to go out after tea, only to be told by

Mum that he had gone to France! This was quite a shock to a young schoolboy at that time, with the result that thereafter the cry at school was, for some time, "See you later Chris – that is, if you're not going to France."

Chapter Eight

BACK TO NORMAL

AT THE end of the year, after news that 'Pic' was going to return to the Channel Islands, Dan Burgess suggested that I might like to take up my position again as Chief Flying Instructor to the East Anglian Flying Club. I was a little uncertain about this because of concern about the attitude of club members and, particularly, the other instructors – but I need not have worried. At a party in the club during the Christmas period, I was left in no doubt that they would be very happy to see me back in harness – they may have caught me when I was a little pickled but it was all jolly-good-fellow stuff and the flattery won me over, so I rejoined the team in January 1966.

FORMATION FLYING

Shortly after my return to the club, some of the members asked if we could teach them some formation flying. Now this is an exercise requiring a lot of training and practice because of the obvious danger to all if anyone made a nasty mistake – unlike service flying, we did not have the benefit of parachutes if the worst should happen.

With the high cost of getting this experience, it follows that there were not many formation flyers among people who had to pay for their flying. Jack Pickrell and I were the only fortunate ones who had learned all of our flying at the taxpayers expense, and fortunately we both liked formation flying.

So the training started, first with the other instructors, then one student at a time formating on a steady leader aeroplane, followed by short spells in different positions and practice in changing stations. Then after we had found a leader who could be trusted, we were able to have two aeroplanes formating on him – and so on until on a great occasion recorded in a photograph, we put up four Austers and one Taylorcraft (very similar to look at) in a great five-plane formation.

The "Silver Sp'arrows' formation team of the EAFC taking off from Ipswich in 1969.

From this marvellous bunch of enthusiasts we produced the "Silver Sp'arrows" our own team of four Austers who performed at many fetes and displays, and at our own 'At Homes'. Names that come to mind include instructors Peter Collier, Jack Pickrell, Bill Wells and members Morley Stevens, Paul Whinney, Eric Hedges, Dick Fox.

'AT HOMES'

The East Anglian Flying Club had a lively social committee who, in addition to the usual dinners and dances and other social evenings also arranged an 'At Home', a rally, fly-in, open day or funday each year, (call it what you wish – they were all much the same) and we worked hard to produce something novel. These events attracted visiting aircraft from all over the country and occasionally we would become 'international' when we had visitors from the continent. These would run to two days with a Grand Ball in between.

Occasionally, visitors would add to the amusement by crashing their aircraft on to our field, but these were never intended as part of our plans, which were themselves sometimes quite hazardous enough. The programmes in the early days included demonstrations of new aircraft by pilots sent from selling agents – imagine the excitement at the sight of those new American aeroplanes made of tin, and sporting the novel nose-wheels!

A typical programme was that for the 'At Home Day' Sunday 28th May 1961 which included the following items:- Demonstration of Bolkow-Klemm K.L.107C by Messrs Flair Aviation Sales Co Ltd: Demonstration of Cessna Skylark and Cessna 150 by Messrs W H & J Rogers (Engineers) Ltd: Demonstration of Jodel Muskateer and Ambassador by Messrs Rollason Aircraft & Engines Ltd: Demonstration of Aircoupe by Messrs Air Rent Ltd: Demonstration of Piper Comanche, Tri-Pacer and Colt by the Oxford Aviation Company Ltd: Demonstration of Crop Spraying by Messrs Airspray Ltd. There were, of course, other interesting and more exciting items as well.

It was at this show that I had my first nose-wheel flight. Pam Klein, a former student of mine when she was a WRAF Officer stationed at Bawdsey, was now a flying instructor at Cranfield and she was the demonstrator of the Cessna 150. After the flight she very much enjoyed pronouncing me fit to fly solo on the type!

With an accident-free record at Ipswich which was an airfield much used for student-flying, you can imagine my disgust whenever a demonstration or show pilot broke his aeroplane. It was normal to assume that pilots sent by companies or recommended by agencies

VIPs at the EAFC's 1966 Annual Dinner – S/Ldr R J Jones (boss of Channel Airways), Mrs Jones, the author and Mrs Dorothy Ward, Norman Jones (boss of the Tiger Club), Derek Southall (Chairman of EAFC), Mrs Southall and Neil Williams (aerobatic champion and test pilot).

Typical "Funday" poster by John Castle.

would be pretty good, but I well remember the demonstration of a Bolkow Junior which was a little metal monoplane with a nose-wheel. From the moment he started taxiing out I could see that he was not a demonstrator – there was nothing clever about this, I had been observing pilots for many years.

True enough, his display was pathetic and he ended up with the nose of the aeroplane buried in the runway. Good stuff from a crowd-excitement point of view, but after a few words with him I was very annoyed. This was conveyed by telephone to the body who had sent him – they apologised sincerely and explained that they had overstretched themselves on that particular day, so rather than let me down had sent this character who was the only pilot available! Who would run an air show?

The Rally of 1965 produced a bit of unexpected excitement – this was my "year out" but I was there as a spectator sitting in the members enclosure watching the flying display with Bert Quinton and Group Captain Charles Gibbs, Commander of RAF Station Wattisham, who was the Guest of Honour – it was common sense that he should be entertained by those who had nothing more practical to do during the Rally.

RAF Wattisham was the home of Treble-one Squadron, commanded by George Black, and they were famous for their flying displays with sixteen Lightnings. They had been at the Paris Air Show and were due back at Wattisham during this afternoon. Charles looked at his watch and turned to Bert, "If you could fly me over to Wattisham now, I could call George by radio and divert the squadron here on their way back." And so started an episode in the Group Captain's life which was to result in a file four inches thick, and questions asked in most places, including the Air Council!

An Auster flown by CFI Pickford had just got airborne at Ipswich with an exciting commentary, when from the south appeared a sight that must live long in the memories of aviation enthusiasts. Sixteen Lightnings in a diamond formation commencing a barrel roll with the Airport as its centre, and there followed the display of formation aerobatics which had earlier thrilled the crowds at Paris. This included the one that breaks away to give a solo display – the squadron's man for this was Tony Doyle who started his proceedings with a .9 Mach (shall we say 650 mph) run at very low level along runway 32 in front of the crowd.

The effect was to see the aeroplane coming without a sound until it was just about level with us, when we were hit by an noise which must be akin to the clappers of hell – and we were at the side. Consider the effect on the unsuspecting occupants of the bungalows which line the boundary of the airport at the upwind end of runway 32, who were therefore directly underneath. Press reports which followed, stated that one man died immediately and one a few days later, while countless other people suffered permanent nervous trouble and a number of chickens laid their eggs prematurely.

The repercussions rumbled on for months, but I don't think that it affected the Group Captain's career very much, because he retired quite honourably with the rank of Air Vice Marshal.

For the Rally on the 13th July 1969, I had the bright idea of a race with an Auster, a car and a motor-cycle. We had two grass runways at Ipswich, 14/32 and 26/08 – both were roughly 1000 metres long and 100 wide – and it appeared to me that with the crowd-line being parallel to 14 and the likelihood that 14, being the 'sea-breeze' runway, would be the runway in use, we could produce quite a novel spectacle for the enjoyment of all.

The intersection of the runways was well to the left of the crowd, so with a start from the right they would see the contestants go by and then turn right down the length of 26 at the end of which they had to do a 180 degree turn to return to the starting point for a second circuit with the finish line immediately in front of the centre of the audience.

We received ready co-operation from John Read, boss of Holbay Racing Engines who used a bright red, hotted-up, 3 litre Capri, and a member of the Ipswich Motor Cycle & Car Club with his grass-track racing motor-cycle, plus me in Auster G-AJUE. We had a full evening of practice, mainly to work out the handicapping necessary to produce a close finish – and it worked. On the day both the car and the motor-cycle had completed their first lap before I moved in the aeroplane, but once airborne I was able to tear around very near to the ground with almost vertical banking in the turns.

With the commentator's help the excitement became quite intense as we hurtled towards the finishing line together. I forget who won but it didn't matter – it was great fun and real entertainment!

On another occasion we had an aerobatic pilot who had been highly recommended, and came from a good stable. He was flying a Jungmeister, a very excellent German biplane considered at that time (1970) to be as good as anything going for aerobatics. He certainly flew it with some panache until he came along close to the crowdline, executing flick rolls at very low altitude. As he arrived exactly in front of the crowd he was clearly running out of height, airspeed and ideas at about the same time so that his aeroplane clipped two others that were innocently parked and then collided rather violently with the ground, leaving a nasty mess of shattered Jungmeister from which he crawled completely unscathed.

It was a pity in one sense that he was not slightly damaged because that might have prevented him from immediately getting into a Stampe owned by a friend, taking off without permission and proceeding to do another aerobatic act overhead. This was the fly-again-immediately-after-a-crash-syndrome much favoured in flying films. But this was not a film – and it was I who got the severe rocket from the airport manager for not stopping him – he could have been suffering from delayed concussion! There was nothing I could do then except hope that he would get down before anything else happened, which fortunately he did without further incident. This was an example of a man who was not as good as he thought he was, and had the arrogance that goes with it.

But of course, we ourselves were not absolutely clear of unplanned happenings, and one such occurred at that same Rally, 5th July 1970 – this was in the days of the novelty of the supersonic boom when opportunists were constantly on the look out for damage-claims against aeroplanes which broke the sound barrier. We had come up with the bright idea of producing a sonic boom using a 1934 DH Hornet Moth G-ADLY owned by a group of four of our members – it was our intention to produce the boom without the shock waves that broke glass and made cows lose their milk or whatever it was that claims were made about.

As an incentive to the Air Training Corps cadets who were selling programmes, it was announced that the one with the highest sales would be given a ride in the Hornet Moth in this display – thereby cleverly killing two birds with one stone. Keith was science teacher at a nearby School so as he knows about these things he was given the job of producing the well-known boom-boom of a supersonic aeroplane.

He duly prepared an oxygen-hydrogen mix and set up his equipment on the roof of the two-storey terminal building, just above the members' viewing area. After due announcement of this exciting event, I taxied out with the lucky cadet aboard, and took off. As arranged I dived the well-wired biplane at all of 140 mph towards the terminal building at the spot where Keith was hidden on the roof, and we passed over the heads of the crowd at about 100 feet. That was all that I had to do, so the happy cadet now followed me through the brief circuit to a nice landing from which we taxied in and parked in the line of the participating aircraft.

As we walked in towards the crowd and the terminal building, a member met us and, agitatedly pointing to the building, exclaimed

"Look what you have done!" It looked like a bomb had hit it. A later survey found that 47 window panes had been broken in the front of the building. Quite a Hornet Moth I thought – perhaps we did go supersonic! A shaken Keith assured me that it was not so – he had merely miscalculated things a bit. His first boom was something of a bang from which he was lucky to survive, as were the people underneath who enjoyed the thrill of the bang followed by the descent of a 20 lb breeze block which actually brushed a sleeve on its way to the ground. Keith did not bother with the second boom!

On many occasions we opened the flying display with a flypast of all the aeroplanes on the field. It took quite a bit of organising but the objectives were to give spectators, particularly the photographers among them, a chance to see all of the many types present, and also to enable visitors who had arrived by air, to take a small part in the entertainment.

Everyone wishing to fly-past had to hand in his name, aircraft type, registration and normal cruising speed from which I had to arrange the order of take-off. Each pilot had a written brief as to how it was to be done, and at the pre-flight general briefing, they and the marshallers and the commentator were advised of the order; the pilots fairly simple task was to remember the aeroplane in front of him – not to get too close to it but never to lose it, from taxi out to touchdown.

I used to lead the take-off, towing an aerobatic glider flown by the incomparable Ernie Cunningham, a delightful man based at Tibenham in Norfolk, who I had towed to and from air meets, and to altitude for displays at many airfields and on many occasions. Of course, there is always at least one story to tell, and this is about one of our take-offs leading the fly-past at Ipswich.

Normal procedure was for me to tow him up to the height he required for his display of glider aerobatics, so that the time taken for the climb would be filled by the antics of the long line of aeroplanes which would level at 1000 feet, now led by my deputy who would take them on a rectangular path in the sight of the crowd. He would control the size of the rectangle to ensure that all of the aeroplanes had taken off before he began the flying past the crowd, not below 100 feet. After each had done the fly-past they would complete another circuit before landing in turn, by which time the glider had enough height to leave me and start his display with no delay in the proceedings.

Well now, on this occasion we were taking off on runway 32 which was directly towards a housing estate which had been built almost up to the end of the runway. Unfortunately, Ernie's glider became unhooked from my aeroplane at about 100 feet over the houses. Nasty – the book says of aeroplanes that if you lose your engine in this position, you stuff your nose down and land straight ahead, turning not more than 30 degrees either way as necessary to avoid anything really hard.

Ernie was not slow to weigh things up – to land straight ahead would demolish his beautiful machine, and more important may damage some folk who were pottering about in the gardens or snoozing in a shed. Behind him was a stream of aeroplanes, but all of them would be airborne long before the upwind end of the runway so that they could clear the houses with plenty to spare. Ernie knew his glider and was experienced in low level display work, so from this height he executed a full 360 degree turn which ended up putting him safely on the ground in the last few feet of the runway, well below the aeroplanes taking-off.

I was later approached by a uniformed RAF Squadron Leader, who clearly knew about these things, expressing the hope that I would be reporting this example of deplorable airmanship to the (then) Minister of Aviation. The Officer had never seen such a blatant disregard of safety as had been demonstrated that afternoon – he concluded with the advice that the glider should have descended straight ahead. I just looked at him – my jaw was probably hanging down.

A GLIDER TOW

There was a considerable whoosh followed by a small thump outside the window of the office, and I looked out to find that a two seat RAF glider had landed on us and with some skill had ended up just there. It could only be one man, Ron, a licensed club member who was also a gliding instructor at a gliding school for Air Training Corps cadets, based at nearby Martlesham Heath aerodrome.

"Sorry to drop in on you like this Stan, but I misjudged things and couldn't get back to Martlesham." As he got out of the glider with his cadet student, he continued, "It will be a hell of a bind to dissemble this and get it transported back to Martlesham. HZ (the Auster) has a tow hook, do you think you could give me a tow back?"

He was quite right, HZ had been used for banner towing at one time and it still had the hook, but it hadn't been used for some time so I had no idea as to its serviceability. Also we had no tow rope. Ah, but he happened to have one in the glider! A bit unusual this, so it was as I had suspected, a deliberate stunt to satisfy his insatiable need for deliberate stunts. He was prepared to risk the hook – I do not doubt that he had an earlier look at this on the aeroplane that he occasionally flew. We tested it with the rope and all appeared to be well.

John Garrod, a young lad who spent a lot of time at the airport and who later became an airline pilot, asked if he could come along in HZ and I agreed – this became an important point later on. Anyway, the glider was trundled to the end of runway 26 and we followed, positioning for the hook-up. I opened the throttle gently taking up the slack on the rope before giving the Lycoming full throttle. Acceleration was very slow and I began to wonder if I had not been a bit generous in trying to get off with the heavy old Sedburgh glider and two people in each of the aircraft.

But the glider came off with the expert Ron flying it accurately and making my job easier, but most of the runway had gone past before HZ decided that she should get airborne. The climb out was to say the least somewhat sluggish but as it was over the river it would not upset anyone on the ground and I suppose that we had struggled up to 150 feet when suddenly everything went very light and John informed me that we had lost the glider.

A turn to look for him indicated also that we had lost the rope – it had become unhooked from us. We watched as the glider manoeuvred over the southern bank of the river and were relieved to see it make a landing in a small field at Woolverstone. It was out of our hands, and after all this Ron had to get on with the job of dissembly and retrieval.

It was the next evening, Sunday, when Graham dropped in to the airport at the time I happened to be in the bar. Graham was an assistant gliding instructor at Martlesham, and we only rarely saw him at Ipswich. "Have a couple of pints," he said, just like that. Not wanting to look a gift horse in the mouth I started on the first without argument, pausing only to ask "What's all this for?" "It would have been half-a-gallon if you had dropped him in the river" he said! "You don't mean to say that you think I dropped him deliberately, do you?" I cried in alarm. "Didn't you?" "Of course not," I pleaded, "John Garrod will confirm that, he was in the aeroplane with me, and would have seen me pull the plug." "Oh well, its worth a pint anyway." Who was not a popular boy?

THE HORNET MOTH

Roy Wilks was the straight man in my stolen aeroplane acts, and he was also one of the group who owned Hornet Moth G-ADLY. He had a daughter living in Paris and he decided to pay her a visit in the Moth, so when he asked me if I would like to go along on a two-night stay, I was not long in accepting. So off we went, non-radio of course, but with no trouble at all via Southend (for customs) to Toussus-le-Noble, on the 10th of June 1970.

A delightful stay in an hotel where, among other things, we experienced a rather strange five minutes in a room full of Frenchmen watching international football on television – England v Czechoslovakia I believe – and they were cheering the Czechs! I don't think I had ever before watched England playing football on TV when the audience was cheering the other side.

But that is not the point of this story – we had a great time, and then on the 12th, duly presented our flight-plan at Toussus for departure to Southend in this very strange aeroplane – but not a half as strange as it must have appeared to them a few minutes later, because as Roy opened the throttle for takeoff from their beautiful hard runway, we started a very violent yawing to left and right with a squealing of tyres until I decided that Roy had gone off his head.

So I took over control, but with no greater success in keeping straight, so I closed the throttle still struggling to keep the aeroplane on the runway. But as the aeroplane slowed it trundelled off the runway, fortunately between two upstanding runway lights, on to the grass beyond. As we came to rest I had expected to see at least three fire engines dashing out to relieve our distress and I am not sure whether we were relieved or disappointed that nobody appeared to be taking any notice of our predicament.

We taxied around a bit and Roy reckoned that we had a bit of wheel-brake trouble but it was a problem only when a lot of rudder was in use – therefore if we were gentle with rudder use we could probably get airborne and at least get to England without having to call for engineering assistance – Francs were in short supply by now. So we taxied gently on the grass, back to the end of the runway, checking all the time that they were not flashing any lights at us from the Tower, and we lined up again for takeoff. With me monitoring the rudder very closely we took off safely, if without elegance, and set course for Southend.

It is better that the landing on the hard runway at Southend is never discussed, but at least we stayed on it and managed to taxi to the apron with some difficulty. I suggested to Roy that whatever the trouble was, we had proved that we could get off reasonably safely from a hard runway – and without going into recriminations about that last landing I was prepared to suggest that with a grass runway at Ipswich and perhaps a little less enthusiastic use of the rudder after touchdown, we might well survive the return to base, where repair services could be a little less costly.

As a part-owner who would have to share any costs, and also a useful handler of tools, Roy saw the sense of this – and we got back to Ipswich without any further surprises.

The Hornet Moth, in common with many aeroplanes that I have flown, has a brake system which assists taxiing by applying brake automatically when coarse rudder is applied. The brake comes on to the wheel on the same side as the rudder used, so that if the aeroplane is reluctant to turn at the rate required when gentle rudder is applied, then coarser rudder is used and the brake assists in sharpening the turn by retarding that wheel. Well that is how it should work, because we found that we had a bolt missing – it must have fallen off while on the ground at Paris. Without going into too much technical detail, the effect was that the brake-activating bar was unable to rotate about the bolt that wasn't there, so it was dragged forward when rudder was applied, causing the wrong brake to come on. The practical effect was that, for example, when right rudder failed to turn the aeroplane to the right, the extra rudder applied left brake. Oh well, at least we didn't break the aeroplane.

THE BEST FLIGHT OF THE DAY

There were one or two delights in being able to give a little show of flying – you knew that you were giving real enjoyment to the crowd and, if you were an exhibitionist like I was, you were having some fun as well. Take the example of the Ipswich Model Aeroplane Club – they used to display at our Rallys so I was happy to oblige their secretary, Bob Wilton who happened to work in the same department at County Hall, when he asked if I could just do a little show for them during their annual competition day on the end bit of a runway at disused RAF airfield at Martlesham Heath.

"Anytime you like" he said, "we'll soon get the models down when we see you coming, so come at any time you are able to, and we shall not expect you to land." So during the afternoon I popped over in an Auster and gave a display of aerobatics and crazy flying. I knew a number of the members, and it looked safe enough, so I decided to land and say hello and best wishes – it is always very pleasant to be the hero of the hour!

A meeting of heads took place while I was there, after which the secretary called the others to order and addressed me thus "This tankard was to be presented to the best model flight of the day, but we consider that there will not be a better flight today than the one we have just seen, so it gives me great pleasure to present it to you." Yes, there is a lot of satisfaction in some quite simple things.

MICHELLE

Peter was an ex-London barman who somehow found himself in the position of barman to the East Anglian Flying Club – and he had a London showbiz girl friend named Michelle, who came down one weekend to visit him. She was quite a corker, young, blonde and all the things you expect of a personality girl. The word soon got around and the bar was well filled on the Saturday evening for one of those spontaneous fun evenings.

After she had captivated quite a number of the male hearts and had done her dancing on the bar top, some wag suggested that she should have a flight next morning, and it was not long before this became an aerobatic flight with the chief flying instructor, overhead the airfield where they could all watch. Oh she would love it, oh yes, oh yes, again and again to all the manoeuvres that were suggested to her. Would I really be prepared to do that for her? – she would love it and Peter would pay for the flight.

Sunday dawned as a beautiful day and Michelle duly appeared, as well as a good number of the revellers of the previous evening. The aeroplane was the Tiger Moth and I gave her a fully professional briefing as to what would be going on. I explained to her that as she had never done any before, there would be no continuous aerobatics, but I would do just a gentle loop to see how she liked it, and then only with her clear approval would there be any more.

She had to be fitted up with a flying suit, helmet and goggles – I made sure that she was secure in her open cockpit seat behind me and that she understood the mouthpiece of the speaking tube for when she wanted to speak to me. So off we went, to the applause of the small assembled company.

I considered that 2000 feet would be enough for the simple loop, and after the necessary checks and assurances, I eased the nose gently down directly in front of the spectators, gaining speed for the loop.

With the greatest care I eased back on the stick to bring the nose up to go around with the minimum of loading as was my normal procedure with beginners, and we had just got to the inverted position when perhaps for the first time in my life I heard from a lady a frantic scream telling me to stop! Well there is no way in which a loop can be stopped from the inverted position on top, you just have to go on around to the bottom. During that, the screams became hysterical and this continued throughout the recovery and the descent which I immediately initiated.

It was really one of the most unpleasant situations that I have experienced in the air – all attempts to talk to her were of no avail and she never stopped screaming into the mouthpiece and thus directly into my ear. She was completely out of control and I feared that she might do something silly like unstrapping herself and even attempting to get out of the aeroplane – there was little that I could do if she started that. So it was with some relief that I felt the wheels touch the ground with her still in the rear cockpit. The girl who was helped out of the cockpit was a very different person from the dancing beauty of the night before!

SONNY

I had flown Sonny over his farm on a number of occasions at times when the crops started to come up – this enabled him to check the efficiency of the seed drilling. The Auster was ideal for this because it was a high-wing aeroplane, slow and easy to turn in small circles. His farm enjoyed an airstrip on which Richard was based – Richard had learned to fly with me at East Anglian after some years as a cadet in the Air Training Corps, in which as Officer Commanding I had tried to teach him "aircrew" subjects some years before.

I was therefore a little surprised, not to say a bit miffed, when I learned that Sonny was learning to fly with an instructor from Luton. It was sometime later when Richard explained that when Sonny had raised the subject of learning to fly suggesting that he would like to come to me, Richard had advised him that he would never reach the standards that I required because, among other snags, he was a bit fond of the bottle or anything else that carried alcohol – I was well aware of his slurred speech during flights with him, when I had also been a little apprehensive about the effect on me of the gin fumes in the cockpit.

I did not realise just how much of a purist about alcohol I had become in those early days, until at supper one evening with a group of friends, one of them commented, "I saw Robert Pask the other day, and he asked after you". Always pleased to hear that I had not been completely forgotten by former students, I replied "Good, how is he now?" "Quite well, but he said that he well remembered an episode with you". "Oh really", I replied," What did he say?" "It appears that you were a bit late with the programme one hot day, so he popped into the bar for a half of bitter while he was waiting. When you eventually arrived, and he had settled into the cockpit, your first remark was: "One of us has been drinking". That was his clearest memory of me – all of thirty years before!

VICTOR

We had a number of incidents with Victor – he was quite a character. He enjoyed a limited sense of humour and was often unaware that folk were pulling it a bit. A serious person, he was tall, dark with horn-rimmed spectacles, dead keen on flying, intense and determined to master the art. I am not sure where he learned to fly nor exactly when he joined the EAFC but my recollection of some of his antics will remain with me forever.

Runway 14 at Ipswich was some 100 metres wide, bordered on each side by open land used for farming by Channel Airways. The runway edges were indicated by white dashes (6 feet x 1) which were made by chalk let into the grass surface, and these were backed up by free standing markers about a foot high made of fabric on a wooden framework, a light construction which would break up easily if an aeroplane ran into them. These were coloured orange and white, so it was reasonable to expect pilots to land between these lines – more so at this time because the grass runway was green in colour while the land to each side was deep brown because the land had recently been ploughed.

Victor had been sent solo to practice something or other and was returning to land at the end of the period. No doubt Victor was satisfied that he had got it right as he descended to the runway because he could see a line of markers on his left, it being the normal thing to look more to the left of the nose of the aircraft during the final stages of the approach. He did not however notice the second line of markers 100 metres further to the left, nor the greenness of the land between them, nor that the landing area he had selected ahead of him was brown.

So he landed in the ploughed area. It must have been a good landing, probably on all three wheels with minimum forward speed and the stick held well back, because HZ was a tail-dragger and anything else might well have resulted in the wheels digging-in and the aeroplane somersaulting on to its back. It is probable that he was helped by the fact that the surface was soft and muddy after recent rain. He came to rest with no damage, but then he made his second mistake of that day by attempting to taxi out of the mud, with the result that the aeroplane became well and truly bogged in the mud.

But Victor was not to be put off, he just increased the power until he had full throttle. It was probably the noise of this that drew our attention to his predicament, because the landing area of runway 14 was quite a long way away from the office, and it is unlikely that we would have been aware that he had landed beyond the runway.

So help now started to weave its way to the scene at about the same time as Victor saw the futility of his attempts to get moving – he shut down the engine.

As the fire tender and the running crowd of interested club members approached the scene, we saw a chocolate coloured aeroplane standing in a sea of mud, and we recognised it as our HZ only by its shape, because all other signs of identity had been effectively covered up by the wet earth thrown up and back by the airflow from the high revving propellor. Oh well, we had better push it out of the mud and back on to the runway where it can be re-started and taxied in.

Can you imagine the mess that a bunch of keen-to-help folk can get into while struggling to push a mud-covered aeroplane out of a muddy field? But they were a good-humoured lot, at least they were until somebody shouted, "Victor, you know who has to clean the aeroplane when we get it back, don't you?" Silence – "Victor! Victor!" Silence. A quick check revealed that Victor was no longer with us, and we did not see him again that day.

Sometime after this, when Victor had gained quite a bit of experience and he had been appointed Chief Flying Instructor to a nearby gliding club, he suffered a nasty prang. Through some misunderstanding he thought that the glider he was towing had unhooked from him at the end of a ferry flight to get the glider and the Tiger Moth tug to another airfield for the night. Unhappily, it was in fact still attached, so while he was holding-off for his landing, the glider whooshed past him pulling his tail around and causing the Tiger to spin in to the ground. Although lucky to escape with his life, he suffered some dreadful injuries.

Friend and aircraft-owner Bert Quinton and I visited him in hospital, and among other things to cheer him up we promised this stitched-up and plastered figure that we would be pleased to take him flying as soon as the doctors would allow it. In due course he came to claim this trip, but because he was not able to bend his knee, we had to manipulate him bodily into the right seat of Bert's Cessna 175 where he lay rather than sat while I got him airborne. However, his morale was high, his nerve was sound, and he voiced his determination to get back to flying as soon as possible.

Behind his back we whispered that he would be lucky! "Not a chance in hell" they would say. "Look at his leg, he'll never be able to bend that again, so how can he fly with a stiff leg?" A short time after this, I received a letter from the Civil Aviation Authority asking me as an examiner if I would conduct a flight test on this chap who had a severe restriction in the use of his right leg. The test was to include recoveries from spins, right and left.

He elected to do the test in a Tiger Moth, which is not the easiest machine to get into, and as I watched his efforts to mount the thing I was filled with advanced regret that I may have to deny him the licence he so dearly wanted to get back.

I had briefed him very carefully to the effect that I would give him clear instructions as to what I wanted him to demonstrate, item by item, and the test would be not unlike the final test that has to be passed before the issue of a Private Pilots Licence, and which he had of course passed many years before. I made it clear that my responsibility during this test was solely to examine his flying ability – his medical or physical condition was not my concern.

In the Tiger Moth, the pilot sits in the rear of the two open cockpits, so I was in the front where, apart from a small see-back mirror fixed to the centre section strut above and to the left of my head, I could not see what was going on behind me, although I was able to see and feel the effect of whatever the pilot did with the controls. So off we went – and to this day, I do not know how he did it with the severely restricted movement of his leg, but he did everything that I asked him to do, including entry to and recovery from full spins to the left and right – manoeuvres which require the use of full rudder.

Whatever I felt about a stiff-legged pilot, I had to report as I found – and his licence was duly restored to him. It could not have been a wrong decision, because he has continued flying aeroplanes and gliders for many years – not without incident I must admit, but these were caused more by finger-trouble than problems with the leg.

A third delightful excitement with Victor came on the 10th of March 1963, on which morning he appeared at Ipswich Airport with another character, asking me if he could borrow the club's Auster HZ, which had a towing hook. I was advised that on Martlesham Heath Aerodrome which was about four miles north-east of us, there was a glider which they wanted to tow back to Whatfield airstrip where Victor's gliding club was based, about six miles to the west. It was all very simple – Victor would fly the Auster to Martlesham, he would then tow the glider piloted by the other chap, over to Whatfield where the glider and the tow rope would be released, and he would then fly the Auster back to me at Ipswich. As they say – a piece of cake!

So why is bloody Ward being so awkward? "What glider towing have you done Victor?" "I've been towing gliders for years". "Have you ever towed with an Auster?" "Well, no, but it's all the same." "It isn't quite you know, Victor. For a start you haven't flown HZ for a very long time, so you need to be checked out just to fly the aeroplane." "All right, if you insist I'll have a checkout." "Now, how about your friend who is to fly the glider, has he done much gliding under tow?" "Jack, meet Stan, the CFI., Stan this is Jack. He has been gliding for years and has considerable experience in being towed, otherwise I would not be asking him to shift this glider for us. No problem here, we can work together with no trouble at all."

Ample nodding all round, even me! But I had already decided that there was no way in which I was going to let these two slope off with my HZ for this trip, but an idea was forming because it was my way to help anybody out if it was at all possible. "Do you know what the wind is Victor?" "Not really, but looking from here I would say that it is something like south-westerly at about 8 knots." "Well, actually it is 180 degrees at 12 to 15. Do you know the runway headings at Martlesham?" "No, I don't for sure." "The only runway that could be used is 22." "That's all right then, not much of a cross-wind, we can cope with that."

I was not so sure – I had not done all that amount of glider towing myself, but I knew that a cross-wind could be a problem on takeoff because the glider gets airborne – and consequently becomes subject to drift – sometime before the aeroplane. If Jack had the experience claimed, he should be able to deal with this, but I would be happier doing it myself because in fact I was satisfied that Victor's sheer enthusiasm for his and Jack's ability was a bit excessive – moreover, before approaching me, he had not even thought out the problems of this particular day, .

"Well Victor, I would like to help you out but I can't let you take the aeroplane away to do a job like this without a bit more evidence that you can cope – especially in these conditions." A pregnant pause. "I can't really check you both out without taking most of the day and it would cost you a lot of money – in any case I have other bookings. But I am prepared to do the towing for you." That went down like a lead balloon, and he commented glumly, "I would have to do the paying, but I would get no flying time." It did sound a bit hard – I knew how poor non-professional pilots were, and how necessary it was to get time in the logbook, especially for a glider man wanting to get air-towing time.

"Couldn't I do the towing with you coming along as check-pilot?" "I had thought of that Victor, but I am concerned that we don't overload HZ, with two aboard plus the glider and pilot." As I spoke I could sense the arguments to counter this – there was a good long run at Martlesham and it was a hard ex-RAF runway, so we would really have plenty of room, even to abort a takeoff, and we could take it gently on the climb and cruise. "On second thoughts, I am prepared to have a go." How easily are the most dreadful decisions taken!

Victor flew me across to Martlesham quite nicely without impressing me, other than sadly, with his attempt to land it on the cross-wind runway. Then they busied themselves with the task of getting the glider in position and duly hooked-on to HZ.

There is a saying which goes "he opened the throttle and released forces over which he had no further control" – unhappily this was largely true about what happened on this takeoff. After a gentle move forward to take up the slack on the tow-rope, Victor opened the throttle fully, and we accelerated along the runway, struggling to keep straight with the cross-wind and the engine-induced yaw both trying to turn us to the left.

A few seconds later the glider left the runway and our ace glider pilot instantly proved his inability to cope with the cross-wind as he drifted to the right. We were still on the runway trying desperately to counter the swing to the left and to get airborne, when the glider's drift to the right pulled our tail with it, and the nose of HZ was hauled towards the left hand edge. It was reasonable to expect our experienced tug-pilot to do something about this but it quickly became clear that reasonableness no longer came into this scheme of things.

Now, a quality expected of any self-respecting flying instructor is the ability to take swift action at a time like this – and on this occasion I was not lacking, probably because the total destruction of the aeroplane and us, and no doubt the glider and its pilot, appeared to be imminent unless something was done.

Our rapidly changing heading to the left would involve us in crossing the runway edge which looked a bit rough, this would be followed by the need to traverse some heathland and gorse bushes, and if we survived this we would be faced with a rather solid clump of woodland. It is a pity that at such moments, we do not have sufficient time to appreciate fully the excitement that is being offered – if only we could analyse the situation so that we could go through all the possibilities that are available during the next few seconds. It must be good for the soul and infinitely beneficial to education and experience.

Unhappily, the sight of death coming through so crystal clearly, blinds one to the beauty of the moment, and all the instructor can do is to grab the controls, state calmly and quietly "I've got her", and then stir the stick and rudder around until something a little more pleasant shows up through the windscreen. Never ask what he actually did, he wouldn't know, but it was probably something very unaerodynamic.

However there we were, airborne but making a very undignified yawing dive/climb towards the trees with our mate behind, who must have been enjoying the full force of the turbulence coming over those trees, just like we were. Except that he had lost the book that would have told him how to deal with it in a way that did not put the tug in such an embarrassing situation. It got so exciting that Victor suggested that we should put a stop to the fun by pulling the plug – that is, releasing the tow rope from the aeroplane. He meant it because his hand went towards the knob, and for a moment we held hands, not in loving friendship but because I did not feel that our old matey behind us had been naughty enough to warrant dumping him into the trees.

That was all. We managed to get some height where the air was a bit smoother enabling him to get a grip on himself, and I was able to take the rest cure by handing over control to this experienced tug-pilot – at least that is what he had told me he was.

Good old Victor!.

NIGHT FLYING

August 3rd 1961 and Alan and I had been on a little day-tour of the low countries from Ipswich via Lympne (for customs), Lille, Rotterdam and Ostend, and that is where things began to get difficult. We had filed our flight plan for the crossing but this was refused on the reasonable grounds that Lympne would be closed by the time we were scheduled to get there. We were in non-radio HZ so our suggested alternative airport had to be contacted by telephone to ensure that they would accept us. They kindly agreed to do so, and off we went along the French coast paying due respect to Dunkirk and Calais as we headed towards Cap Griz Nez for the then-mandatory Channel crossing lane. We landed with no problems, but daylight was now running out fast, and it was then that we made the dreadful mistake of asking Customs if they could hurry things up so that we could get to Ipswich before dark!

It is not often that I have had to strip an aeroplane down for inspection but we had to this time, and you could not really blame them. Here were two smart-Alecs, using an airport not normally used by light aircraft, certainly not for Channel crossings with Lympne just across the way and always ready to receive the non-radio tiddlers – and then trying to rush their way through Customs! Not surprisingly, suspicions were aroused.

It was just after sunset when we took off from their beautifully lit-up runway. I had quickly but carefully weighed-up the problem – we had no night facilities at Ipswich and therefore no runway lighting – a telephone call to the Manager asking for car headlights or something would probably have resulted in a negative and a veto of any attempt to land there. After all, Channel Airways could hardly be expected to enter the business of helping an illegal night flight – but Alan had to get back that evening. Although the night was very dark the cross-country would not be difficult with the large lighted towns, and coastlines which usually showed up quite clearly. HZ did at least have navigation lights although we could not say how long the battery would last, given our many start-ups during the day and the fact that we had no generator.

As we passed over Southend with its magnificent array of runway and taxiway lighting I felt a twinge of envy of the pilots using this, while I had still had that little worry about getting into Ipswich – it was not the landing so much as being able to find the runway. The airfield was easy enough to recognise by the fact that it was the darkest patch of ground to the south-east of the town, and after a few minutes of deep concentration downwards I was able to identify Nacton Road and to follow the street lights along past the bus terminus to the point where they were dimmer. This was where the very high lamp-posts gave way to lower posts to reduce the obstruction to aeroplanes on the approach to runway 26.

The high poles stopped at the northern edge line of runway 26 so that gave me the clue I wanted – the wind at Lydd had been quite light so regardless of its direction I decided that 26 with this excellent indicator of its right hand edge would be the best runway to land on. It was not really difficult – as I rounded out for the landing I got a flashing glimpse of the upstanding edge markers which were positioned at about 100 yard intervals along the runway. These confirmed that I was on the runway and they helped me to judge our height so that I was able to produce quite a reasonable landing.

During July of 1965 I had done some night flying from Wattisham in a Cessna 175 belonging to Sonny Waller of Whatfield – this was the first night flying for me since reserve-service days, except for the flight from Lydd to Ipswich in 1961. During the rest of 1965,

Bert Quinton and I did quite a bit in his 175, mostly using RAF Wattisham where the aeroplane was based. A lot of this was a matter of returning from somewhere after dark, but we also did a lot of show-off trips like giving passengers the thrill of seeing the lights of London at night.

Dorothy and I used to spend many evenings with Bert at his bungalow in Stowmarket, especially after flying on a Saturday, and I was not averse to sipping some of Bert's whisky. So it was surprising that I had not touched a drop on the evening when the great George Black, at that time Commander of Treble-one Squadron Lightnings at Wattisham, telephoned very late to say that he had just been notified that his wife was due to arrive at RAF Lyneham from Cyprus at about midnight. He would like to get her home that night. Bert asked me if I would do it, so I had the pleasure and honour of checking-out this outstanding pilot in the art of night-navigating a Cessna – and we got there – and back!

It was in July of 1965 that Dan Burgess told me that there was a set of gooseneck flares at Ipswich, and that he would be prepared to set these out whenever we wanted them.

Goosenecks are like watering cans filled with paraffin oil: the wick comes out of the spout and when lit they give a flame that can withstand half a gale. Set at about 100 yard intervals along the side of the runway, they provided effective lighting for takeoffs and landings. Gooseneck flares had been used extensively during the war, and I had flown with them on many occasions both then and afterwards in the RAFVR. The big snag was in setting them out and collecting them again because this was one of the messiest jobs imaginable – Dan's offer to do this for us was therefore a very generous one indeed.

One amusing incident concerned a trip we did with the ladies from Ipswich, where the flarepath had been laid for us. The weather forecast was acceptable so we went off to Southend to buy the ladies alcoholic drinks while we drank lemonade. At that time Ipswich had no navigation aids so we just had our mark one eyeballs, but we did have Tom who was Air Traffic Controller-cum-Barman.

As we came out to the aeroplane at Southend for return to Ipswich I was a bit concerned to see that the visibility had reduced considerably since we went in, and it was evident that it would not be long before Southend would be closed-in. This meant that if we got airborne it might be a little difficult to get back, so I decided to check the weather at Ipswich. On the telephone Tom assured me that everything was clear with a beautiful moonlit sky. So off we went.

It was the dreaded sea fog that was causing the trouble and we went into it almost immediately after takeoff, so we continued the climb and broke out into the beauty of a clear sky with the moon lighting up the white sheet of fog below us. The ooos and aaahs were a delight to hear as I gave Bert a heading to steer, and worked out the time to Ipswich where we expected that we would be able to see the ground again. On a guestimate of our position I advised Southend that we were north of their zone and wanted to leave their frequency to contact Ipswich – they said "Roger, clear to change to Ipswich, goodnight."

The instant that I selected Ipswich's frequency I heard Tom calling GOLF ALPHA ROMEO MIKE NOVEMBER. That was a bit ominous – the normal procedure is for Air Traffic to wait to hear from you. So with mighty dread clutching at my stomach or somewhere, I told him to go ahead. What do you know – they had some sea-fog, full cover and visibility down to something quite horrid and rapidly getting worse. We did not have headsets which would have kept such messages secret from the passengers, so I was aware of some excited whispering from the rear seat – it is always a bind having to appear brave and unruffled at such a time.

But I wasn't too frightened because we could divert to somewhere inland if we were unable to get into Ipswich so we carried on, and things were fairly quiet in the cabin. At Manningtree, with about eight miles to run, I was able to get a misty sight of the ground from which it was possible to recognise where we were. With this and an occasional sighting I was able to plan an approach to the airfield, and accordingly with a skill and coolness that surprised even me, we crept in and touched down. Tom, whose assessment had been a little more dismal than necessary, was tickled pink, and I was the ladies' hero of that hour and perhaps of many more after.

A FAMILY NOTE

My Father was proud of his often-stated claim that he would go flying with me at any time so long as he could keep one foot on the ground, and he was not shamed into having a go even when my dear Mother and his Sister flew with me in an Auster, which adventure they had both thoroughly enjoyed.

My son Rob and his wife had made me a Grandfather in 1966 – this quite pleased me except that it meant I was now married to a Grandmother. However, knowing that my Father was, like me, fond of a bit of publicity, I approached him with the idea that the local press would be pleased to make something of a photograph of four generations flying in one aeroplane. The thought of his mates reading all about this in the 'paper' was too much to pass up, so he agreed.

Arrangements were made for the 26th of August 1966, the news editor was pleased, Bert Quinton lent me his Cessna 175, the press photographer arrived and duly took pictures of Great Grandad, Son me, Grandson Rob and Great Grandson Jeremy sitting in the cockpit before the flight. Details were duly taken in shorthand, as to what I intended to do on the flight – and then they left us to get on with it, while they hurried away to another news event.

Father now came up true to form with the remark that as they had got the pictures and the report, we need not really do the flight! But he was not able to get away with that, because the combined disgust of the assembled family was too much for him – and away we went. There was nothing particularly exciting about the trip down to the coast and over Harwich and Felixstowe, but he spent most of it looking back to where he thought the airport was, with a sort of longing expression, and the relief as we touched down must have been felt on the other side of the town.

The sequel to this is that I started to look forward to the day when Jeremy would make me a Great Grandfather, so that I could fly the four

Four generations go flying – author's father, son and grandson, August 1966.

generations as a GG pilot – but it was not to be because I failed my medical and lost the licence before Jeremy or any other Grandchild had got around to becoming a parent.

It was at about this time that a news report concerning a flying display, carried the statement that Stan Ward was without doubt the best Auster pilot in East Anglia! You might think that I would be unbearably smug about this, but in fact I was not at all flattered – you see, the East Anglian was the only club still flying Austers, and if I was not the best pilot in the club then it was a poor-old-do.

THE END OF CHANNEL AIRWAYS

Channel Airways went into liquidation in 1972, possibly because of the excessive variety of aeroplanes that they were operating, or possibly because of the pressures of package- holiday charters, but there can be no doubt about the difficulties consequent upon the breakdown of, say, the single Trident airliner, which would require three DC3s to pick up its stranded passengers. What is in doubt is the accuracy of a press report which claimed that the cause was the low rates charged for flying the four little Austers in their flying club at Ipswich!

However, we had to face it, the lease of Ipswich Airport together with the club aeroplanes were put up for sale by tender and the whole set-up was taken over by Lonmet(Aviation) Ltd. The East Anglian Flying Club and I survived for just six months because the new owners had ideas of an expansion into which four Austers with a part-time chief flying instructor did not fit.

During this period we saw a remarkable change in refuelling habits which had been followed in aviation circles for a long time – certainly since I had started flying. Whenever an aeroplane went to the fuel installation for a fill-up, it was a normal courtesy and safety action that the refueller would check the level of the oil in the engine.

When Jack Squirrel, our engineer, went to check the oil in the aeroplane which our new boss had just flown in, he was jumped upon from a great height, and firmly instructed that never again was a refueller to go near to the oil in this machine or in any other in the future. It was pointed out that is how you can get sand in your oil! We were not accustomed to this sort of thing at Ipswich. It followed therefore that after I had glided Auster G-AJUE to a safe landing on runway 08 at Ipswich when we had lost the use of her engine because of a broken con-rod over Shotley, the boss's first comment was to ask who we thought had put the sand in the oil!

A full-time professional CFI was appointed for the new British School of Flying and I worked alongside him for a short time as our Austers were phased out in favour of Cessna 150s – we also acquired a Cessna 172 and a Bolkow Junior. But life for me became increasingly difficult with the new management, so that when my position was formalised by the offer of a part-time job as an assistant flying instructor I had no hesitation in declining, although the farewell to my students was quite a wrench.

This move did not involve any loss of flying for me, because private owners were pleased to be able to get me for advanced training, and to check-out other pilots to fly their aeroplanes.

Chapter Nine

MONEWDEN, ETC

FOLLOWING THE change of management at Ipswich, a number of flying strips appeared on local farms, and flying groups were formed to operate various aeroplanes. I was soon engaged to instruct pilots who were already licensed, in techniques such as short-field work, conversions to different types of aeroplane, and instrument-flying with simulated approach aids.

I was particularly involved at Monewden near Woodbridge, where the farmer, John, was a former student of mine. He had laid two strips of grass at right angles, the main one being some 1500 feet long and 75 feet wide – but a hedge at one end and an electricity cable at the other frightened me a bit. The site also had a small idiosyncrasy in that the centre which was also the intersection of the two strips was the lowest point of the field, so the start of all take-off runs was downhill and the end of all landing runs was uphill – not a bad thing once you got used to it.

Jodel G-BBAR which opened John Wright's farm strip in July 1973 – author flying from right-hand seat.

John announced that he had bought a Jodel D117 G-BBAR, and he asked me to go with him to fetch it from Hazeleigh Grange near Maldon in Essex, which we did on the 10th of July 1973. The D117 is an all-wood two-seat aeroplane of French design and construction – a low wing tail-dragger with a 90 hp Continental engine, it cruised at about 90 mph and approached to land at 55.

I was a little apprehensive as we cleared the cables on the approach to Monewden because there were no wheel brakes on my side of the aeroplane, but she settled nicely and came to rest with a bit to spare. I was however a bit more dubious about its ability to get off the ground and clear the hedge with me and John's 230 lbs aboard, so I did the first take-off alone: she leapt into the air with such gusto that I had no hesitation in taking John on the next one. The fact that she cleared the hedge was a credit to the high power-to-weight ratio of the D117, but for future comfort we agreed that a gap must be cut in the hedge.

The fear of hitting electricity cables is a very real one, so that most pilots when approaching over them will allow more clearance than is necessary, with the result that these high approaches involve touchdowns well into the field – not good if the field is a bit short. However, after the expected arguments and delay, John eventually got Eastern Electricity to put the vital section of the electricity cable underground.

To help John to continue operating his aeroplane, the Monewden Flying Group was formed and I was kept busy introducing the pilots to the Jodel, and to the different techniques required at a small field. Flying from the farm strips came as a bit of a shock to those whose experience covered only level runways 1000 metres long and 100 wide.

It was shortly after this that the Civil Aviation Authority used their powers to issue regulations under the Air Navigation Act, making it illegal to teach flying for the issue or renewal of a licence or rating, from an unlicensed airfield. Licensing laid down various minima concerning obstructions and lengths and widths of strips, so this was claimed to be a safety measure.

Whether or not this really had anything to do with safety or the quality of flying training, is not clear, but it certainly did benefit the bigger clubs (or more truthfully – schools) who operated under the "approved course scheme". This scheme enabled them to knock five hours of expensive flying time off the minimum hours to licence, but conditions of the scheme required that they had to employ a commercial-licensed chief flying instructor and operate only from licensed airfields. Licensed airfields charged landing fees – so whatever else this regulation did, it certainly ensured that every student pilot now had to pay landing fees.

Monewden, like most of the strips, was unlicensed and would never have met the requirements for licensing so the group was accordingly classed as a "non-training" one. I was nevertheless the Chief Flying Instructor, and it has to be said that it might have been a poor old set-up without the training and checks that members were put through, because I still took my job seriously.

A problem with this regulation then arose – John had three sons, and he wanted them to be taught to fly by me. He had an aeroplane, he had me, and he had a farm strip. So what would you do? The justification for the new regulation was that it was necessary to stop 'cowboys' from teaching flying from the boot of a car on a meadow. It was considered that there was something wrong with this and that these naughty boys may be taking money from their clients without giving a proper service.

I had never accepted that this was anything other than the simple fact that the 'cowboys' did not have to pay the landing fees, parking charges and rents for accommodation on licensed airfields which the more-formal organisations had to pay, and that accordingly they had to be stopped from providing cheaper flying training in competition with their bigger and more influential brothers. This ignored the fact that the 'cowboys' had to be qualified and licensed to teach flying, and that the reduction in overheads enabled many more "ordinary" people to take up flying. And nobody ever provided me with any evidence indicating that their product was in any way inferior to the others. In fact I will go further by suggesting that their product was superior to that of a number of "approved" organisations, where the training was often in the unsupervised hands of assistant instructors, while the commercial CFIs were away earning their comparatively high salaries by flying as air taxi drivers.

Well now, if I was teaching the sons of the owner of the field in his own aeroplane, they could hardly accuse me or John of operating to make an illegal profit out of the world's greatest sucker – the student pilot!

I explained to John that it was possible that when the logbooks were sent with the licence applications, up to the Civil Aviation Authority they might disallow the flying from his unlicensed airfield – the fact that I might also get a drubbing did not I am afraid worry me at all.

So away we went. One of them decided that he was happier on a farm tractor but the other two completed the course with no difficulty. I took obvious precautions like using a licensed airfield for their first solos and using only licensed airfields for their test cross-country flights which had always been a requirement, for good reasons like certification that they had actually been there.

Their logbooks were of course made up correctly showing that the training had been carried out at Monewden, and it was something of a relief that their licences were issued without question. I do not believe that either suffered any handicap from their training – in fact, some years later one of them made a successful forced landing after an engine failure, with no damage to the four of them on board – the aeroplane was not quite so lucky. The other completed an incredible round-the-world flight with his wife in a Jodel D140A Musqueteer in 1990.

The height of absurdity however was that the regulation regarding training from licensed airfields applied also to training for the issue and the renewal of the IMC (Instrument Meteorological Conditions) Rating. I was quite busy with this sort of work at Monewden before the regulation was adopted. However, Ipswich had no more facilities for instrument training than did Monewden – i.e. none, but Ipswich was a licensed airfield and was accordingly acceptable for such training.

Therefore to be legal I should have required my instrument-students to take-off and fly to Ipswich, (15 minutes of flying plus the landing fee) so that we could then take-off for the instrument flying lesson: on completion, we should have landed back at Ipswich, and paid a second landing fee. That would have constituted a legal IMC training session. After that we would have to fly back to Monewden (another wasted 15 minutes of flying).

The necessary practice and examination in the use of approach aids had to be carried out at an airfield which had them – such as Southend, Norwich or RAF Wattisham, regardless of whether we were flying from Ipswich or Monewden. Well now, I was never one to obey rules mindlessly, so I took no notice of this one, and carried on training for IMC ratings and renewals at Monewden – and on completion of the courses, the Civil Aviation Authority issued the ratings without question!

Monewden was the scene of one or two amusing incidents. One of these indicates the fact that you should not ignore the happening of something unusual. John had told me that while flying his Jodel G-BBAR he had suffered the odd occasion of momentary loss of power from the engine which had righted itself, but the experience had been a bit unnerving. I was doing quite a bit of flying on the aeroplane at that time so I merely advised that I would watch for it.

One evening when I was giving some dual to Nick, the youngest son of his lady, Marjorie, I climbed up through a layer of cloud with a base at 500' and tops at 1500'. This was not particularly easy in the Jodel because the turn indicator was driven by the suction from the inlet manifold of the engine – car drivers from the early days may recall that windscreen wipers were driven similarly, and they, like the turn indicator, ceased to function at full throttle. So the climb was a bit protracted at reduced power, and like all good airmen, I applied carburettor heat frequently during the climb, although this gave none of the usual indications of carburettor-icing.

Surprise, surprise therefore when, as I levelled off in the clear air above the cloud, the engine ceased firing. Nasty! All appropriate actions were taken to no avail, during which we had re-entered the cloud so I was in effect faced with a forced landing from 500'. Mental navigation was duly applied in the hope that the strip would be in sight when we came below the cloud and would you believe it, it was, so I was able to demonstrate a successful forced-landing-without-power to my incredibly relaxed student.

The propellor continued to windmill until the hold-off prior to landing, when the engine stopped. I waited a few minutes then switched on again and pulled the starter – the engine fired and we taxied in. Clearly, the trouble had been carburettor-icing and if it had been anyone else I would have accused the pilot of failure to use carb-heat properly. But I was the pilot and I knew that heat had been applied meticulously. So why had ice formed?

The answer came the next day when engineer Bob Hammond came over to look at it. He inspected the heater box through which induction air is passed when the pilot selects hot air in conditions that might cause icing. To the amazement of all, Bob found that there were so many holes caused by corrosion in the heater box that air passing through received scarcely any heat.

John was lucky that the icing he had experienced had been minor, and had not developed, and luck had favoured the many of us who had been spared any real icing – but then there were few like me who would fly in cloud in an aeroplane so inadequate for instrument flying. Carb icing is possible outside cloud but it is less likely, and I had never encountered it in the Jodel. One of the pre-takeoff checks is to ensure the effectiveness of the carb heat system by noting the loss of engine power when heat is applied – in my ignorance, I had frequently demonstrated to pilots that there was scarcely any loss of power when carb heat was applied to this engine!

Another funny moment came about with Dave, a long-time student-pilot on Austers at Ipswich. He knew that he was never likely to qualify as a pilot but he enjoyed flying dual with me, and this continued after the move to Monewden. The Auster had a quadrant throttle lever, requiring a rotational movement to open it – upward and forward, whereas the Jodel had a simple push forward into the dashboard.

It was on the approach to Monewden, and I considered that we were getting a bit low so I called "Power" quite quietly, meaning that I wanted him to open the throttle a little to reduce our rate of descent. Nothing happened so I called again a little more urgently. Again nothing happened, and I considered that things were now getting a bit serious so I bellowed "Power". Dave responded in an urgent manner, but his right hand reverted to the Auster movement – and with great strength he pushed the throttle lever up, with the result that the rod bent through about seventy degrees at the point where it entered the dashboard.

Now, nobody could apply power – "I have control" and for once that merely meant that I was now responsible for the aeroplane, but I had little control except to fondle the elevators and squeeze the last bit of flying out of the tortured wing – our guardian angel must have been watching over us very closely that day because by rights we should have landed well short of the strip to finish up in the ditch at the threshold, but somehow we just reached the edge of the field and landed without any damage.

On the 13th of June 1985 a temporary member of the Group was refuelling Jodel D117 G-BBAR at Monewden by himself using Jerry cans – first he filled the front tank which he reached by standing on a box. The filler point to the rear tank was on the right side of the fuselage, and this he reached by standing on the right wing, pouring the fuel through a plastic funnel. It would probably not have occurred to any of us that there was any real danger in the fact that he was wearing a nylon summer shirt, but it did occur to him a little too late as he saw a tiny flame in the neck of the funnel. He reckoned that it took less than one minute for the fire to consume the right wing, and within four minutes the whole aeroplane had been completely destroyed.

What had been a perfectly serviceable aeroplane had become a grotesque heap of bits of metal and charred, smoking wood. There was a peculiar pattern of the control wires all leading from the dual control columns, the engine was lying at a strange angle to everything else, and the undercarriage legs had the bare brakes still attached.

The aeroplane was a write-off, and John had no intention of replacing it – he had long ago obtained a fine Robin DR300. There followed a lot of talk which ended up with the group operating two Jodels, although we did barely enough flying to justify one.

It was decided to sell one of the Jodels, a D119 G-BAAW, so the time came when I was required to demonstrate the aeroplane to each one of a group of three flyers who were interested in a joint purchase, to show them what a beautiful machine it was. The field at Monewden was damp and greasy but presented no problem, and the first flight went off very nicely.

On the second, the pilot did a competent three-pointer touchdown but after that, the aeroplane started to nose to the right. I interfered by pushing on full left rudder. Still we went to the right. "Come off the right brake", I bellowed in the kindest possible way. "I'm not using any brake". I believe that at this stage I used that expletive which is so commonly used by airmen. We were now heading for the edge of the grass runway beyond which was a big drop to the newly ploughed field. It was too late to open up and try to get airborne again so disaster was imminent.

"I've got her" – not much point really, it was more of a habit than anything else but I probably felt that I might be better able to minimise the damage. I did get the switches off to stop the engine and it looked as if we might stop before we ran off the runway, but no such luck – we slid softly and silently off the edge, whereupon the wheels stuck in the mud and the aeroplane went smoothly up on to its nose.

Plenty of hands arrived to help us get out of the cockpit, and these were used to get the tail down and to lift the aeroplanes back on to the runway. There appeared to be little damage, even the propellor was intact. We found later that the shock on the undercarriage legs in the fall over the edge had pushed both back a bit, requiring expensive replacements. So what had caused all this? Even before engineer Gary arrived on the scene, we found that the right wheel was locked solid, and we could see that some brake lining was protruding through the back plate – these were internal expanding drum brakes. I traced the wheel marks back to where the skid had started – they indicated that immediately after touchdown, the light weight on the wheels had enabled the rudder to keep the aeroplane straight, but as the aeroplane slowed and the weight increasingly transferred from the wings to the wheels, the drag of the locked wheel skidding in the mud had pulled the aeroplane to the right.

After Gary had removed the wheel, taken out the brake and lining from the drum, and replaced the wheel, I was able to taxi the aeroplane back to the hangar. The lining which is normally glued to the brake shoe had come away and jammed between the shoe and the drum. After all the repairs had been carried out I asked if it could happen to the other brake. My concern was that we had been lucky on this occasion, but I frequently flew into Framlingham and it was clear to me that if the left brake failed like that on the hard runway 24, which was in fact the comparatively narrow former perimeter track, the aeroplane could topple at high speed over the edge to a drop on the left side: from that it would probably nose over on to its back with serious consequences for those in it.

I was however assured that the left brake was perfectly sound – and the end of the story is that a few weeks later the left brake did fail in the same way, except that (i) I was not in it and (ii) my doom-laden forecast did not happen because it occurred during taxiing at low speed. But it does show what a slender thread our lives sometimes hang on.

BALLOONING

Brian Ribbans telephoned me during an afternoon at Monewden to ask if he could come and fly his balloon from the field. He was an old friend, living at that time near to Felixstowe, but I had not had a lot of contact with him recently, although I heard that he had bought a hot-air balloon. He had flown a little dual with me in Austers at Ipswich, so I knew of his enthusiasm for flying and that this was limited by his lack of readies.

There was no reason to refuse, in fact I was sure that the Group members at Monewden would welcome the change in aviation

Ballooning with Brian Ribbans.

entertainment. Brian appeared without much delay whereupon we all got down to unloading his truck and laying out its burden of balloon, basket, burner, and gas bottles.

The intention, he advised, was to go up to about 300 feet with the balloon tethered to the truck. Then we spent some time in deciding where to attach the rope, and in the consideration as to whether or not the truck was heavy enough to retain everything. I should have been warned by this evident lack of experience, but otherwise the preparation appeared reasonably efficient, and the details of what the bystanders were required to do were explained quite clearly.

The burner was lit and some hot air was blown into the balloon so that it was soon wallowing about on the ground, partly inflated. It was then that Brian spoiled my whole day by suggesting that I might like to go along with him. What can the Chief Flying Instructor reply to that when it is all said within earshot of a dozen members of the flying group. I quickly weighed up the gains and losses involved in saying yes and no, and decided that, against appearing chicken and having to watch some less-fearing member taking my place, I would go – it was after all a tethered flight so we could only go 300 feet away, and therefore help if required would always be near to hand!

So I climbed aboard, and quite enjoyed the excitement of the further inflation which lifted the balloon off the ground while the ground-handlers held the basket down. At Brian's call they let go and we hovered about the ground for a few moments until the burner heated the air enough for us to rise steadily and, in the quiet wind conditions, almost vertically.

And there we hung, silently, 300 feet above the ground, and with the burner shut down, able to chat with the folks below. This was indeed a new adventure and I liked it. I am glad to say that the descent was controlled and we landed quite reasonably. "Gosh", I said breathlessly, "that was my first flight in a balloon". "Yes", said Brian calmly, "and mine"!

This did not immediately put off the bystander-helpers, but the next landing did bring ballooning to an end for that day. Morley was the passenger this time, and there he was looking down at us over the edge of the basket, but the descent now was rather less than controlled – the thing was obviously coming down much too fast. The fleeting picture that I had, and I can still see it to this day, was of Morley's face – there one moment and completely gone the next. The impact with the ground was such that his knees crumpled and he disappeared into the bottom of the basket.

Fortunately neither he nor Brian was injured, but the reluctance of the potential passengers from then on was, I do believe, shared by Brian.

He later went for his commercial ballooning licence and I helped him with the technical subjects like aviation law, navigation and meteorology which were similar to the requirements for the Private Pilot's Licence. He taped a number of my one-to-one talks so that he could go over them again as required – the one on meteorology became a must for most of the balloonists in his group.

The time came when he kindly offered me a flight that was to be free in both senses, and I decided that he must by now have gained sufficient experience to make this a fair risk. We met at Shrubland Park on a morning when the wind was a bit more than was ideally desirable. He was also a bit short on ground-handling aid, having only his ever-keen wife Anne and young daughter Suvann'e. We used the shelter of some trees for the take-off, but it also really needed a considerable weight of bodies outside to hold the basket on the ground until a clean lift-off could be achieved.

Anne's basic job was to drive the retrieve vehicle, while Suvann'e had come along for the flight. Anne was therefore the only anchorman available, and while she would not claim to be a light-weight, she was not sufficiently heavy to hold us down for long enough in the gusty wind conditions, with the result that we left the ground prematurely.

Anne wisely let go at once, but we were floating only temporarily, our movement being horizontal rather than vertical, and it was not long before we came to earth again. But the balloon was moving with the wind, so the basket was dragged along the ground causing a bit of what is beautifully described as "dog-kennelling" – that means that the open top of the basket becomes the open bottom with everything, and everybody, being scraped along the earth.

Brian cut the power immediately and opened the dump valve to deflate the balloon, and so collapse it on to the ground. Nobody and nothing was damaged, although this was not a particularly inspiring start to my first free-flight. However, no-one was ruffled except me and I tried to hide it, so we started again. This time, apart from a bit of scraping of the basket bottom, full burner-power got us airborne at a shallow angle, going northwards.

Flying generally at about 300 feet above the ground, with the need for only an occasional burst of burner, it was rather fun to float along above back-gardens from which the odd occupant would wave and even shout back friendly, morning greetings. It all seemed so much more civilised than a noisy low-flying aeroplane, when what sometimes appeared to be a wave was more likely to be the shaking of a clenched fist.

Above us, the formation of some cumulus cloud indicated rising air, so it was not surprising that we started to climb without the aid of the burner. Now, I did not really know anything about ballooning, but it occurred to me that for a balloon like this to stay in the air it must be kept warm, and that meant that the burner must be kept in use – but back-seat drivers are a bit of a menace – so I held my tongue.

It was at 1500 feet that we lost the influence of that bit of rising air, and the descent started! And what a descent! Full burner-power came on but we continued going down and down – there was no way of calculating whether our rate of descent was reducing, and if it were, whether it would get to zero before we reached the ground. On dear me, what a way to go – after all those exciting aeroplane flying hours, where was the justice?

The passage of time may have blurred the memory, but I would swear that we got down to less than fifty feet before the descent ceased, and you may think that I was now able to grin cheerfully, pretend that I had not had a single moment of qualm, and perhaps congratulate Brian on his fine judgement. But no – as we raced at high speed along the ground, it was clear that we now had a problem of getting the beast to go up because just a short way ahead of us stretched a line of steel pylons complete with their high tension cables. It was now all a matter of angles – of the angle created by our speed over the ground against our rate of climb, which at first sighting was a bit small.

However, as in all stories written by the endangered one, I survived along with Brian and Suvann'e, because the laws of physics had ordained that full burner-power would create an angle of ascent that would clear the cables.

The rest of the story will seem to be an anti-climax now, involving as it did the fact that we were a bit concerned about the evident increase in the wind speed and the problems that this would create for the landing. We over-shot the first landing site because of our high speed over the ground, and then approached another like a bat out of hell. There then followed our second experience of "dog-kennelling" in that day, but we finally skidded safely to a halt in a field just a few miles west of Framlingham.

With thirteen and a half thousand flying hours, I do believe that in the 50 minutes of that flight, I enjoyed more moments of terror than in any block of fifteen hundred hours anywhere in that career.

That all happened many years ago when, like all of us, Brian was making the mistakes which, provided we survive them, add to the knowledge and experience essential to all good pilots. Brian has long been one of those, and I would not hesitate to fly with him again at any time.

THE ARV SUPER TWO

It was as a result of our displeasure at the high cost of a small part for the American built engine of one of the Jodels that the Group decided in March of 1986 to buy a kit and build the much advertised ARV Super Two. This was a side-by-side two seat, all metal, high wing, tricycle undercarriage aeroplane boasting 125 mph cruise and 800' per minute climb on a 75 hp, three cylinder, two-stroke, liquid cooled engine. But it was all British and we were very proud to be one of its first buyers.

The enthusiasm was great in the early days and the planned progress with careful job allocation was aimed at completion in three months – August 1986. The fact that the first test flight took place on the 21st of May 1989 speaks for itself, and this was achieved only by employing professional help to complete it. The costs went wrong as well, rather like Concord, except that the Super Two rose from an estimated mere £20,000 to nearer £30,000.

Although I was not involved in the assembling of the aeroplane, I did all of the test flying as well as the preparation of Pilot's Notes, and the training of the other group members. How come, you might say, when I lost my licence in 1982? The answer is that some members,

ARV Super Two – with test pilot and some of the builders at Monewden – author, Chris Allen, Keith Cockrill and Rex Belton, May 1989.

including me, felt that their interest in the aeroplane would be best protected if I were in it during these uncertain times – I could of course fly only as passenger. The pilot on the first flight was Stevie Wallis who won the contest for the position on the basis that he was the lightest of the bunch, and at such a time you don't want too much weight added to my 172 lbs! On some of the following test flights, I was accompanied by heavier members, but all went well and the aeroplane continues to fly as a group machine.

NAYLAND A B & C

After the changes on the departure of Channel Airways from Ipswich in 1972, one of the airstrips opened by refugees from Ipswich was on a piece of land hired from a farm at Nayland, just across the border in Essex – it was a fine level site but to avoid too much interference with the farm it was positioned to the side of a field alongside a hedge with a tree or two in it. I was doing some check-out flying from here and we could cope with this, but shortly after we started to use it, the farmer next door indicated his displeasure by building a huge haystack on the boundary of his field where it coincided with the threshold of our strip. This was unkind because we then had to approach over this, effectively reducing the already rather short landing distance available.

The owner received more complaints from other neighbours, and the local planning office started to show an interest. I believe that he wanted to keep on the right side of those sort of people, so Nayland "A" folded up.

It was then that Nayland "B" appeared – the lettering becomes necessary to avoid confusion. This was just a meadow, well sprinkled with cowpats and enjoying a delightful fall away to a pond at one corner. As if that were not enough, the approach boundary was littered with very awkward-looking trees. There was certainly plenty of supervised flying required by low-hour pilots so I was kept quite busy, mainly on behalf of Richard Neale for whom I used to do the check-outs on pilots who wanted to use his aeroplane back in the Ipswich days. When like so many others, he saw the need to move away from Ipswich, I moved my services with him.

Nayland "B" did not survive for long, although we somehow managed to survive without any accidents.

It was then a simple matter to transfer to Nayland "C" as we then christened the farm-strip owned by Tony Harris (a pilot trained at the EAFC) which was actually at Wissington near Nayland. I had been there to the odd barn-dance party in a real barn, and, on at least one occasion had entertained the crowd with a crazy flying display when it had been possible to take advantage of the undulating nature of the site to appear suddenly from low level or to disappear equally suddenly down into a valley. Suffice it to say that it later became commonly known as the ski-slope, on which landing is uphill and take-off is downhill, regardless of wind direction.

Tony is one of nature's gentlemen who had provided this facility on this unlikely site, way back in the sixties and in the nineties had to fight expensive legal battles against people recently moved into the area who have been able to arouse the opposition of others who had not previously noticed that the strip even existed. Such are the problems in maintaining flying facilities in the climate of the nineties.

THE IPSWICH SCHOOL OF FLYING

My departure from Ipswich Airport in 1972 upset the members of the East Anglian Flying Club more than it did me, and a great deal of publicity was given to their disagreement with the new management. The only other unit there, the Ipswich School of Flying, which had opened in 1971, had a hard time to keep going, maintaining their position only by the legal right to operate on the airfield because it was licensed for public use.

The poor old East Anglian FC, later misnamed the East Anglia Flying Club, slowly faded away but, after the loss of government contracts, the need to increase revenue brought about a change of heart by the management who now encouraged the establishment of other flying organisations, so the Suffolk Aero Club was born in 1976 followed by the Horizon Flying Club in 1980.

I was not fully occupied with flying activities at Monewden and elsewhere, so when John Thurlow of the Ipswich School of Flying invited me in May of 1978 to do some work for them I was pleased to accept; I could help here and also continue to fly at Monewden and anywhere else that I may be required.

MOLESWORTH

It was 1979 and I had been asked to do my crazy flying act for the Shropshire Aero Club in their Whit Monday display at Sleap aerodrome. They must have liked the act because this was my second year with them. Auster Autocrats were now in short supply but my friend Leo was ever ready to let me use his Alpha, which was the modified version using a Gypsy Major engine.

Many folk believe that because a man owns an aeroplane, he must be pretty well off, but the opposite is very often the case. It is precisely because he owns an aeroplane that many a man hasn't a bean for anything else – even, regrettably, for flying the wretched thing. Leo was such a man, so he was more than a little pleased with the idea of a trip from Elmsett in Suffolk where he kept the Auster, to Sleap in Shropshire, because he knew that he would be able to fly it there and back. Roy Wilks, my straight man, would be quite happy to sit in the back.

The essential flight planning on the morning of departure soon indicated that with the north-westerly wind blowing at the time, we would not be able to get to Sleap non-stop with our 15 gallon fuel tank and consumption of 7 gallons per hour. Quite simple old chap, you just drop in and pick up some fuel at an airfield en route. Yes, but the only field reasonably available was Leicester East. Now there is nothing wrong with Leicester East but we are short of time because I want to get to Sleap by 1300 hours to get myself organised and view the site. I needed to select the best places to position the aeroplane and the bicycle, and the points to take-off from and to get back on to. With a bit of luck I might be able enjoy the free lunch that would be provided by courtesy of the Shropshire Aero Club.

You see it is just not an easy matter to pop in for fuel. The Auster had no radio so this meant that we would have to carry out the protracted non-radio circuit-joining procedure and then after landing, first find the re-fuelling point without any taxiing instructions, and then try to find someone who is remotely interested in supplying an Auster with fuel. When this is achieved we would then have to find somewhere to pay for it – and this could be a two mile walk from the place where we had to book in, pay the landing fee and book out. Then we would have to agree a way of getting the Auster out to the pre-takeoff point and then after starting the engine, wait for light signals as appropriate to taxi and to takeoff. Oh no, we didn't have time for all that – there must be a better way.

We need only a little drop, and that mainly as a safety measure so five gallons would see us laughing. Leo had a five gallon jerry-can left over from the days when he kept his Auster on a field which had no refuelling facilities – in those days he would pick up five gallons from the local garage on his way to the field. I know that the Civil Aviation Authority would not like that very much, but feel sure that they would not go after Leo at this late stage just because of my revelation.

"But how are we going to put it into the tank?" I heard an anguished cry although the penny must already be dropping with one or both of them. "We will have burned off five gallons after about 45 minutes into the flight so beyond that we look out for a suitable field to land on, pop in the fuel and away we go before anyone realises that we are there – remembering always that this is a Sunday morning so there won't be all that number of people about. If all else fails we can still land at Leicester East but I don't think that will be necessary." After all, the early pilots often did this sort of thing, even landing near to garages – but of course the CAA would not like that nowadays, especially if we did not have the permission of the landowner. However, with a bit of luck the CAA would not get to know about it and I don't think that they will come after me now.

So off we go, navigating with compass. watch and a half-million scale map until we estimate that the fuel tank would be prepared to accept the five gallons being nursed by Roy in the rear seat. Now we are looking for a suitable field, when just past the American-operated base at Alconbury we passed a disused airfield which looked pretty deserted, and it had a roughly east-west hard runway with a very useful extension bit at the east end. "Where's that?" came a cry, "Molesworth" shouted those who wanted it to be known that they knew where they were, "it might be a satellite of Alconbury." "Yes, but it looks pretty quiet – let's have a closer look at it." I took over control now and hauled the Auster around to the left, letting down gently so as not to attract attention on the ground. The surface of the extension looked quite serviceable and blessed be, this jutting out part of the runway appeared to be screened from the hangar area by a line of bushes on the north side. "Looks good to me, I'm going in if you all agree." They seemed quite enthusiastic.

Nice and wide so that even if anyone did bother to look up at us they would never guess that we were approaching to land at Molesworth – not until the last moments anyway, when we would be very low. The noisy Gypsy engine was now throttled reasonably well back to give us a steady descent so that after a long creeper approach I touched down on the very end of the runway, and with gentle braking we came to rest only a short way along and well out sight of any of the buildings. I had already stopped the engine so we now went into action with the pre-planned order of doing things. Leo was out and lifting the back of his seat to receive the jerry-can while Roy followed. I was out at the other (right) side with the funnel, removing the filler cap just in front of the windscreen and inserting the funnel. By this time Roy was up, standing on the wheel receiving the jerry-can from Leo who continued to support the weight – refuelling had commenced!

As it became evident that with the can getting lighter, Roy could cope on his own, Leo got back into his seat to prepare for start-up. Pouring five gallons seemed to take ages – you could never be sure that there was not somebody about on a Sunday morning who might just have seen our stealthy approach and who, suspecting a drop of illegal Pakistani immigrants, was doing his civic thing and attracting attention, so speed was the thing. At the last drop of petrol Roy dropped off the wheel to get back in the rear of the Auster while I replaced the filler cap. He had to get in by lifting the back of my seat, so by the time I got there my seat back would be in place.

But I still had another job to do – restarting a hot engine by hand was not always easy, but I did know the Gypsy Major which was much kinder in this situation than the Lycoming engines with which many Auster V's were fitted. "Switches off, throttle wide", "Switches off, throttle wide" Leo repeated faithfully so I was now able to "blow out" – a kind term to describe the process of hand turning the propeller the wrong way in order to get rid of the excess of petrol vapour which floats around the innards of a hot engine. About a dozen pulls seemed to me to suffice, so I called for "Brakes on, fuel on, switches off, throttle closed". Leo repeated to confirm, so I was able to request "throttle set, contact", with a thumbs up signal.

Confirmation from Leo again – now it all depended on his idea of 'throttle set'. Too much or too little could mean disaster, a word that I ought not to use in this context, but failure to start in this situation would not be far short of that – perhaps I am given to some exaggeration – caused in this case by a lot of experience of many unhappy propeller-swinging hours. However, we were in luck – one good sharp swing of my right arm and the engine burst into noisy life. Leo knew his engine.

With a dash round to the right hand seat I was strapped in seconds. A quick glance indicated that Leo had done the pre-takeoff checks, or at least he had set the tail trimmer and flaps so with an "I've got her" I opened the throttle to full in a reasonable two seconds. Purists will complain that I did not do a pre-flight run-up to check the magnetos – correct, but the engine was making a noise and in the circumstances, I would have gone even if it had been doing this on only one magneto.

As we lifted off the runway my fears were confirmed for there was a car, rapidly approaching across the apron from a lighted hangar. In a moment he would have a sight of our registration letters on the side of the fuselage so I did a bit of practice for the crazy flying display by weaving into an under-banked turn to the left (we also have letters painted on the underside of the wings). Now the problem was to keep our tail pointed at the car without giving a view of the wing surfaces, and this was achieved by giving the country folk for about three miles south of Molesworth the sight and sound of an Auster at very low level. We continued on that heading for about five miles so as not to give any indication of our path to destination, before resuming our heading to the north-west.

I don't believe that I lost too much sleep after this but there was some relief when a month had gone by without any communication from the police or the CAA. It was some time after this that we learned that our Government had selected Molesworth as the second site on which to base Cruise Missiles for the defence of the nation against something or other. How were we to know that in 1979?

AFTER RETIREMENT

In February 1981 I reached the ripe old age of 60 and was therefore able to retire from my employment as Principal Administrative Officer to the Suffolk County Architect's Department. I then gleefully started a life of full-time flying, although I did not contract myself to any one school, and accordingly was able to fly freelance with anybody and any organisation.

As a pilot approved by the CAA to carry out test flights for the issue and renewal of Certificates of Airworthiness for light aircraft, I had, until 1972, done the air testing of aeroplanes maintained at Ipswich, but after leaving Ipswich and particularly after retirement I was more readily available to other engineers. Bob Hammond at Framlingham found me very useful with his considerable level of work, and I enjoyed the opportunity to fly many different types of aeroplane, generally with Bob as my test observer.

But you meet some strange situations even in air testing. One aircraft engineering firm some way away, were very pleased to come across me because they had been having the greatest difficulty in obtaining the services of a test pilot for the aeroplanes that they maintained, and I would be particularly useful because I was skilled on Austers and there were not many test pilots around there with tail-dragger experience. My first appointment with them was for an Auster and a Ercoupe. I did the Auster first with no trouble at all, but the Ercoupe failed to achieve anything like the scheduled rate of climb, in spite of five test climbs.

With all the allowances possible, the shortfall was so great that I had no alternative but to fail it, and although I gave all the advice I could as to what should be done, this did not exactly make me the flavour of the month. Surprise, surprise, but I learned that the aeroplane had been successfully test flown by somebody else within two days, and I was never again called upon to help that organisation. Another engineer who stripped that engine down sometime later, told me that the faults he had found would have reduced the power output by a quarter!

It was getting into 1981 when Tim Painter approached me at Framlingham with two problems – he was completing the building of an Evans VP2 under the supervisory eye of Bob Hammond – first he wanted someone to do the first and subsequent test flying, and then because the VP2 was a taildragger he wanted instruction in flying a taildragger.

Thus it was that on the 3rd of August 1981, I taxied out at Framlingham in this tiny, incredibly ugly but beautifully built open-cockpit two seater. There was nothing particularly exciting about the 15-minute first flight except that the perspex windscreen buckled – I was not aware until after landing that the top of the fuselage behind me had caved in, but that part was not load-bearing, and only the smooth line had been altered.

On ferrying the VP2 over to Coddenham where the rest of the test flying was to be carried out, it became clear that we had an engine cooling problem and a rate of climb which left a bit to be desired. All of these little problems were cleared up by Tim between test flights and we came to the required Vne (maximum permissible speed) and spinning tests. I considered that with an untried aeroplane it would be reasonable to carry a parachute just in case.

It was clear that there was not room for a seat type parachute normally worn in small aeroplanes so I went along to Tony Knight who operated the excellent Parachute Centre at Ipswich Airport, and he lent me a back pack. Tim and his wife met me at Coddenham at the arranged time, and I shall always remember the lady's look of absolute horror which greeted my mention of the parachute – but I shall never know if this was caused by fears for my safety or the possibility that I might leave this aeroplane – the result of six years of combined constructing effort – to destroy itself.

However, my attempt to get into the tiny cockpit with the back pack was fruitless – I hid my terror and climbed aboard without it – smiles all round again, and I stayed close enough to the airfield for them to see the successful Vne dive and the spin and recovery. The postscript to this is that shortly afterwards, the FAA, (the VP2 is an American design) in consequence of one or two unfortunate accidents, banned all spinning in the VP2.

Although the VP2 has two seats, its permissible maximum all up weight dictated that the two people must either be slightly below average weight (and indeed, size) or if one is average then the other must be quite tiny. At our weight and size, Tim and I could not possibly fly together so I could only recommend an ultra lightweight female instructor, but he did not find this at all acceptable.

So we had to borrow a two-seat Condor which was the closest resemblance to the VP2 that I could think of, and I used that to convert Tim to the tail-dragger. The story ends with the fact that after a meticulous briefing, I sent him off on his first flight in the VP2 of his own construction – even to making the propeller. The couple came within the weight restriction, so after gaining a bit more experience, Tim was able to introduce his supportive wife to the delights of their joint enterprise.

The ISF was initially equipped with Cessna 150s but in June 1981 they bought two Piper PA 38 Tomahawks, which were purpose-built trainers, low-wing, side-by-side two seaters with Lycoming engines.

Compared with the Cessna 150, the Tomahawk was an aeroplane requiring more positive handling, and was perhaps not quite as forgiving, so that it helped to produce pilots who were a bit more ready to deal with the surprises they would have to encounter in aeroplanes they might convert to in later years.

Just before this acquisition, some publicity had been given to two fatal crashes involving instructor-student combinations practising spin recoveries – well – failures to recover. In my usual, I am afraid, attitude to such accidents I was ready to blame the instructors rather than the aeroplane. This type of accident had occurred once before in my recollection.

Both the Tiger Moth and the Cessna 150 were so gentle in the spin that they would recover with the minimum forward movement of the stick. This did not conflict with the standard recovery action which requires that the stick be moved forward until the spinning stops. But if you had been instructing exclusively on these aeroplanes, you could get used to the recovery coming with as little as a three-inch forward movement – indeed, I say "three-inch" here because to my horror I actually saw this stated in the Pilot's Notes of a 150! Now some aeroplanes, and here I will name the DH Chipmunk and the Piper Tomahawk, require more than this. Unhappily, this can come as a nasty shock to the pilot who has forgotten the wording of the standard recovery action.

When this type of accident happened to a Chipmunk instructor-student combination in the RAF, after a full inquiry orders were issued that every Chipmunk pilot from the CFI downwards had to undergo spin recovery instruction which required a climb to 7000' from which height a fully developed spin had to be entered and sustained until the flat spin developed. At this stage, the separate controls are completely ineffective, so that only the correct sequence of control movement would result in recovery – and this involved moving the stick as far forward as you could reach.

I suppose not surprisingly, the students of at least one rival flying club were well informed about the Tomahawk spinning accidents, and they would expound on this at great length to all and sundry, until I decided that something had to be done. The ISF had a competition evening coming along, so I took advantage of this to put in a bit of flying with a commentary coming from the aeroplane via the radio-telephone to loud speakers on the ground, during which I described what I was doing while the spectators observed two full spins with recovery, overhead the airfield, to the left and to the right, starting from 1500'. Most people had never seen a spin that close, but it stopped the prattling.

I hasten to add that there was nothing irresponsible or dare-devilish about this exhibition – as with all of my display flying, I had earlier in the day climbed to an adequate altitude to check the maximum loss of height involved, so there was not much risk.

THE LOST LICENCE

It was at 3 pm on Tuesday the 12th of October 1982 that I attended for the electro-cardiograph examination by Doctor Barry. This was a test in advance of the full medical examination for the renewal of my Private Pilot's Licence which was to be with Doctor Burges on the following day. Barry asked some unusual questions, and he did not finish with his usual comment in a rich Irish accent, "Well I'll be passin' yer on this occasion – on the one condition that you make sure that you won't ever be flyin' over my house." There was something wrong!

On the following day Doc Burges revealed that I had a heart problem, and there was no point in continuing with his examination until this had been investigated further. With the help of a pilot friend who also happened to be a medical secretary, a private appointment was made with a heart consultant for Thursday the 15th. After his examination, we got into a discussion which involved my age of 61 years and a question about how long I expected to continue the life of a flying instructor.

I meekly suggested perhaps another five years and referred to a chap named Cyril Pascoe who was still instructing at 71 years of age. This got me nowhere, because the Doc now said quite clearly that at the age of 61, I would have to forego the glamour of my present life and seek a quieter hobby.

Doc Burges who had been my GP for many years and was fully familiar with my activities at Ipswich Airport did everything possible in trying to keep my licence in the knowledge of how important it was to me that I should be able to continue flying. But the only course now was to appeal to the Medical Department of the Civil Aviation Authority, with his supportive letter.

I duly appeared at CAA House in London for a full clinical examination on the 15th December after which the following conclusion was written by the consultant physician, an Air Vice Marshal, "I feel that the combination of his age, atrial fibrillation and the fact that he has had an episode of ventricular tachycardia, means that he should not be granted any medical certificate. I have indicated this to him and naturally he is disappointed but I think he must now seek other interests." The CAA Medical Officer concurred.

In discussion with the Air Vice Marshal immediately after the examination, I learned that I was not to be allowed even the privilege of flying as a pilot with the safeguard of a safety pilot beside me. Strictly only as a passenger. "What about aerobatics in that capacity?" "That is the last thing I would contemplate." "Then how ill am I?" "We shall have to keep an eye on you." This involved my becoming a user of digoxin for the remainder of my time, with two-monthly check-up visits to my local doctor.

And that is how a flying career is ended – but was it? There is a term "riding shotgun", which implies that you have a guy (pardon the cowboy expressions that figure in this) sitting there keeping an eye open to safeguard the pilot-in-charge. No, it is not an official flight crew position and consequently there is no licence for it. He has no authority and may not interfere with the operation of the aircraft – he is in fact, a passenger.

Ah now! that is something that the man said I could be. It did not take long for some licensed pilots to grasp the opportunity to do a bit of flying alongside perhaps the most experienced instructor for many miles around, with the possibility of collecting some of those gems of wisdom for which he was so famous – and all the time they would be flying as captain of the aircraft. Some of these people also enjoyed some increased confidence as a result of such flying.

However, my reputation for high quality teaching of the technique of getting into and out of small strips took a nasty beating on an occasion when I was flying for the Ipswich School of Flying, on a trip advising Keith in their Cherokee 140. With a passenger in the rear seat we had landed at the farm airstrip at Coddenham just as a thunderstorm arrived, so we had to shelter for some time in the barn/hangar. A second strip had recently been laid and was now considered fit for use, so we elected to use that for take-off as it was a bit closer to the wind direction and did not have high trees at the upwind end like the old strip had.

Silly me! It was evident as Keith opened the throttle that our acceleration was not all that it should be – the recent heavy rain had softened the comparatively new surface. But the Cherokee was a good bird and I was confident that we would sneak off the end of the runway without any difficulty. It was not to be so because just as I reckoned we were about to lift off, we hit a pool of surface water which slowed us like we had trodden on the brakes. It was then obvious that we were not going to get off and it was equally clear that we were not going to stop before we ran out of runway – and you didn't have to be very clever to guess that the boundary of this field was a good, healthy, wide and deep ditch.

I was reasonably able to make quick decisions, so before Keith had time to consider whether or not to keep going, I had mouthed the famous words "I've got her", very shortly after deciding that a high speed slither into the ditch could have nasty after tones. Now, I must point out here that I just did not have time to consider the fact that it was quite illegal for me to take over control – one can operate the controls of an aeroplane only if one is appropriately licensed or if one is accompanied by a licensed flying instructor. However I do believe that if I had time for that consideration, I would still not have hesitated to take over, on the basis that my neck was in imminent danger, and I reckoned that licensed or not I was better able to deal with the situation in which we found ourselves.

The problem with which I was now faced was to keep going at full power, try to bounce the aeroplane across the ditch, and hope to continue the take-off in the adjoining field.

With incredible judgement or luck, as could be seen from the wheel marks afterwards, I lifted the nose at just the right moment, so that the nosewheel passed over a small mound at the edge of the ditch, and only the main wheels hit it. The aeroplane literally bounced across the gap, which proved to be no less than 12 feet wide, but any thought that we were going to keep flying were quickly dashed as the Cherokee sank like a lead balloon into a field of standing barley. Deceleration was now fairly rapid as I struggled to save the noseleg from the violence of the ridged surface, and in anticipation of such a failure, I stopped the engine to reduce the chance of damage to that and probably also to the propeller.

But we came to rest about fifty yards into the field with the noseleg quite intact! I do believe that any vexation shown by the School's proprietors was not so much with my misjudgement, but more because I had not taken the heaven-sent opportunity to write-off the aeroplane which happened to be due for some very expensive maintenance work! They felt this even more so when faced with the cost of recovery from the field because with no evident damage, there was no insurance claim – in addition to this, the next-door farmer would not allow removal before payment of £100 for the anticipated damage to his crop.

In fact, the job of moving the Cherokee back to the airstrip was done by volunteers from the school, supervised by engineer Bob Hammond, including the construction of a temporary bridge across the ditch. Bob carried out a careful inspection of the aeroplane and was able to declare no damage and fit to fly – then the farmer agreed to reduce his charge to fifty pounds.

Regarding riding 'shotgun', it was not long before an irate chief flying instructor from another club put his foot down with the proprietor, demanding that I should cease acting as adviser to their licensed pilots – just before this, I had flown with a pilot who was building hours for an instructor's course, and we had done some actual instrument flying in cloud before and after aerobatics. It was a bit unfortunate that the lad, without reference to me, had suggested to the proprietor that he would like to do a lot more flying with me!

So that ended that at that club, but the boss was a close friend of mine so I continued to hang around when I had nothing better to do, and there were little jobs that I could do when nobody else was available, like the occasional ground lecture, flight briefing, answering the telephone or greeting visitors.

But there were snags, such as this in the mid-eighties – "We've got a spare seat Stan, would you like to come up to Shipdham with us? We're just going for lunch". "Yes, I'd love to come, thank you very much". "There's only one condition". "Oh!" "You are to sit quietly in the back, and not say a word to either of us". Thus began a minor incident which had the final laugh on me.

The two chaps who invited me to go along with them were both licensed pilots and both had suffered instruction from me before I lost my licence in 1982. They were aware that I was always ready with a bit of advice, whether or not it had been requested, but this was a trip that they had done many times before without my assistance and, quite rightly, they did not want any interference from me during what they were looking forward to – a pleasant fly to lunch – but they were happy that I should fill the spare seat, the fourth being occupied by a youngish lady.

So off we went in a Cessna 172 to Shipdham, a former war-time airfield some 38 nautical miles to the north-west, and now a licensed civil airfield operated by Arrow Air Services who generously charged no landing fee to aircraft which used their services – like having lunch in their rather nice bar-restaurant.

If I had any silent criticisms of my friends' airmanship or navigation on the way up, they cannot have been very serious because I cannot remember any now, but as we positioned for joining the circuit pattern for landing, things changed. They did not use the radio but that was understandable because at that time, although Shipdham had an air-ground facility they did not always have it manned, so quite often you did not get any reply to your call, and they did not mind non-radio arrivals.

However, whenever students or pilots approached such airfields with me in radio-equipped aeroplanes, I would normally suggest that calls be made in the usual positions around the circuit, so as to give other aircraft that may be around, some idea of where we were and what we intended to do.

But I had made the vow of silence so I just kept a good lookout as any airman would, and my mouth remained firmly shut. The entry into the circuit pattern seemed to be a bit ponderous and it was some time before I could understand what the intentions were – and then, gradually, a tiny suspicion was aroused, and it was not long before the awful truth dawned upon me that we were positioning for a 'wrong-way' approach. The wind-sock obviously favoured a landing on runway 02, and more importantly the landing 'T' confirmed that this was the runway in use!

It was however quite clear that we were now hell-bent to land on runway 20. I had been in this position many times before, indeed, I had even landed on one occasion. Normally I could quietly draw attention to the pilot's silly error and all would be quickly put right. But here, I had given my word not to interfere – I might not have been here, in which event they would have had to work it out by themselves. Please do not accuse me of irresponsibility – I believe that had it been a case of my spotting flames licking around somewhere which they had not noticed, I am sure that I would have made some comment. This was not that serious – Shipdham was not normally all that busy, and certainly the circuit appeared to be clear of other traffic. So I remained silent, but my eyes were standing out like chapel hatpegs looking for law-abiding folk who may be going the other way.

By now we had entered base leg, and we appeared to be a bit high – the throttle came back fully, leaving us in the glide, and 20 degrees of flap came down before the turn on to final approach. We were now clearly very high, and the following wind was making our glide angle that much flatter, so we had a full 500 feet as we passed over the runway threshold. Half-way along the runway, the decision was taken to go around, and power came on gradually to full throttle to give us an alarmingly small angle of climb. An animated conversation was going on in the front seats but I was not privy to it.

Then it became clear that another attempt was to be made! At this I could no longer constrain my desire to follow the habit of a lifetime – to complain – even if it did mean the breaking of the vow, and the probability that I would never again be invited to lunch. "I'm sorry to interfere but you were down-wind". Two heads moved quickly around the sky, ground and cockpit before the startling comment, "That's peculiar, when I rang them this morning they told me that they were using runway 20". I could not help thinking, voicelessly, – "Oh dear, the wind really ought not to change like that"!

Unhappily, that was not the end of it for me. I was fairly well known as an instructor because of many visits to Shipdham, so try to imagine my discomfort as I entered the quite busy bar-restaurant to be greeted by Nigel the proprietor, with "Hello Stan, you got down then – which runway did you finally land on?" You cannot really start explaining the whole story to an eating and drinking crowd, can you?

In 1987 I was invited by Tony Knight, boss of the Ipswich Parachute Centre, to do a dual free-fall parachute drop. It was to be a publicity exercise, co-ordinated with a similar drop by Jane Lockwood, a 23-year old stewardess. I was 66 at the time, so maybe it was to be a case of the young and the old or maybe of beauty and the beast. After one sight of the beautiful Jane I was sure that I knew which body would be strapped to the boss; and so it was that the very competent instructor Brian Pushman was instructed to deal with me, while the boss took care of the young lady.

With a lot of experience of dropping parachutists, I had long wanted to do one myself, but I had lacked the courage – now was the opportunity to have a go at sky-diving without having to do all the training necessary for a solo effort. In their next edition the Ipswich Evening Star made a lot of it – "sprightly pensioner" and "from 10,000 feet at 120 miles an hour before opening" and all that. I thoroughly

Author goes sky-diving with instructor Brian Pushman, April 1987.

enjoyed every minute of the exercise, and the quote of my comment was true "It was fabulous, it really was – I recommend all OAPs to have a go".

My grandson Neil had taken up parachuting at the Centre with such enthusiasm that he was elected "Most progressive sky-diver of 1987" by the British Parachute Association. The Star reported this at some length in January 1988 under the headline "Parachutist keeps it in the family...". The photograph of grandfather, son and grandson referred to Robert's 21 jumps in the 1960s, Neil's 79 in 1987 and my solitary debut in the same year, describing us as "the three daredevil generations"! (Robert's parachuting is described in Chapter 7).

It was 1989 before I went back to Ponca City Oklahoma where they had taught me to fly 46 years earlier – it was a private visit in May, but I went again in the September, and again in October 1991. I know of none of the various RAF units on which I served during the war that I would give tuppence to re-visit once, so why all this?

I am not sure, perhaps it had something to do with the fact that this was where the flying adventure really started for me – but I don't really

Son Robert, grandson Neil and the author, described by the press as "three daredevil generations" of parachutists, January 1988.

The author crossing Grand, the main street, on a visit to Ponca City in 1989.

believe that. It was surely the memory of the kindness of the people of that city – I have commented earlier upon the unstinted hospitality that we enjoyed, and the manner in which homes were opened us. This was experienced again as soon as I arrived on that first return, and we were to see much more of it during the later visits.

Many ex-cadets have re-visited a number of times before me, in fact at least two returned immediately after the war to settle down and become American Citizens. The No 6 British Flying Training School (Ponca City) Association had been formed with sections in both the USA and the UK, on the initiative of Mrs Lillian Taylor who was one of our very attractive Link Trainer Instructors during the war, and who still lives in Ponca City and graces the office of President of the Association.

When Enid Bishop and I arrived in May 1989, the local newspaper kindly put a notice on the front page to ask if folk who remembered me would get in touch, via Lillian. In that way I was able to meet retired Assistant Superintendent of Maintenance, Farrel Watson, who was the gentleman who found me and my aeroplane on that night of the blizzard in March 1943. We were equally pleased to meet each other again, and he showed me the torch with the aid of which he had first spotted the wreckage – it was double-length flashlight, which he had made by welding two barrels together.

The local press, radio and T/V were most interested in all of this, and he became a celebrity overnight. The newspaper also printed a full-page article about the RAF cadet who had returned after 46 years. With my ready assistance they shot the full "line-shoot" about the crash, the production of the 'Vaudeville', and my Wings Examination result. Fame at last! It was rather pleasant to find that people recognised me in the shops, thanks to the media attention and my plummy accent.

I had a number of photographs that had been taken in the air and on the ground during the period of training in 1943, so it seemed a good idea to take similar pictures in 1989 in the same locations. This included hiring a Cessna 172, to fly from my Alma Mater for the air shots. The pictures were entered in an album dedicated to that visit, and it was perhaps a little unkind to match photographs of some of the ladies who had befriended and hosted us in those far off days, with pictures of the same ladies taken on this visit – the passage of 46 years had of course taken its toll, but nobody objected!

During that visit Lillian Taylor persuaded us to come back in September, when it was planned to dedicate a full display in the basement of the City Library, on the transfer of her memorabilia of 6 BFTS which had formed a small museum in her husband's office block. Not only that, but this would coincide with the dedication of a permanent exhibition of the "RAF in Oklahoma" in the Air & Space Museum of the prestigious Kirkpatrick Centre in Oklahoma City. (There had been a second BFTS, No 3, based at Miami, Oklahoma). At Lillian's request, I donated a number of bits of my memorabilia to the Air & Space Museum.

The visit in September 1989 was something of a mini-reunion of USAAC and RAF ex-cadets, during which I renewed acquaintance with a number of the Americans who had been on the same flying course as I was in 1943. Many of these have visited us in Ipswich – in particular, we have enjoyed holidays with Whitney Sullivan and his wife Ginger in Westcliffe in Colorado, Ipswich in Suffolk and at other reunions.

That September visit started with a display of the ex-cadets to the people, in a 'motorcade' through the main street of Ponca City, led by a formal USAF Colour Guard with the Stars and Stripes. We went next day to the exhibition in Oklahoma City, where it was something of a shock to find that a large section had been devoted to me. Flattering though it was, and we all love that, it might have been more appropriate to devote the main display to the bravery and dedication of those who did not survive.

When Don Finch, Curator of the Air & Space Museum, saw the 1943-89 album, he immediately asked for it to add it to the display, and I promised him that instructions to this effect would be left in my Will. Later on, during a speech to the assembled company and spectators, this gave me the opportunity to raise a laugh on the subject, with the lie that his response to the promise that he would get it on my death, was that he would look forward to that!

On that subject, it may be interesting to note that from opening in August 1941 to closing in April 1944, some 1113 RAF and 125 USAAC pilots were trained at the School. By April 1993, the Association's nominal roll totalled 180 – representing all of the known survivors from the war and the years between.

October 1991 saw a reunion organised to attract ex-cadets from both the RAF and the USAF, for a full five days of festivities in the hands of our hosts, the people of Ponca City. The Mayor issued a Proclamation declaring those five days to be known as "Darr Days", a reference to the fact that 6 BFTS was operated at the Darr School of Aeronautics.

The people had excelled themselves in planning a reunion we could never forget, which included exhibitions, picnics, visits, dinners and entertainment of all descriptions. A breakfast organised at our airfield was followed by a fly-in of, among others, seven PT17s (Stearmans) and five AT6s. These aeroplanes were flown by their owners, and most of them were available to ex-cadets for nostalgic joy-rides – the Conoco Oil

Company having generously sent a tanker of aviation fuel for free refuelling.

I went for the Stearman, and enjoyed an incredible reunion with the aeroplane and the landscape so familiar 48 years before. Again, this gave me the opportunity during a later speech of appreciation, to relate that my benefactor, Dick Darnell, had commented about my handling of the aeroplane to the effect that the only time the balance indicator was central was as it passed through from fully one side to fully the other – I was lying of course.

At first, after the loss of my licence, I did quite a bit of work in tidying-up the aerobatic ability of a number of pilots. It was a sad thing to observe the clear indications of failure by instructors to instil in their students many of the simple basics of the art. Unfortunately, although I very much enjoyed aerobatics, it was this part of the Air Vice Marshal medico's advice that soon had to be taken, because I began to notice that after an hour of being tossed around, which is one of the more unpleasant aspects of accompanying learner-aerobaticists, I became exhausted for the rest of the day! So I had to give that up.

There were however, many other areas where my companionship was sought, and I was kept busy advising on beacon flying, instrument approach aids, conversions to different types of aircraft, and the use of radio-navigation equipment. This also involved extensive navigation trips including a lot of cross-channel adventures, as well as some attempts to increase the self-confidence of many pilots. It was

Through the generosity of Dick Darnell from Oklahoma City (rear seat), the author flies in Dick's Stearman PT17 at Ponca City again, in October 1991 – 48 years after.

surprising how many pilots wanted me to tidy up their flying by putting them through a flight test similar to that required for the issue of the Private Pilot's Licence – sadly, those who asked for this were generally just the people who had no difficulty in "passing" it.

The sort of flying I was doing was quite legal, but it was not too popular with some instructors who were, after all, earning their living, and were not slow to suggest that I was taking the bread and butter out of their mouths. There was therefore little for me to do in the Schools at Ipswich Airport, so this sort of flying became confined to private owners and groups, some at Ipswich but mostly from farm-strips nearby.

It was in 1993, eleven years after the loss of my licence, that I retired from flying, and I had logged 13,590 flying hours – not a lot when compared with medium and long-haul airline pilots but a fair figure when it includes thousands of trips of an hour or less. In fact, during an idle moment I calculated that about 9,000 were done at Ipswich Airport alone, during which I had made some 22,500 landings on that lovely grass. I had hoped that in view of this they might have re-named it Stanley Ward Airport rather like John F Kennedy at New York and Will Rogers at Oklahoma City, but it was not to be – the Borough Council decided to close it!

It is possible that the Guinness Book of Records and perhaps the CAA Medical Branch will be interested to know that since I was found to be medically unfit to hold a licence, I have flown 2,238 hours "riding shotgun".

Happy picture of author and Enid Bishop (private pilot) to whom this book is dedicated, 1994.